Richard Brathwaite

Natures Embassie

Divine and Morall Satyres; Shepheards Tales, Both Parts; Omphale...

Richard Brathwaite

Natures Embassie

Divine and Morall Satyres; Shepheards Tales, Both Parts; Omphale...

ISBN/EAN: 9783337023058

Printed in Europe, USA, Canada, Australia, Japan

Cover: Foto ©Thomas Meinert / pixelio.de

More available books at **www.hansebooks.com**

Brathwaite's
Natures Embassie.

Only 400 copies printed, and 50 on Large Paper.

This is No.......

Natures Embaffie

Divine and Morall Satyres: Shepheards
Tales, both parts: Omphale: Odes,
or Philomels Tears, &c.

BY

R. BRATHWAITE.

BOSTON, LINCOLNSHIRE:
Printed by *Robert Roberts*, Strait Bar-Gate.
M.DCCCLXXVII.

LIFE AND WRITINGS

OF

RICHARD BRATHWAITE,

Author of "Natures Embassie."

 IF the Life and Works of RICHARD BRATHWAITE, the author of the present volume, all that it is now desirable or possible to know has been told by Haslewood* with such copiousness of detail, that the writer of any new memoir has rather to sift and winnow what has already been gathered and gleaned, than to glean anything new of his own.

Richard Brathwaite, the great-grandfather of our author, lived at and was owner of Ambleside, in the barony of Kendal, in Westmoreland. His grandson, Thomas Brathwaite, the father of the poet, purchased of John Warcop, after a family possession of more than

---

* *Barnabæ Itinerarium, or Barnabee's Journal; by Richard Brathwait, A.M. With a life of the Author, a Bibliographical Introduction to the Itinerary, and a Catalogue of his Works. Edited from the first Edition*, by Joseph Haslewood. Lond. 1820 (only 125 copies printed).

b

three centuries, the manor of Warcop near Appleby, and resided there probably until the death of his own father, Robert Brathwaite, when he became possessed of the paternal estate of Burneshead. He married Dorothy, daughter of Robert Bindloss, of Haulston, Westmoreland. Of this marriage our poet, RICHARD BRATHWAITE, was the fourth child and the second son.* He is supposed to have been born about the year 1588, at his father's seat of Burneshead, above-named, in the parish of Kendal. In two or three copies of verses addressed to the Alderman, to the Cottoneers, and to the Worshipful Recorder of Kendal,† he alludes to the latter place as the locality of his birth. He may therefore be considered as

---

* Fuller particulars of the names, order of birth, and marriages of the poet's elder brother and five sisters are subjoined for those who are interested in them :—

1. Agnes, who married Sir Thomas Lamplew, of Downby, Cambridgeshire.
2. Thomas (afterwards knighted), married Elizabeth, daughter of Sir John Dalston, of Dalston, Cumberland.
3. Alice, married Thomas Barton, of Whenby, Yorkshire.
4. Richard, the poet.
5. Dorothy, married Francis Salkeld, of Whitehall, Esquire.
6. Mary, married John Brisco, of Crofton, Esq.
7. Anne, married Alan Askoughe, of Richmond, Yorkshire.

Brathwaite's *Description of a Good Wife*, 1619, was inscribed "to his five equally affectionate Sisters, all vertuous content."

† *A Strappado for the Diuell*, 1615, pp. 173-210. These pieces contain some very curious local allusions.

one of the worthies of Westmoreland, and the father of the Lake Poets of that country, though he had little else but the accident of his dwelling-place in common with the three or four distinguished writers who two centuries later were destined to bear that designation.

In 1604, at the age of sixteen, Wood states that BRATHWAITE became a gentleman-commoner of Oriel College, Oxford. Having graduated here, and been very successful in a college exercise, he was desirous of accepting the encouragement and preferment that seemed to open out to him, and to continue peacefully in those hallowed cloisters the study of literature and poetry. His parents, however, desired him to pursue the profession of the Law,* and after a short stay at the sister University of Cambridge, where his tutor was Lancelot Andrews, afterwards bishop of Winchester, he began to devote himself rather distastefully and reluctantly, to its 'brawling courts' and 'dusky purlieux.' This restraint, however, instead of forcing him into the vortex of dissipation, seems to have rather deepened his love of literature, and his

"Faith in the whispers of the lonely Muse."

In his *Spiritval Spicerie* (1638), he writes as

---

* He seems to allude to this in some speeches of Technis, in the first Eglogue of his *Shepheards Tales* (see pp. 190-191 of the present volume).

follows:—"Amidst these disrelishing studies, I bestowed much precious time in reviving in mee the long-languishing spirit of Poetrie, with other morall assayes; which so highly delighted mee, as they kept mee from affecting that loose kind of libertie, which through fulnesse of meanes and licentiousnesse of the age, I saw so much followed and eagerly pursued by many. This moved mee sometimes to fit my buskin'd Muse for the Stage;* with other occasionall Presentments or Poems; which being free borne, and not mercenarie, received gracefull acceptance of all such as understood my ranke and qualitie. For so happily had I crept into opinion by closing so well with the temper and humour of the time, as nothing was either presented by mee (at the instancie of the noblest and most generous wits and spirits of that time †) to the Stage, or committed by me to the presse; which past not with good approvement in the estimate of the world."

From the Inns of Court BRATHWAITE seems to have adventured for a time among the merchants, and finally to have left Court and City to turn country squire, his parents having settled a sufficient estate upon him.

* No dramatic piece of Brathwaite's of this early period is known to be extant.

† William Shakespeare, perhaps (who was still living), or 'rare Ben Jonson.' Who knows?

This resolution was taken soon after the death of his father in 1610; an event which probably led to an arrangement by which possession was given, at no very distant period, of the landed property limited and assigned for his use. Certain it is, the death of BRATHWAITE'S father created some family differences, that were only set right by the prudent intervention of friends. BRATHWAITE specially refers to this subject in the dedication to his uncle—a certain Mr. Robert Bindloss—of his earliest known printed work,* when speaking of "the troubled course of our estates and the favourable regard you had of our attonement, which is now so happily confirmed." In addressing his elder brother he also alludes † to the same subject :—"Our ciuill warres be now ended, vnion in the sweete harmony of minde and coniunction hath prevented the current of ensuing faction," &c.

The full-title of BRATHWAITE'S maiden publication is as follows :—

1. *The Golden Fleece. Whereto bee annexed two Elegies, Entitled Narcissvs Change. And Æsons Dotage. By Richard Brathvvayte*‡

---

* *The Golden Fleece*, by Richard Brathvvayte, *Gentleman*, 1611, p. 176.

† *Ibid*, p. 178.

‡ It may here be remarked that the name of Brathwaite was spelt by his contemporaries with as many capricious variations as those of his more illustrious contemporaries Dekker and Shakespeare, *e. g.*—Braithwaite, Braythwait,

MEMOIR OF

Gentleman. London, Printed by W. S. for Christopher Pursett dwelling in Holborne, neere Staple Inne, 1611. Octavo. Sig. G. 8.

The Dedication, as we have seen, is to his uncle Bindloss. The principal poem of *The Golden Fleece,* including the *Pieridum Invocatio,* &c., extends to forty pages, in six-line stanzas, and annexed the two Elegies, of similar measure. At sig. E. 3 appears a new title-page ; this later portion of the work containing "Sonnets or Madrigals. With the Art of Poesie annexed thereunto by the same Author," and being dedicated "to the worship-fvll his approued brother Thomas Brathwaite, Esquire." It is probable that while BRATHWAITE'S "first-birth" was printing, the "pensive tidings" announced the death of his father ; and two stanzas follow addressed by "the Authour to his disconsolate Brother." The Sonnets or Madrigals are seven in number.

On the last page of sheet G the catch-word 'The' appears ; and there can be little doubt the *Art of Poesy* was printed. In the two copies, however, referred to by Haslewood, it

---

Braynthwayt, Branthwait, Braythwayte, Brathvvayte, (as in the title cited above), Brathwaite and Brathwait. The spelling of his autograph is perfectly clear for "Brathwait" in three extant specimens of 1629, 1663 and 1672 ; though in a fourth specimen of the last-named date he has added a final *e*, and writes it "Brathwaite." Between these two forms then, it would appear, lies the choice : the rest are all incorrect.

was deficient, nor does it seem to have since turned up in any.

Three years later (1614) BRATHWAITE published

2. *The Poet's Willow : or the Passionate Shepheard : With sundry delightfull, and no lesse Passionate Sonnets: describing the passions of a discontented and perplexed Lover. Diuers compositions of verses concording as well with the Lyricke, as the Anacreonticke measures; neuer before published: Being reduced into an exact and distinct order of Metricall extractions. Imprinted at London by John Beale, for Samuel Rand, and are to be sold at his shop at Holborne bridge,* 1614. Sm. 8vo, 48 leaves.

The work is dedicated to one William Ascham, a fellow-collegian, in six seven-line stanzas signed with the author's name. Then follows an Elegy on the death of Henry Prince of Wales, which had been the theme of so many of the poets of that time. *The Poet's Willow*, which gives its name to the volume, is a pastoral in forty-four eleven-line stanzas, preceded by a prose argument. Amatory poems to Eliza and Dorinda form the remainder of the collection : the " Pensive thoughts of Gastilio," in sapphics, is remarkable for its novelty of measure.

His next book, published in the same year (1614), Haslewood calls "an excellent little work, written in animated language, and evidently from the heart." Its full title is :

3. *The Prodigals Teares* : *or his fare-well to Vanity. A Treatise of Soueraigne Cordials to the disconsolate Soule, surcharged with the heavy burthen of his sinnes : Ministring matter of remorse to the Impenitent, by the expression of Gods Iudgements. By Richard Brathwait. London, printed by N. O. for T. Gubbins, and are to be sold at his Shop, neere Holborne Conduit,* 1614. Small 8vo. pp. iv. 139.

Again in the same year was published BRATHWAITE'S fourth work—

4. *The Schollers Medley, or an intermixt Discourse vpon Historicall and Poeticall relations........By Richard Brathwayte Oxon. London, printed by N. O. for George Norton, and are to bee sold at his Shop neere Templebarre,* 1614.* 4to, 63 leaves.

It is in this work (p. 31) that BRATHWAITE speaks of the intention then entertained by his friend Thomas Heywood, the dramatist, to write a general though summary description of the Lives of the Poets.

There were two works published by BRATHWAITE in 1615 :—

5. *A Strappado for the Diuell. Epigrams and Satyres alluding to the time, with diuers*

---

* This original edition is now become very rare. The book was reprinted, with additions and corrections, in 1638 (and again in 1652), under the title of "A Survey of History."

measures of no lesse delight. (12mo, 16 unnumbered pages of prefatory matter, and 234 numbered pages.)

The title is followed by "the Authors Anagram RICHARDE BRATHWAITE. Vertu hath bar Credit." We have already had occasion to quote from some pieces in this work, as verifying the fact of the author's birthplace being at or near Kendal. Mr. Payne Collier says there is no work in English which illustrates more fully and amusingly the manners, occupations and opinions of the time when it was written. In the lines "Upon the General Sciolists or Poettasters of Britannie" there is an interesting passage of encomium on George Wither and William Browne. One of the most amusing pieces in the collection, partly from its humour, but more from its allusions, is entitled "Upon a Poet's Palfrey, lying in lavander for the discharge of his provender:" it reminds us in some degree of the Italian artist Bronzino's stanzas upon a horse given to him by one of his patrons, but never delivered. He alludes in the first stanza to Richard III's exclamation of "A horse, a kingdome for a horse" in Shakespeare, and later on to Don Quixote (Shelton's translation of the first part of which had recently been published) and his Rozinante, and to Tamburlaine's exclamation,

"Holla, ye pamper'd jades of Asia,"

in Marlowe's play. Altogether *The Poet's Palfrey*, with its refrain

 "If I had lived but in King Richards dayes,"—
 "If I had lived but in Don Quixotes time," &c.

is one of BRATHWAITE'S liveliest and happiest productions.

6. *Loves Labyrinth: or the true-Louers knot: including the disastrous fals of two star-crost Louers Pyramus & Thysbe. By Richard Brathwayte.* 12mo, 104 numbered pages and 5 supplementary unnumbered pages "To the Reader." The pagination is distinct from that of the previous work, but the printer's signature is continuous. The imprint is the same in both : "*At London printed by I. B. for Richard Redmer and are to be sold at the West dore of Pauls at the Starre.* 1615."

In some verses prefixed to Humphry Mill's *Night's Search*, 1646, is a curious allusion to the popularity of the earlier portion of this double volume :—

> If Dekker deckt with discipline and wit,
> Gain'd praises by the *Bell-man* that he writ;
> Or laud on Brathwait waiting did abound,
> When a *Strappado for the devill* he found,
> Then may this Mill of Mills, by right of merit,
> Equall, if not superior fame inherit.

Love's Labyrinth is a long poem in easy heroic numbers ; and Haslewood pronounces that whatever may be its imperfections, it is "not discreditable as the production of early youth."

BRATHWAITE first married in 1617, Frances daughter of James Lawson, of Nesham, near Darlington. The licence was dated May 2nd, 1617, and the marriage ceremony took place at Hurworth, a village about three miles from Darlington, and in the parish of which Nesham is situated. Six sons and three daughters were the issue of this marriage; John, the youngest of the nine, was born 19th February, 1630. BRATHWAITE wrote of him in his *Whimzies** as follows:—

"Thou art my ninth, and by it I divine
That thou shalt live to love the Muses nine."

Whether this truly *whimsical* prophecy was fulfilled or not, we cannot say.

To continue our list of the works of BRATHWAITE. Two extremely curious volumes from his pen issued from the press in this year of his first marriage. The title-page of the first is in itself a curiosity, and runs as follows:—

7. *A Solemne Ioviall Disputation, Theoreticke and Practicke; briefely Shadowing the Law of Drinking; together with the Solemnities and Controversies occurring: Fully and freely discussed according to the Civill Law. Which, by the permission, priviledge and authority, of that most noble and famous order in the Vniversity of Goddesse Potina ; Dionisius Bacchus*

* See Art. 17.

being then President, chiefe Gossipper, and most excellent Governour, Blasius Multibibus, alias Drinkmuch. A singular proficient and most qualifi'd Graduate in both the liberall Sciences of Wine and Beare; in the Colledge of Hilarity, hath publikely expounded to his most approved and improved Fellow Pot-shots; Touching the houres before noone and after, usuall and lawfull..... Faithfully rendred according to the originall Latine Copie. OENOZYTHOPOLIS, *at the Signe of Red eyes.* CIƆIƆCXVII. 12mo.

Prefixed is a spirited and minute engraved title in two compartments, by Marshall, exhibiting Wine-drinkers and Beer-drinkers.*

8. *The Smoaking Age, or the man in the mist: with the life and death of Tobacco. Dedicated to those three renowned and imparallel'd Heroes, Captaine Whiffe, Captaine Pipe and Captaine Snuffe... Divided into three Sections.*

1. *The Birth of Tobacco.*
2. *Pluto's blessing to Tobacco.*
3. *Times complaint against Tobacco.*

OENOZYTHOPOLIS. *At the Signe of Teare-Nose.* CIƆIƆCXVII.

Prefixed is another engraved title from the masterly *burin* of Marshall. There is a poem at the end of this volume entitled " Chavcers incensed Ghost," in which allusion is made to

---

* This was afterwards used as a frontispiece to the *Antidote against Melancholy*, 1661, and a facsimile of it is given in Ebsworth's *Reprint of Choice Drollery*, 1876.

some Comments "shortly to bee published" on "The Miller's Tale" and the "Wife of Bath"; but which BRATHWAITE does not seem actually to have published until nearly half a century later.*

At the end of Patrick Hannay's poem of *A Happy Husband* (1619) appeared the following piece by BRATHWAITE :

9. *The Description of a good Wife: or, a rare one amongst Women. Together with an Exquisite discourse of Epitaphs, including the choysest thereof Ancient or Moderne. By R. B. Gent. Printed at London for Richard Redmer, and are to be sold at his shop at the West end of Saint Pauls Church.* 1619. 12mo.

The Essay on Epitaphs, in which he anticipated by nearly two centuries his fellow countryman and poet of the Lake District, William Wordsworth, bears a separate title, with BRATHWAITE'S full name, and an imprint of the previous year—"*By Richard Brathvvayte Gent. Imprinted at London by John Beale.* 1618." Among the obituary verses is " a funerall Ode" in memory of his elder brother, Thomas Brathwaite.

His next publication was :—

10. *A new Spring shadovved in sundry Pithie Poems. London, Printed by G. Eld, for Thomas Baylie, and are to be sold at his Shop in the middle-row in Holborne, neere Staple-*

---

* In 1665. *Vide infrà.*

Inne, 1619, 4to (containing E in fours, last leaf blank).

There is a curious woodcut on the title, representing a Well enclosed within spikes, and various persons, male and female, filling their pitchers from it. Besides some spirited and harmonious lines entitled "Bound yet Free," the collection has several small Poems, some serious, some jocose. Haslewood considered it "on the whole, a curious and entertaining tract."

In 1620 appeared :—

11. *Essaies vpon the Five Senses, with a pithie one vpon Detraction. . . By Rich. Brathwayt Esquire. London, Printed by E. G. for Richard Whittaker, and are to be sold at his shop at the Kings head in Paules Church-yard.* 1620. 12mo. 76 leaves.

At the end of this volume is the character of "a Shrow," which is omitted in the Second Edition, "revised and enlarged by the author," published in 1635.

12. *The Shepheards Tales. London, Printed for Richard Whitaker,* 1621. 8vo, 25 leaves.

This was separately and subsequently published, and is very rarely found bound up with the work of which a facsimile reprint is now offered to the reader, and in which a continuation of *The Shepheard's Tales* appeared, viz.

13. *(a) Natvres Embassie : or, the Wildemans Measvres : Danced naked by twelue*

Satyres, with sundry others continued in the next Section.

Wilde men *may dance* wise measures; Come then ho, *Though I be wilde,* my measures *are not so.*

(b) The Second Section of Divine and Morall Satyres: With an Adivnct vpon the precedent; whereby the Argument with the first cause of publishing these Satyres, be euidently related.

(c) The Shepheards Tales.*

(d) Omphale, or, the Inconstant Shepheardesse.

(e) His Odes: or Philomels Teares.

These all bear the same imprint, "*London, Printed for Richard Whitaker.* 1621."

The Satires are divided into two sections, the first containing twelve and the other eighteen, levelled against the common vices of society, with illustrative examples from ancient history. In the first satire on Degeneration as personated in Nature, the following stanza must clearly allude to one of the writings of his contemporary, George Wither :—

> But I will answer thee for all thy beautie :
> If thou wilt be an Ape in gay attire,
> Thou doest not execute that forme of dutie,
> Which Nature at thy hand seemes to require :
> Which not redrest, for all thy goodly port,
> Thou must be *stript, and whipt,* and chastisd for't.

* He alludes in the Dedication to "a former part as yet obscured." See ART. 12.

The "Sir T. H. the Elder, Kt.," to whom *Natures Embassie* is dedicated, Sir Egerton Brydges* conjectures to be Sir Thomas Hawkins, of Nash Court near Faversham in Kent, the translator of Horace, or his father.

The 12th & 13th Articles, *i. e. Natures Embassie* with the addition of the separately printed first part of *The Shepheards Tales*, were reissued together in 1623 with a new title-page running as follows:

Shepheards Tales, containing Satyres, Eglogves, and Odes. By R. B. Esquire. London, Printed for Richard Whitaker. 1623.

The four other title-pages in the course of the volume remain unaltered and severally bear the date of 1621 as before. *Shepheards Tales*, however, appears to have been considered by the stationer a more taking title than *Natures Embassie* to work off the copies still remaining on his hands two years after the original publication of that volume. Mr. Payne Collier considers that "the volume displays much talent and possesses much variety," and he selects for special commendation, as a most lively and attractive performance," *the Shepheards Holy-day, reduced in apt measures to Hobbinolls Galliard, or John to the May-pole.* The opening of this Musical Dialogue is very spirited, and proceeds through many stanzas,

* *Archaica*, Part vi. (Lond. 1815, 4to.) p. xvii. of Preface to the reprint of Brathwaite's *Essays upon the Five Senses*.

all very animated, and pleasantly descriptive of country-life. In one of her replies the Shepherdess is rather bold in her invitation, and free in her talk. The book, and especially this part of it, contains many allusions to May-games and other country sports, and to ancient customs, proverbs, &c., and is therefore important to students, as throwing some light on the England of Shakespeare's time.

A song in the Third Eglogue of the second part of *The Shepheards Tales* is characteristic of that period, and preserves the names of several tunes or ditties now obsolete.

>   Roundelayes,
>   Irish-hayes,
>   Cogs and rongs and Peggie Ramsie,
>   Spaniletto,
>   The Venetto,
>   Iohn come kisse me, Wilsons fancie.*

The Odes *(e)* were reprinted in 1815, with modernized spelling, at the Lee Priory Press, by Sir Egerton Brydges.† As the impression, however, was limited to eighty copies, this cannot be said to have hitherto much affected the rarity of the original. In a short preface the accomplished Editor asserts that all BRATHWAITE'S poetical productions having

---

* Page 259 of the present volume.

† *Brathwayte's Odes; or Philomel's Tears. Edited by Sir Egerton Brydges, Bart. Kent: Printed at the private press of Lee Priory; by Johnson and Warwick*, 1815, pp. xii. 36.

become very rare, this short specimen of his genius was selected for revival. "And if the Editor's taste," he adds, "be correct, it will prove him not to have been without merit, either for fancy, sentiment, or expression. *Readers of narrow curiosity may think such revivals of forgotten poetry useless ; and the superficial may deem them dull : the highly cultivated and candid mind will judge of them far otherwise !*"

Passing now from the work which the reader holds in his hands, the next publication of BRATHWAITE'S we have to notice is

14. *Times Cvrtaine Dravvne, or The Anatomie of Vanitie. With other choice Poems, Entituled ; Health from Helicon. By Richard Brathvvayte Oxonian. London Printed by Iohn Dawson for Iohn Bellamie, and are to be sould at the south entrance of the Royall-Exchange.* 1621, 8vo, 100 leaves.

The collection entitled "Health from Helicon," which forms the second section of this volume, has a separate title, with the same imprint, running as follows :—

Panedone : or Health from Helicon : containing Emblemes, Epigrams, Elegies, with other continuate Poems, full of all generous delight ; by Richard Brathvvayte, Esquire.

Two hitherto undiscovered works of BRATHWAITE, alluded to in his other writings, claim to be briefly mentioned here. In his *Survey of History*, 1638, speaking of the Earl of Southampton, he says "A Funerall Elegy to his precious memory was long since extant; being annexed to my *Britains Bath*, Anno 1625."

In his *English Gentleman* (Art. 15), p. 198, he says, "What more admirable than the pleasure of the Hare, if wee observe the uses which may bee made of it, as I have elsewhere *(in a Treatise entituled The Huntsmans Raunge,)* more amplie discoursed?"

In 1630 BRATHWAITE published:

15. *The English Gentleman; Containing Sundry excellent Rules or exquisite Observations, tending to direction of every Gentleman, of selecter ranke and qualitie; How to demeane or accomodate himselfe in the manage of publike or private affaires. By Richard Brathwait Esq. . . . . . London, Printed by Iohn Haviland, and are to be sold by Robert Bostock at his shop at the signe of the Kings head in Pauls Church-yard.* 1630, 4to. pp. 487.*

A brief analysis of the contents of this volume, for the purpose of detecting imperfect copies, may not be unacceptable. In conjunction with the "Compleat Gentlewoman," which forms a second part, no work of that age can have been more uniformly read or more highly appreciated. On opening the

---

* A second edition of *The English Gentleman* appeared in 1633.

volume it exhibits a glowing specimen of the burin of Robert Vaughan, in ten compartments, for the frontispiece, with a folding broadside prefixed as an explanatory draught of it. The printer's title is followed by nine leaves of Dedication, copious tables, and other matter. After p. 456 is a sheet without pagination, under signature *N n n*. The first two leaves have "The Character of a Gentleman," another has an "Embleme," recto, and reverse "Upon the Errata," and fourth leaf blank. Then follows a new title :—

Three Choice characters of Marriage, fitly sorting with the proprietie and varietie of the former Subject: Having especiall relation to one peculiar Branch shadowed in the Sixt Observation.

These characters complete the volume with p. 487.

A sort of sequel or complement to the above work is another published in the following year, and entitled—

16. *The English Gentlewoman, drawne out to the full Body: Expressing*

 What Habilliments doe best attire her,
 What Ornaments doe best adorne her,
 What Complements doe best accomplish her.

By Richard Brathwait Esq. ... London, Printed by B. Alsop and T. Favvcet, for Michaell Sparke, dwelling in Greene Arbor. 1631, 4to, pp. 221.

The Frontispiece in compartments, intended as a companion to the one before the *English Gentleman*, is engraved by W. Marshall, and has a folding broadside prefixed explanatory of the subjects. After the printer's title twenty-two leaves of Dedications, and a table. After p. 221 is the character of "A Gentlewoman," four leaves, not paged, the "Embleme" and "Upon the Errata" two more. Some copies have an "Appendix upon a former supposed Impression of this title," consisting of five leaves, with signature in continuation, but not paged.

In the same year appeared

17. *Whimzies: Or, a new Cast of Characters. London, Printed by F. K. and are to be sold by Ambrose Rithirdon, at the signe of the Bull's-head, in Paul's Church-yard.* 1631. 12mo, 117 leaves.

Notices of this little volume will be found in Dr. Bliss's edition of Earle's Microcosmography,* and in Sir Egerton Brydges' Restituta;† but neither of these celebrated antiquaries and bibliographers seems to have been aware of its authorship. If the presence of the usual irrepressible note "Vpon the Errata's" did not alone suffice to authenticate it, some verses, at the end of the volume already quoted,

* Lond. 1811, p. 282.
† Vol. iv. p. 279. This notice was written however by Thomas Park.

'Upon the Birth-day of his sonne John,' certainly would.

The last 24 leaves of this book have a new title,—thus :

A Cater Character throwne out of a Boxe by an Experienc'd Gamester. London, Imprinted by F. K. and are to be sold by R. B. 1631. 24 leaves.

In both sections of the book BRATHWAITE assumes the name of "Clitus Alexandrinus," and both are dedicated to Sir Alexander Radcliffe.

On 7th March, 1633, after a married life of nearly sixteen years, BRATHWAITE had the misfortune to lose his wife, whom it seems he tenderly loved, and whose death he piously and sincerely mourned. In veneration of her memory, and as a public acknowledgment of her worth and virtues, he published for several years verses as the *Anniversaries upon his Panarete ;* and when reprinting the *Essays on the Five Senses* in 1635 he availed himself of the occasion to deliver a moral admonition to their youthfull offspring by introducing therein "Love's Legacy, or Panarete's blessing to her children," which is framed as if delivered in her very last moments, forbearing to speak of marriage as a matter beyond the apprehension of their tender years.

The first of these elegiac tributes appeared in the year following his wife's death, and is entitled :—

18. *Anniversaries upon his Panarete.* . . . *London, Imprinted by Felix Kyngston, and are to be sold by Robert Bostock, at the Kings Head in Pauls Church-yard.* 1634. 8vo, (containing 24 leaves not numbered—signature A, B, C.)

"To the indeered memory," the text begins, "of his ever loved, never too much lamented Panarete, M^{ris} Frances Brathwait," and he celebrates with much earnestness and eloquence her virtues, her person and her birth.

In 1635 BRATHWAITE published

19. *Raglands Niobe: or Elizas Elegie: Addressed to the unexpiring memory of the most noble Lady, Elizabeth Herbert, wife to the truly honourable Edward Somerset Lord Herbert, &c. By Ri. Brathwait, Esq.* 12mo, 14 leaves.

The imprint is substantially the same as that of the last article. At the end was appended a continuation of the *Anniversaries upon his Panarete.*

In the same year appeared

20. *The Arcadian Princesse; or the Triumph of Ivstice: Prescribing excellent rules of Physicke, for a sicke Iustice. Digested into fowre Bookes, and faithfully rendred to the originall Italian Copy,** *By Ri. Brathwait Esq. London, Printed by Th. Harper for Robert Bostocke.* 1635. 12mo.

Prefixed is an engraved title, by W. Marshall, of the figure of "The Arcadian Prin-

---

* By Mariano Silesio.

cesse" seated on a throne holding the scales of Justice, wherein an old man labelled "*forma pauperis*" weighs down another well clothed, labelled "*Ira potentis.*" Other sentences appear in several labels, and on the foot of the throne "by Ric. Brathwait Armig." Dibdin bestows high praise in his *Bibliomania** on the poetical portion of this volume. "Whoever does not see," he says, "in these specimens, some of the most powerful rhyming couplets of the early half of the seventeenth century, if not the model of some of the verses in Dryden's satirical pieces, has read both poets with ears differently constructed from those of the author of this book."

21. *The Lives of all the Roman Emperors, being exactly collected from Iulius Cæsar, unto the now reigning Ferdinand the second. With their births, Governments, remarkable Actions, and Deaths. London : Printed by N. and J. Okes, and are to be sold within Turning-stile in Holborne.* 1636. 12mo. pp. 384.

An engraved title, by W. Marshall, gives several medallions of the Roman Emperors, and a small one of the author, of nearly similar representation with that prefixed to the Paraphrase of the Psalms.

22. *A Spiritual Spicerie: Containing Sundrie sweet Tractates of Devotion and Piety. By Ri. Brathwait, Esq. London, Printed by I. H.*

---

* Lond. 1811, pp. 395-7.

for George Hutton at his shop within Turning stile in Holborne. 1638. 12mo. 247 leaves.

The section of this volume entitled "Holy Memorials" contains some interesting autobiographical details, from which we have already quoted, respecting the author's early life.

23. *The Psalmes of David the King and Prophet, and of other holy Prophets, paraphras'd in English : Conferred with the Hebrew Veritie, set forth by B. Arias Montanus, together with the Latine, Greek Septuagint, and Chaldee Paraphrase. By R. B. London, Printed by Robert Young, for Francis Constable, and are to be sold at his shop under S. Martins Church neere Ludgate.* 1638. 12mo. pp. 300.

This little volume has an engraved title by Marshall, representing in three-quarter figures (miniature ovals), Moses, David, Asaph, Heman, and Æthan. Various instruments of music, as improving psalmody, are hung against a pedestal upon each side of the title, which is given in an oval tablet as "by R. B. Esq." Beneath the title, in another small oval, is a portrait of BRATHWAITE, subscribed *Quanquam δ*. It has been contended that this version of the Psalms has been wrongly attributed to BRATHWAITE, and that the initials "R. B." belong to some other writer of the time. But collateral evidence is not wanting. That of the portrait, which, though it represents him with the gravity of advanced years, still bears a resemblance easily traceable to the more youthful likeness, has been already mentioned; there is the further evidence of the use of the digit or index (at p. 284) used also in *The Survey of History* and in *Barnabee's Journey;* and of the never-failing Apology for the Errata, found in all BRATHWAITE'S books.

After remaining a widower for six years BRATHWAITE married again in 1639, taking for his second wife Mary, daughter of Roger Crofts, of Kirtlington, in Yorkshire; who was well jointured, being seised in her own right of the valuable manor of Catterick. He describes her in *Panaretes Triumph* as a widow and a native of Scotland. Their issue was one son—the gallant Stafford Brathwaite, who was afterwards knighted, and killed in the ship "Mary," under the command of Sir Roger Strickland, during an engagement with the "Tyger" Algerine man of war.

Some time after his second marriage he quitted Burneshead, probably to occupy the Manor house at Catterick. The fevered state of the times might partly cause him to quit the old family residence. BRATHWAITE was "a subject sworn to loyalty" and not likely at that period to escape the common wrack of power. Lavish hospitality in support of the Royal cause on the one hand, and contributions imperiously demanded and violently enforced in the name of either the Parliament or the

Army upon the other, would serve equally to impoverish his hereditary property, and to make a removal to the newly-acquired estate at Appleton a matter of convenience to prevent shading family honours. His possession of the Manor is confirmed by several documents, and it is probable that with the family of Crofts he had been, long before his second marriage, in close or neighbourly intimacy.

We continue our list of BRATHWAITE'S publications.

24. *Ar't asleepe Husband? A Boulster Lecture; stored with all variety of witty jeasts, merry Tales, and other pleasant passages; Extracted from the choicest flowers of Philosophy, Poesy, antient and moderne History. Illustrated with Examples of incomparable constancy, in the excellent History of Philocles and Doriclea. By Philogenes Panedonius.** London, Printed by R. Bishop for R. B. or his Assignes. 1640. 8vo. pp. 330.

A frontispiece engraved by Marshall represents a man and wife in bed, the female—a Mrs. Caudle of the seventeenth century—delivering her admonitions to a deaf ear. To the strong internal evidence of this work being the production of BRATHWAITE may be added as two convincing and independent proofs forming an absolute confirmation of his title, 1. A

---

* The second section of his *Times Cvrtaine Drawne*, 1621, had been entitled " Panedone: or Health from Helicon."

reference which occurs at p. 201 to one of his acknowledged pieces, the Comment upon the Wife of Bath ; and 2. the introduction into the present volume of two or three pieces of poetry that first appeared in the *Strappado.*

25. *The Two Lancashire Lovers: or the Excellent History of Philocles and Doriclea. Expressing the faithfull constancy and mutuall fidelity of two loyall Lovers. . . . By Musæus Palatinus. . . . London, Printed by Edward Griffin, for R. B. or his Assignes.* 1640. 8vo. pp. 268.

There is an engraved title, and at p. 247, a second embellishment, which is found also in some copies of the *Boulster Lecture.*

In 1641 appeared a new edition of BRATHWAITE'S English Gentleman and English Gentlewoman, in one volume, folio, with the addition of a piece entitled *The Tvrtles Triumph.* In an engraved title there is an interesting display of the principal subjects discussed in the two works, after the manner, but not precisely copied from the titles to the earlier editions. The figures are nearly all changed, the mottoes omitted, and much of the garniture altered. Whether this deviation from the original designs obtained the sanction of the author seems doubtful, unless he was too indolent to revise the broadside containing an explanation of the frontispiece, as the two sheets of the first edition are here printed together without alteration.

Haslewood attributes the following work to BRATHWAITE on account of "the mannerism of style, which his many unacknowledged publications now compel us to confidently rely upon :"—

26. *The Penitent Pilgrim. London, Printed by Iohn Dawson, and are to be sold by Iohn Williams at the signe of the Crane in Pauls Church-yard.* 1641. 12mo. pp. 445.

It has an engraved frontispiece, by our author's usual artist, W. Marshall, of an aged man journeying barefoot with bottle and staff, scallop shell in his hat, his loins girded, and beneath his feet the legend: " Few and evill have the dayes of my life been." On the last leaf a quaint couplet occurs before the

Errata.

"No place but is of Errors rife
In labours, lectures, leafes, lines, life."

27. *Mercurius Britannicus. Tragi-Comoedia Lutetiæ, summo cum applausu publicè acta.* 15 leaves. 4to. (no place or date.)

Mercurius Britanicus, or The English Intelligencer A Tragic-Comedy, At Paris acted with great applause. Printed in the yeare 1641. 17 leaves. 4to.

This was a political squib; and considering the ready pen of BRATHWAITE, and his unceasing desire to attain popularity, we may conclude it was not the only time-serving piece he put forth at that eventful period. It is interesting also as an earlier exhibition than *Barnabee's Journal* of his facile skill in using the Latin tongue.

28. *Astræa's Teares. An Elegie Vpon the death of that Reverend, Learned and Honest Judge, Sir Richard Hutton Knight; Lately one of his Majesties Iustices in his Highnesse Court of Common Plees at Westminster. London, Printed by T. H. for Philip Nevil, and are to be sold at his Shop in Ivie Lane, at the signe of the Gun.* 1641. 12mo. sig. H. 2. (55 leaves).

A frontispiece, with all the strength and spirit of Marshall, contains a whole length figure of the Judge in his robes, in a reclining posture. It is an excellent portrait, and of the greatest rarity, not being noticed by Grainger. As early as 1614 our author dedicated *The Prodigals Teares* to Richard Hutton, Sergeant at Law, and *The Shepheards Tales* in the present volume were inscribed seven years later "To my worthie and affectionate kinsman Richard Hutton, Esquire, Sonne and Heire to the much honoured and sincere dispenser of judgement, Sir Richard Hutton, Sergeant at Law, and one of the Iudges of the Common Pleas."

Sir Richard Hutton died February 26, 1638, so that this Elegy did not appear until three years after that event. In a marginal note in this volume there is a reference to the 5th Anniversary upon his *Panarete*, and he therefore seems to have continued these yearly celebrations of his first wife (to have written, at any rate, if not to have published them) at least until the year of his second marriage.

29. *Panaretes Trivmph; or Hymens heavenly Hymne. London, Printed by T. H. for Philip Nevil, and are to be sold at his Shop in Ivie Lane, at the signe of the Gun.* 1641.

The poem begins at the back of the title:

" Remove that funerall-pile ; now six whole yeares
Have beene the nursing mothers of my teares."

He then describes the necessity of foregoing funeral tears during another nuptial, and they are to be preserved for those who cannot weep; as "spritely blades—some widows—profuse gallants," whose necessity in that respect is interestingly described. His moral reflections conclude as the bell tinketh: he married a second time a lady of Scottish extraction, which occasions his introducing "Calliopees expostulation with the Calidonian Nation." A "courteous Curtain Lecture" is also delivered by his wife and a florid description is given of her person and manners.

We now come to the famous volume of doggerel rhymes by which BRATHWAITE is chiefly remembered outside the narrow circle of scholars and students. Though as voluminous a writer both in prose and verse as his contemporary Wither, by this one work, or rather happy *jeu d'esprit*, he is now chiefly known to the general world of English readers. This unique and curious publication is written both in Latin and English, the double title being as follows :—

30. *(a) Barnabæ Itinerarium, Mirtili & Faustuli nominibus insignitum: Viatoris Solatio nuperrimè editum, aptissimis numeris redactum, veterique Tono Barnabæ publicè decantatum. Authore Corymbœo.*

(b) Barnabees Journall, Under the Names of Mirtilus & Faustulus shadowed : for the Travellers Solace lately published, to most apt numbers reduced and to the old Tune of Barnabe commonly chanted. By Corymbæus.

The date of the original edition has never been precisely ascertained, but is supposed to be about 1648-1650. The authorship of this anonymous book, after long remaining unknown, was settled upon BRATHWAITE by Haslewood by means of a chain of laborious and irrefragable evidence, both external and internal. The internal evidence is alone conclusive; such as the reappearance in Barnabees Journal of stories told in BRATHWAITE'S other works ; thus the story of hanging the cat at Banbury had originally appeared in a short poem in the *Strappado*, p. 109. The story of Grantam *(Grantham)* spire is introduced in the *Arcadian Princess*, with the name of "Grantam" transposed into *Margant*. There are allusions also which are evidently autobiographical, such as those to Kendal and to Nesham, where BRATHWAITE wooed and won his first wife. In describing Lancaster he alludes to John a Gaunt, and he does the same at the opening of his *Two Lancashire Lovers*, 1640. Other similarities of versification mottoes, proverbs, Apology for Errata, &c., complete the internal evidence.

"It was reserved," says Southey, "for famous Barnaby to employ the barbarous ornament of rhyme so as to give thereby point and character to good Latinity."*

We know from his other writings that BRATHWAITE was an excellent Latin scholar. The external evidence of BRATHWAITE'S authorship is threefold. 1. Thomas Hearne the antiquary says in a manuscript note: "The book called Barnabas's Rambles, printed in Latin and English, was written by RICHARD BRATHWAITE, who writ and translated a vast number of things besides, he being the scribler of the times. Anthony-à-Wood does not mention this amongst his works. But Mr. Bagford tells me that Mr. Chr. Bateman (an eminent Bookseller in Pater Noster Row) who was well acquainted with some of the family, hath several times told him that BRATHWAITE was the author of it."†

---

* Quarterly Review, No. xxxv. p. 32.
† *Hearne's MS. Collections for the year* 1713, vol. xlvii. p. 127.

2. In a copy of the second edition, 1716, that belonged to Edward Wilson, Esq., of Dallam Tower in Westmoreland (a descendant on the maternal side of the elder branch of the Brathwaites), was written the following note: —"*The Author I knew* was an old Poet RICH. BRATHWAITE, Father to Sir Thomas of Burnside-Hall, near Kendall in Westmorland."

3. There was sold by Messrs. Leigh and Sotheby at the sale of the Library of John Woodhouse, Esq., 12th Dec., 1803 (lot 24) a copy of the original edition of Barnabee's Journal, with a poem in manuscript copied on the fly-leaves undoubtedly by BRATHWAITE, entitled: "*Rustica Academiæ Oxoniensis nuper reformatæ Descriptio, &c.* CLƆDCXLVIII."

Here is a weight of cumulative evidence that is irresistible.

It is evident, however, that though the *Journal* was probably not published until about the middle of the century, the earlier portions of it at least had been written many years previously. "Many circumstances," says Haslewood, "unite to confirm the belief that the *Itinerary* was the lapped and cradled bantling of years, scarcely in the author's own opinion pubescent, until himself might be believed past the age of such waggery. It may be characterized as a seedling planted in the spring of youth; nourished and pruned in the summer of his days; courted to blossom amid evergreens that circled his autumnal brow, and which formed the wreath of fame that adorned and cheered the winter of his age, and remains unfaded."

The next work on our list is

31. *A Muster Roll of the evill Angels embatteld against S. Michael. Being a Collection, according to the order of time, (throughout all the Centuries) of the chiefe of the Ancient Heretikes, with their Tenets, such as were condemned by Generall Councels. Faithfully collected out of the most Authentike Authors. By R. B. Gent. London, Printed for William Sheers, and are to be sold at his shop in S. Pauls Church yard at the sign of the Bible.* 1655. 24mo. pp. 94.

Then follows:

32. *Lignum Vitæ. Libellus in quatuor partes distinctus: et ad utilitatem cujusque Animæ in altiorem vitæ perfectionem suspirantis, Nuperrimè Editus. Authore Richardo Brathwait Armigero; Memoratissimæ matris, florentissimæ Academiæ Oxoniensis Humillimo Alumno. Londini, Excudebat Joh. Grismond.* MDCLVIII. 12mo. pp. 579.

This volume has an engraved title by Vaughan, crowded as usual with Latin sentences applicable to the figure and design. It is divided into three parts, and at the end of the second is a piece of Latin poetry of forty stanzas that corroborates the appropriation already made of Barnabee's Journal.

33. *The Honest Ghost, or A Voice from the Vault. London, Printed by Ric. Hodgkinsonne.* 1658. 8vo. 169 leaves.

The book consists of two subjects and is distinguished by these two titles, 1. The Honest Ghost. 2. An Age for Apes. Each of these has a frontispiece by Vaughan; the latter begins at page 115. There are some Latin rhyming couplets at p. 319, exactly in the style and metre of the Itinerary:

> "Neque dives, nec egenus,
> Neque satur, neque plenus;
> Nec agrestis, nec amœnus,
> Nec sylvestris, nec serenus;
> Palmis nec mulcendus pænis
> At in omni sorte lenis."

At the Restoration of Charles the Second, BRATHWAITE, who had always been loyal to the King's cause, published some gratulatory verses:

34. *To his Majesty upon his happy arrivall in our late discomposed Albion. By R. Brathwait, Esq. London, Printed for Henry Brome, at the Gun in Ivie-lane,* 1660. 4to. 8 leaves.

In this poem he declares himself to have been a resolute sufferer for both sovereign and country, and depicts the very impaired state of his fortune.

35. *The Captive-Captain : or the Restrain'd Cavalier. Drawn to his full Bodie in Eight*

Characters. Lond. Printed by J. Grismond, 1665. 8vo. 98 leaves.

36. *Tragi-Comoedia, Cui in titulum inscribitur Regicidium, Perspicacissimis Judiciis acuratius perspecta, pensata, comprobata ; Authore Ri. Brathwait, Armigero, utriusque Academiæ Alumno. Londini, Typis J. G. & prostat venalis in officinâ Theodori Sadleri, in Strandensi &c.* 1665. 8vo. pp. 192.

Last, but not least, among the publications of BRATHWAITE comes his Commentary on Chaucer, planned and probably written many years before.

37. *A Comment upon the Two Tales of our Ancient, Renowned, and Ever Living Poet Sr Jeffray Chavcer, Knight. . . . . The Millers Tale and The Wife of Bath. Addressed and published by Special Authority. London, Printed by W. Godbid, and are to be sold by Robert Clavell at the Stags-Head in Ivy-lane,* 1665. 8vo. pp. 199.

In perusing the foregoing voluminous list of works the reader will not fail to be struck by the strange alternation they exhibit of buffoonery and jesting, and of piety and sanctity. That the same author should have successively written books so dissimilar in character would seem almost incredible to any one unacquainted with the fashions and temper of that age, and with the numerous other and more illustrious instances of the same curious medley or conglomeration. In some of his earlier plays—in the Blind Beggar of Alexandria, A Humorous Day's Mirth, Monsieur d'Olive, The Widow's Tears, might we not equally say that we fail to recognise the grave translator of Homer, and the Christian pietist who paraphrased Petrarch's Penitential Psalms? If the sins of his youth are forgiven to George Chapman let them not be too heavily remembered against the less famous RICHARD BRATHWAITE.

BRATHWAITE "left behind him," says Wood, "the character of a well-bred gentleman and good neighbour," and to this might be added, of a Christian and upright man. A description of his person has descended orally, by which the trim fashion of his green years added comeliness to his gray hairs. Tradition reports him to have been in person below the common stature; well-proportioned, and one of the handsomest men of his day; remarkable for ready wit and humour; charitable to the poor in the extreme, so much so as to have involved himself in difficulties. He commonly wore a light grey coat, red waistcoat and leather breeches. His hat was a high-crowned one, and beyond what was common in those days when such hats were worn. His equals in life bestowed on him the name of 'Dapper Dick.' In disposition he was as admirable as in person; and he always took a conspicuous part in his neighbourhood in promoting the festivities of Christmas; so that in those good old times he was long the darling and favourite of that side of the country.

The death of RICHARD BRATHWAITE took place at East Appleton, a small township of and adjoining to Catterick, on 4th May, 1673, in the eighty-sixth year of his age. He was buried in the parish church of Catterick, where a monument was erected to his memory on the north side of the chancel.

The present is a literal Reprint; all the peculiarities of spelling being carefully preserved; even the innumerable blunders in the Latin and Greek marginal notes have been exactly reproduced, although, from the blurred and indistinct manner in which many of them are printed, it has been almost impossible sometimes to decipher them.

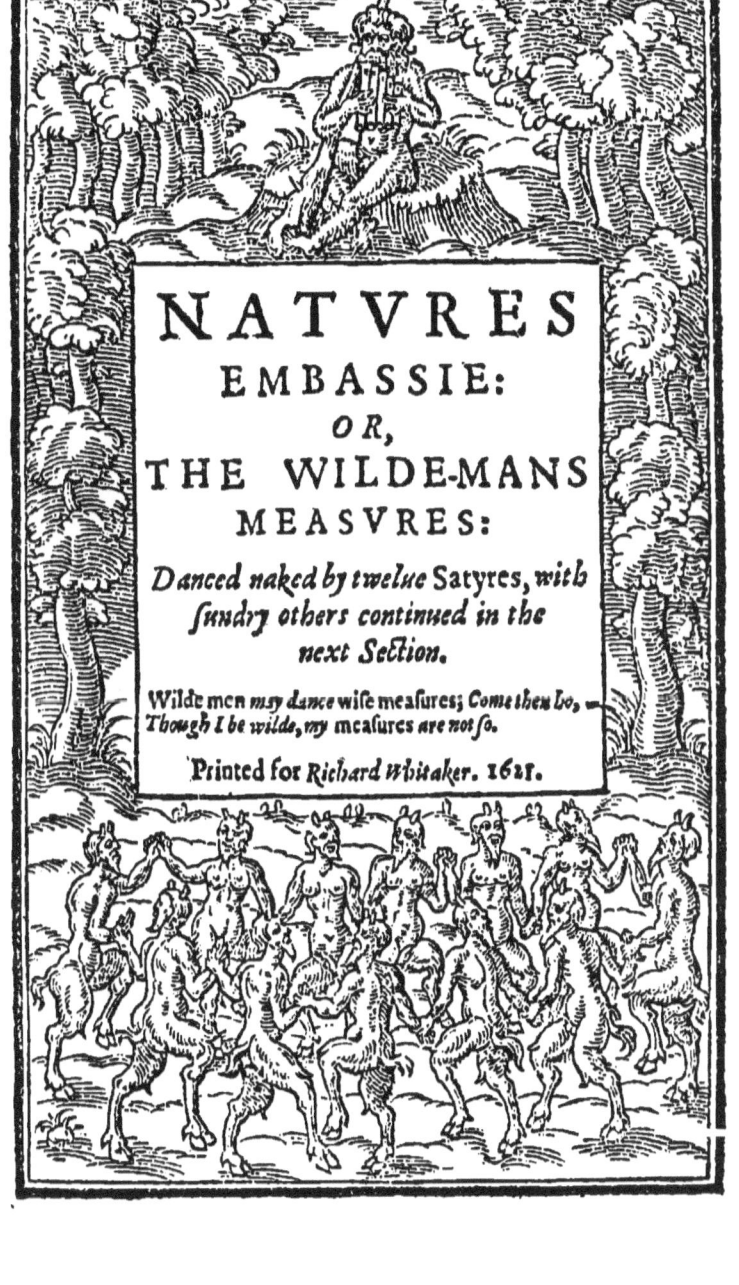

NATVRES
EMBASSIE:
OR,
THE WILDE-MANS MEASVRES:

Danced naked by twelue Satyres, *with sundry others continued in the next Section.*

Wilde men *may dance* wife measures; Come then ho,
Though I be wilde, *my* measures are not so.

Printed for *Richard Whitaker.* 1621.

TO THE ACCOM-
PLISHED MIRROR OF TRVE
worth, S^r. T. H. the elder, knight, pro-
feſſed fauorer and furtherer of all free-
borne ſtudies : continuance of
all happineſſe.

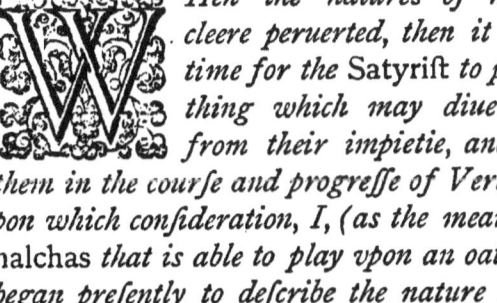*Hen the natures of men are cleere peruerted, then it is high time for the* Satyriſt *to pen ſom-thing which may diuert them from their impietie, and direct them in the courſe and progreſſe of Vertue ; vp-pon which conſideration, I, (as the meaneſt* Me-nalchas *that is able to play vpon an oaten pipe) began preſently to deſcribe the nature of* Men, *made ſo farre good by obſeruation, as my weake and immature iudgement could attaine vnto ; meaning to make the Poets verſe an Axiome :*
Scribimus indocti, doctiq; poemata paſſim.
This thus diſcuſſed and weyed, I was long in doubt to whom I ſhould dedicate this vnfruit-full vintage, rather gleanings, or whō I ſhould

flie

The Epistle

flie vnto for sanctuarie, if the sinister Reader (as who euer wrote without his Detractour) *should carpe at my labours. Wherefore standing longer in suspence then the matter required, I picked forth your selfe, most able to weaue an Apologie for your friends defects.* Let not therefore the maleuolent censures of such men whose chiefest eye-sores be other mens workes, and whose choisest content is to blemish them with imperfections, receiue the least countenance from you, whose iudgement by giuing these my labours approbation, shal be a greater argument of their merit, then their partiall censures shall argue their want. Hiparchion *was graced as well as* Musæus, *though the best of his measures was but piping to the* Muses. *For the paines of well-affected Authors neuer faile of patrons (at least amongst ingenuous men) to protect thē, of fauorites to second them, or guardians during their minoritie to foster them. And such is your integritie and true loue to learning, that the meanest sheepheard if he flie for refuge vnder your shelter, shall be accepted aboue the measure of his deserts, or meanes of his hopes. For without question, if your acceptance did not far exceed the height and weight of my Discourse,* Quid hic nisi vota supersunt? *there would nothing remaine for me, but to fall to my prayers,*

in

Dedicatorie.

in beseeching the kind & vnkind Reader (like our penurious pamphlet Orator) to commiserate my Treatise, and in stead of a narration, to make a publike supplication: but being protected by the singular care and prouiding eye of your fauours;
—Maior sum quàm cui potuit fortuna nocere.

I haue penned this short Discourse, interwouen with history as well as poesie, for two things summarily, and especially for the first thereof. The first is the iniquitie of this present time wherein we liue: so that Nature *had either time now to send an* Ambassage *or neuer: since*

* Mulier formosa superne
definit in piscem—

* Atq; homines prodigia rerum maxima.

Such is the course of degenerate Nature, *that in a conceipt of her selfe she thinks she can mend her selfe by being adorned with vnnaturalized ornaments, which* Nature *neuer apparelled her with. The second reason is the motion of a priuate friend of mine, whose pleasure may command my whole meanes, yea my selfe to the vttermost of my abilitie. These reasons haue I alledged, lest my Preface should seeme naked of Reason, which were ridiculous to the reasonable Reader, and to you especially, whose maturitie in arguments of this Qualitie, hath gained you a deserued Opinion, enabled by Iudgement, of power to counteruaile the censures of others lesse iudicious.*

The Epistle Dedicatorie.

iudicious. Thus tendring you the fruites of my Reading compiled, and in manner digested, not out of selfe-conceit, but aime to publique good intended, I rest. From my studie. May 24.

Yours to dispose

Richard Brathwayt.

The diſtinct ſubiect of euery Satyre, *contained in either* Section: *with an exact ſuruey or diſplay of all ſuch* Poems, *as are couched or compiled within this Booke.*

1. Degeneration, perſonated in *Nature*. [1]
2. Pleaſure, in *Pandora*. [5]
3. Ambition, in the Giants. [11]
4. Vaine-glory, in *Cræſus*. [16]
5. Crueltie, in *Aſtiages*. [22]
6. Adulterie, in *Clytemneſtra*. [27]
7. Inceſt, in *Tereus*. [31]
8. Blaſpemie, in *Caligula*. [34]
9. Beggarie, in *Hippias*. [41]
10. Miſerie, in *Taurus*. [49]
11. Hypocriſie, in *Claudius*. [51]
12. Exceſſe, in *Philoxenus;* with three funeral *Epicedes*, or Elegiack Seſtiads. [55]

The ſecond Section.

1. Sloth, in *Elpenor*. [77]
2. Corruption, in *Cornelia*. [82]
3. Atheiſme, in *Lucian*. [86]
4. Singularitie, in *Steichorus*. [94]
5. Dotage, in *Pigmalion*. [98]
6. Partialitie, in *Pytheas*. [106]
7. Ingratitude, in *Periander*. [108]
8. Flatterie, in *Terpnus*. [114]
9. Epicuriſme, in *Epicurus*. [127]
10. Briberie, in *Diagoras*. [134]

In-

11. Inuention, in *Triptolemus*. [136]
12. Difdaine, in *Melonomus*. [141]
13. Idolatrie, in *Protagoras*. [144]
14. Tyrannie, in *Eurysteus*. [148]
15. Securitie, in *Alcibiades*. [155]
16. Reuenge, in *Perillus*. [160]
17. Mortalitie, in *Agathocles*. [165]
18. In *Nafonem* Iuridicum. Mythologia. [168]

Two fhort moderne Satyres. [170]
Paftorall tales, or Eglogues. [175]
Omphale, or the inconftant fhepheardeffe. [263]

ODES.

1. The Trauellour. [289]
2. The Nightingale. [292]
3. The Lapwing. [293]
4. The Owle. [295]
5. The Merlin. [297]
6. The Swallow. [299]
7. The fall of the leafe. [301]

With two conclufiue Poems, entituled *Brittans Bliffe*. [305]
And an *Encomion* to the *Common Law*: or Aretenomia. [307]

The firſt Argument.

Ature the common mother (to vſe an Ethnicke induction) breedeth diuers effects, according to the conſtitution of each particular bodie, being compoſed and compacted of that *Matter* wherto we ſhall returne, being *Earth*. Now though *Nature* (as with the Morall Philoſopher I may ſay) neuer is deceiued, as ſhe is conſidered in her owne *frame*, bringing forth alwayes men able to the performing of humane functions, faire in proportion and ſtate of their bodies, apt for the atchiuing of anie matter either publike or priuate : yet notwithſtanding, manie times by euents and accidents, diuers deformities & blemiſhes appeare, which by *Nature* were not decreed to be : and like are the maleuolent affections ariſing from the diſtempered qualitie of the minde. And whereas many in the corruption of their erring opinions and reaſonleſſe arguments, have auerred how *Nature is the primarie mouer, conſeruer and preſeruer*, yet Seneca will tell you, that it is God that worketh theſe things which we aſcribe to a fained Deitie ; and that *Nature differeth no more from God or God from Nature*, then *Annæus* from *Seneca : [* Vide Epiſt. ad Lucil.]

as he speaketh in his naturall Questions, and in his bookes of Benefiting. But this was the opinion of such as had not the supreme light of deuine knowledge to them reuealed, but such as worshipped whatsoeuer they thought was a guider or director of them, or by custome (how ridiculous soeuer) was traduced to them. So we may reade in the ancient historians, of the Egyptians who adored whatsoeuer they thought comely, as the Sunne, the Moone, the starres and inferiour lights. Others worshipped trees, stockes, stones, and venimous serpents. Thus did the brutish affections of vnnaturall men shew their Gods by deciphering an heauenly power or influence, in Branches and such workes of Nature. But these though in no wise excusable, may admit some reasonable defence, forasmuch as their conceipt could reach no further. For as *Zenophanes* saith, *If beasts could paint, they would pourtray God to their owne shape and feature, because they could conceiue no further.* And this is the cause why the Heathen adored their plants, starres, and such creatures, inasmuch as they could not reach nor attaine to the knowledge of an higher Deitie. But to conferre them, that is, the Heathen and prophane people with the now-being Christians, it will seeme wonderfull, if I make manifest by relation had to their liues, how the depraued conditions of our Christians now adayes (whose knowledge giues them assurance of Eternitie) walke in as great blindnesse and palpable darknes as euer the Heathen did. And since the matter is most apparent,

as

Marginalia:
Vide Episto Alexand. de situ & statu Indiæ.

Zenophanes.

The occasion of this Treatise.

high time it is for *Nature* to fend her *Embaſſie* to this *Age* for her *Reformation.*

THE FIRST SATYRE.

*Hou wicked lumpe in a deformed guiſe,*
Tripping like Hymen *on his wedding day,*
Nature thy former Inſolence *defies,*
Saying thou erreſt from her natiue way:
For all thy fooliſh wayes are baits to *ſin,
Where vertue droupes, and vice comes dancing in.

* Prima eſt quaſi tittillato delectationis in corde, ſecunda conſenſio, tertium factum eſt conſuetuda. *Aug. Serm.* 44.

Doth not thy habite ſhew thy wanton mind,
Forward to all things but to vertuous life :
Paſſing thoſe bounds which Nature hath aſſign'd,
Twixt Art and Nature by commencing ſtrife ?
I tell thee, Nature ſends me to repreſſe
Thy fooliſh toyes, thy inbred wantonneſſe.

But thou wilt ſay, Nature hath made me faire,
Should I rob Beautie of her proper due ?
Should I not decke her with * embroidred haire,
And garniſh her with Flora's *vernant hue ?*
I muſt, I will, or elſe ſhould I diſgrace
With a rent maske the beautie of my face.

* Venuſtas tribuitur à natura, corrumpitur ab arte.

But I will anſwer thee for all thy beautie :
If thou wilt be an Ape in gay * attire,
Thou doeſt not execute that forme of dutie,
Which Nature at thy hand ſeemes to require :
Which not redreſt, for all thy goodly port,
Thou muſt be ſtript, and whipt, and chaſtiſd for't.

Nature hath sent me to forewarne thy wo,
Lest thou secure of thy distresse, reioyce:
If thou wax * proud, then where so ere thou go
Thou shalt decline: this resteth in thy choice,
Whether to die branded by Infamie,
Or to preserue thy life in memorie.

<small>* Sequitur superbos vltor à tergo Deus.</small>

This thus obserued, wilt thou yet be proud?
And grow ambitious, bearing in thy brow
The stampe of honour, as if thou hadst vow'd
No grace on thy inferiours to bestow?
Proud minikin let fall thy plumes, and crie
Nature, I honour will thy Embassie.

It was a good time when Eue *spun her threed,*
And Adam ** digg'd to earne his food thereby:*
But in this time Eues *do their panches feed,*
With daintie dishes mouing luxurie.
That was the golden age, but this is lead,
Where vice doth flourish, vertue lieth * dead.

<small>* Pastinatio deuinum opus. *Hesiod.*</small>

<small>* Damnosa quid non imminuet dies? ætas parentis peior est auis, &c.</small>

This therefore is my message pend by Truth,
Erected in the honour of Dame Nature,
Inueying gainst Pride, whose aspiring grouth
Disfigureth the beautie of the creature:
Thus haue I spoken that which Nature mou'd me,
Directed to thee, for Dame Nature lou'd thee.

The

The Argument.

H*Efiod* reporteth how *Pandora* was fent from *Iupiter* to deceiue mankind, at leaſt to make triall of his frailtie, by the free proffers of her bounty, fending her, full fraught with all Pleaſures, to the end ſome thereof might enſnare and infenſate the minds and affectiõs of the then liuing and inhabiting *Arcadians*, to whom her meſſage was principally addreſſed, as appeareth in the firſt booke of his *Opera & dies.*

This *Pandora* is voluptuous, (though her name ſignifie munificence, or an vniuerſall exhibitreſſe of all gifts) ſent to enthrall and captiuate the appetites and affections of men, to the intent they might yeeld themſelues vaſſals and bondſlaues to all ſenſuall deſires, foments of impietie, or agents of immodeſtie. And *Pandora* ſeemeth to make this ſpeech or oration vnto them, as an introduction formally handled, for their pleaſure & delectation. Louing Arcadians, if this ſpacious world now ſo ſpecious (whilome an indigeſted *chaos*) were firſt ordained for a place of libertie, do not you make it a cage of reſtraint. It was the will of Nature, who not onely founded but diſpoſed of this vniuerſe as you ſee, that *Men* the hope of her loines and ioy of her life, ſhould liue delicioufly, and not be enfeebled by ſtrict & rigorous abſtinence the

Mother of difeafes, feeding and nourifhing many groffe and maleuolent humours, whereby the health vfeth to be empaired, and the whole ftate of your bodies diffolued. Wherefore *Iupiter* as your common prouider, forefeeing thofe miferies which were incident before my coming to all mankind, hath now appointed *Me* as *Deputie* to bring this meffage vnto you, that from henceforth you fhould wallow in pleafures and delights according to your owne defires and affections. Let not fruitleffe *Abftinence* be a meanes to reftraine you, or *Temperance* a chaine to withhold you, but like *Talaffioes* companions bid continencie adieu, and make hafte to lafciuious meetings: for to make recourfe to the principall delight of a knowing man, *Contemplation*, is it not tedious to spend a mans time in ftudie or endleffe fpeculation? Yes certainly, nothing can be worfe then to wafte mans life like *Epictetus* lampe; nothing better then to cōfume mans daies in *Polixenus* cell. And though *Epictetus* may fay, *Semper aliquid difcens fenefco*, alwayes learning I grow aged, yet *Polixenus* may auerre a matter though of leffe confequence, yet a practife of more felf-forgetting chearfulneffe,—*Semper aliquid bibens, nihil extimefco*, alwayes drinking I am cheered. So that nothing can abafh *Polixenus*, nothing can difmay him: for his daily practife exempts him from meditation of griefe, being as remote from danger as he ftands fecure for honour, making euery day his owne prouider, and ftanding as refpectleffe of pofteritie as he is careleffe in hoording Treafure.

He

He is happie, and free from dangers menacing abroad, or afpiring thoughts (Ambitions fubtileſt traines) vndermining at home. But *Epictetus* feare proceedeth from the height of his knowledge, fearing Death the abridgement of knowledge: yet feareleſſe of Death it ſelfe, for it is nothing; but the iſſue of Death making his knowledge nothing. *Polixenus* none can diſturbe; for his minde is fixed on that obiect, which is placed before him; ſince Nature hath alotted him meate, drinke and apparell, he respects no more. Yet as rich as *Bias*, for he can ſing,—*Omnia mea mecum porto*. But ſimple *Epictetus*, who repoſeth ſo great truſt in his Contemplatiue part, whereto auailes his ſtudie? whereto tendeth this Speculation? ſince Art hath made him no wiſer then to make no difference betwixt wine and water. Neither hath Art made him any thing the richer: for his *Lanterne* is of more value then all the reſt of his ſubſtance. Then as you will haue regard to your eſtate or to the health of your delicate bodies, ponder the effect of my Oration, and reape thoſe ſenſible delights made yours by fruition, in contempt of Stoicke and ſtrict contemplation.

When *Pandora* had made this plauſiue Oration, mans minde (by an inbred appetite to what is pleaſant) was ſoone addicted and inclined to the premiſes; exclaiming with *Herodian*, that it was a difficult thing to ſubdue a mans affections. Wherfore no ſooner was *Pandora* gone, but preſently they * began to caſt off the reines of diſcipline, expoſing themſelues to follie and all recreancie.

* Subſidebat autem in imo vaſe, ſpes.

8   OF PLEASVRE.

Now fee into the Morall hereof, how Man is moft addicted to that which in it owne nature is moft depraued, alwayes faying with *Medæa* in the Tragedie,—*video meliora probóque Deteriora fequor.*

Such is the crookedneffe of mans nature, that he is prone to the worfe part, and confequently like foolifh *Epimetheus* readie to receiue *Argicida's* rewards, fubiects of impietie and lafciuious defires, as * *Hefiod* reporteth of him. *Iupiter sent cunning Argicidas to Epimetheus,* with intent to enfnare his affections with the faire fhew of fuch pleafant * rewards as he brought with him; namely tempting obiects like *Athalantaes apples,* whereby fhe was deluded, her fpeed fore-flowed, becoming a prey to *Pomæis* that fubtile courfer as he himfelfe wifhed.

Such are the gifts of Nature, which oft bewitch the mind of the receiuer. So that *Elpenor* was neuer more deformed (whofe feature became the prodigie of Nature) then *He* who fuffereth his minde (the light of his body) to be by thefe gifts befotted. For firft he takes a view of them; then he defires them, and after the defire he entertaines them. Which receit is no fooner made, then *Cyrces* with her Cup, or the Syrens with their voyce, inchant thefe poore companions of *Vliffes*: but he who *Vliffes*-like ftands firme, and not to be remoued by any fond alluremēt, carrying with him that * *Moli* or herbe of grace by which all charmes are fruftrated, fhall be a fpectator of his Companions mifery, in himfelfe fecured while they are

fplit-

* Ad Epymerhea Iupiter mifit inclytum Argicidam, munera ferentem deorū celerem nuncium, &c.
* Floremiuuentutis non deciduum.

* Homerus in Odiff.

OF PLEASVRE. [9]

splitted, which I, in this second Satyre briefly and compendiously collected (as well by reading as obseruation seconded) haue by a morall inference in some sort declared.

THE SECOND SATYRE.

Pandora the inchantresse.

Pandora, *shall she so besot thy mind,*
That nothing may remaine for good instruction?
Shall she thy mind in chaines and fetters bind,
Drawing thee onward to thy owne destruction?
Be not so foolish, lest thou be oretaken,
And in thy shipwracke liue as one forsaken.

For though that Nature which first framed thee,
Seeme to winke at thy crimes a day or two,
Yea many yeares, yet she hath blamed thee
For thy offences, therefore act no more.
Though she delay assure thee she will call,
And thou must pay both vse and principall.

She smileth at thy locks brayded with gold,
And in derision of thy selfe-made shape,
Who would beleeue (faith * she) this is but mold,
Who trips the streets like to a golden Ape?
Nature concludes, that Art hath got the prize,
And she must yeeld vnto her trumperies.

For I haue seene (faith Nature) what a grace
Art puts vpon me, with her painted colour:
How she * Vermillions ore my Maiden-face,

* Bella es nouimus & puella, verū est: & diues: Quis enim potest negare? Sed dum te nimium laudas, nec diues, neque bella, nec puella es. *Martial in Epigram.*
* Nonne vulgatum est bonas formas cerussa deuenustare? *Pic. Miran. in Epist.*

Now

Now nought so faire, though nought before was fouler;
Indeed I am indebted to her loue,
That can giue moueleſſe Nature meanes to moue.

Thou black-fac'd Trull, how dar'ſt thou be ſo bold,
As to create thy ſelfe another face?
How dar'ſt thou Natures feature to controle,
Seeking by Art thy former to diſgrace?
By heauens I loath thee for thy Panthers skin,
Since what is faire without is foule within.

Indeed thou art aſhamed of thy forme:
And why? becauſe of beautie thou haſt none;
Nay rather grace, by which thou may'ſt adorne
Thy inward part, which chiefly graceth one;
,, Complaine of Nature (graceleſſe) and deſpaire,
,, Since ſhe hath made thee foule, but others faire.

* Talis ornatus non eſt Dei.

But yet thou wilt be faire, if * painting may
Affoord thee grace and beautie in thy brow:
Yet what auailes this fondling? for one day
Painting will ceaſſe: though painting flouriſh now;
,, Itch not then after faſhions in requeſt,
,, But thoſe that comelieſt are, eſteeme them beſt.

Yet for all this, I pittie thee poore foule,
In that Dame Nature hath not giuen thee beautie;
Hang downe thy head like to a deſart Owle,
Performe in no caſe to her ſhrine thy dutie
Vnto her altar vow no ſacrifice,
Nor to her deitie erect thine eyes:

Thou

Thou haſt good cauſe for to lament thy birth;
For none will court thee ſmiling at thy feature,
But prize thee as the refuſe vpon earth,
Since on my faith thou art an vglie creature,
Yet ill wine's good when it is in the caske,
And thy face faire oreſhadow'd with a maske.

O be contented, with thy forme, thy feature,
Since it is good enough for wormes repaſt,
Yeelding thy due vnto the ſhrine of Nature,
The faireſt faire muſt yeeld to death at laſt!
Thinke on thy mould, and thou wilt ſeriouſly
Receiue the charge of Natures Embaſſie.

The Argument.

IF I ſhould intreate of ſuch affaires as rather conferre vnto a warlike diſcourſe, then reforming of the multiplicity of errors raging & reigning in this Age, ſtrangely depraued, and in the vniuerſall ſtate of her body diſtempred, I might ſeeme to make an vnprofitable meſſenger in this weighty Embaſſie: but to that end haue I choſen ſuch matter as may be a motiue for the furtherance of this mine aſſay. When this — *indigeſta moles*, this vnſeaſoned peece of matter had firſt receiued ſome forme or faſhion, then preſently as it increaſed in yeares, ſo it began to adorne it ſelfe with a comely preſence, fence, attired modeftly without affectatiõ, feemely without curiofitie, fimply without the vanitie of Art, knowing what was fhame without an artificiall blufh.

So that thofe dayes well deferued the name of —golden Age: for—*redeunt Saturnia regna.* But afterward by a degenerate, rather vnnaturall courfe (as what is not corrupted in time, if we confider her originall puritie) *A certaine kind of people*, as extraordinarie in proportion for their greatneffe, fo of vnbounded mind for their ambition and boldneffe, began firft to wage battell with the gods immortall: till the gods perceiuing their ftout and afpiring natures, ouerthrew them in their own practifes: for they did—*Imponere Pelion Offæ.* Tumble mount *Pelion* vpon *Offa*, whereby they might reach euen vnto heauen: but the gods made thofe mountaines the Giants fepulchers; where they lie (vnder thofe vaft hils) and euery feuenth yeare, as the Poets faine—*Sub tanti oneris immenfa mole corpora fubleuantes, & eorum opera perperam aggreffa execrantes*, they lie vnder the weight of fo great a burthen to giue them a fenfible touch of their former ambition. Not without an excellent morall inclufiuely fhadowed, and fitly applied to fuch ambitious heads who are alwayes afpiring high, till with the Giants they be caft downe, leauing no other monument to pofteritie, faue difhonour, the due guerdon of their impietie. And furely who fhall but confider the diuerfe fingular ends and purpofes wherto those pregnant fictions of the Poets were addreffed, wittily and emphatically

The Giants. Cæus, Iapetus, Typhæus.

OF AMBITION.

cally expreſſing *their* feuere and impartiall iudgements, iuſtly inflicted on offendors, ſhall ſee in them a wonderfull inuention, and a continuall diſcourſe, proceeding forward without any alteration, tedious digreſſion, or materiall difference in the relation. Againe, to obſerue the reuerence which euen the Pagan Authors vſed toward their gods, beginning no worke of what conſequence ſoeuer, without inuocation of their fained deities, would moue in vs a more ſerious admiration. So that as *Valerius Maximus* ſaith, *Ab Ioue optimo maximo or ſi ſunt pꝛiſci oratores: The ancient Orators vſed alwayes to begin their works* in their forme of pleading, with an auſpicious *Iupiter*, whereby their workes might haue good ſucceſſe and proceeding. So may I ſay, by a preſent application had to theſe times, *that as our beſt-promiſing labours become fruitleſſe, vnleſſe the Almightie proſper and giue them ſucceſſe: ſo by neceſſarie conſequence*, whoſoeuer falleth into contempt and deſpiſing of God immortall, ſhall haue his purpoſes defeated, and vtterly vanquiſhed with the forenamed Giants. Wherefore my third *Satyre* ſhall inueigh againſt ſuch as in contempt of God (giantlike) practiſe not onely to pull him from his *throne* by violence, but blaſpheme him through a forlorne and godleſſe inſolence, and as though God had not the power to reuenge, will extenuate his power and leſſen his maieſtie.

THE

THE THIRD SATYRE.

THou wicked Caitiffe proud of being nought,
    Wilt thou prouoke thy God to strike thee downe,
Since he with care and labour hath thee sought,
And diuerse fauours in his mercy showne?
Do not draw downe the viols of his ire,
Lest he reward thy sinne with quenchlesse fire.

Thou sillie worme compact of slimie mud,
Which shalt returne to earth from whence thou came,
Thou which conceiued was of corrupt bloud,
Thou wormlin, how dar'st thou reuile his name?
Farwell thou gracelesse Impe, thou saplesse branch,
Borne to contemne thy God, to cram thy panch.

Thou Epicure, that liu'st in liuing ill,
Liuing by louing to stretch forth thy gut,
Taking more pleasure thy deep panch to fill,
Then in thy maker confidence to put:
Thou for thy feeding shalt receiue thy food,
Amongst such vipers as shall sucke thy bloud.

It is the nature of the viperous brood,
To be the author of their parents death;
Like an * Hyrudo they do sucke their bloud,
And take away that breath, which gaue them breath,
Thou * viperlike disclaimes thy parents name,
As though to vtter him thou thought it shame.

Shame on thy naming, if thou wilt denie
Him, who first gaue thee breath and vitall spirit,

Him,

* *Horse-leach.*

* Vipera viperæ mortem adfert. Plin. in natur. Hist. dum pario, perio. ibidem. Præmorso Maris capite parit vipera.

OF AMBITION.

Him, who can giue thee true tranquillitie,
Him, who will shew thee meanes how to inherit ;
Leaue off thy foolish fantasies, be wise,
Lift vp thy eyes to him who gaue thee eyes.

But if (vngratefull wretch) thou feele his grace,
Yet wilt not yeeld him thanks for all his loue,
Be sure he will auert his diuine face,
And all his wonted mercies cleane remoue ;
So thou the swine that breakes the acorne-shell,
Regardest not the tree from whence they fell.

Be warn'd by Cœus, who with Giants power,
Thought with his fellowes to * clime vp to heauen,
But vanquish'd by his power doth all deuoure,
Vnder the ruggie mountaines are laid euen,
Therefore beware, aspire thou not so high,
Lest thou lie low, where those same Giants ly.

* *Saying with Tiridates* in *Tacitus*: Sua retinere, priuatæ domus, de alienis certare regia laus est.

Thou art a shadow, God the substance is,
Yet insubstantiate, whose Deitie
Doth comprehend all things, for all are his,
Yet he is not * contain'd most certainely,
For he is infinite in qualitie,
Endlesse in loue, boundlesse in quantitie.

Auicen. Thom. in quest. Aug. in Pelag.

* Continet omnia tamen non continetur ab aliquo.

As for his presence, it is euery where,
On * sea, on land, and in the depth of depths,
His prouidence in each place doth appeare,
His mercie is for generations kept,
Wilt thou (fond foole) contemne his heauenly power,
Who gouernes thee, point, moment, minute, houre.

* Terræ Marique Deus est, nec terræ Mariue homo est, qui nouit vbi Deus non est.

What

What though so many will entice to euill,
And in plaine tearmes denie the Deitie?
Let them remaine as fuell for the diuell,
Confeſſe thou ſtill his power effectually:
Looke in the Planets, and the ſtarres, whoſe light,
Giues record of his power, ſignes of his might.

If thou looke vpward, bodies there be manie,
Yet trouble they not one anothers motion,
If thou looke downward, there the *Sea doth moue thee,
Beating the ſhores, while ſhores beate backe the Ocean:
Looke to the earth, and thou wilt wonder there,
To ſee a Ball ſo firmely hang in Aire.

* *Threatning earth with inundations, yet bounded in with her banks as with a girdle.*

But if theſe motiues limit not thy will,
Then I'le endorſe this in thy forlorne brow,
How with thine owne hand, thou thy bloud doeſt ſpill,
The fruites whereof thy puniſhment ſhall ſhow,
Denie not him who neuer did deny,
For thy default vpon the Croſſe to die.

The Argument.

IT is reported of *Crœſus*, that he ſent for *Solon*, well perceiuing that he was eſteemed the wiſeſt in Greece: to the intent he might ſee him placed in his maieſty, pompe, and great ſolemnity. When *Solon* was come, he demanded of him, whom he
thought

OF VAINEGLORIE.

thought to be the happieſt man in the world; not doubting but he would conclude him to be the happieſt, conſidering the magnificence of himſelf, the admiration of his attendants, & the ſecurity of his ſtate, grounded on ſuch powerfull alliance. *Solon* (contrary to his expectance) replyed, He could iudge none truly happie before his death,—*Neminem ante obitum fœlicem eſſe arbitror.* Yet *Crœſus* would not let him go ſo, but demanded further: whom he thought then liuing to be the happieſt; whereto anſwered *Solon, Tellus;* & who next ſaith *Crœſus?* Next to *Tellus* do I eſteeme *Cleobis* & *Biton* (who died in the very performance of parentall obedience:) & ſo forward without the leaſt mention made of *Crœſus* felicitie. Whereby it ſeemed that *Crœſus* was much offended, though he cōcealde his anger for that preſent time, leſt the fooliſh conceipt of his ſelfe-eſteemed happineſſe ſhould become palpable. But within ſhort time afterward *He* found *Solons* ſaying moſt true : for being taken priſoner by *Cyrus* the Perſian king, he was grieuouſly puniſhed, & reſtrained by ſtraite ſeuere impriſonmēt, till ſuch time as a day was appointed for *Crœſus* death : & being to be ſet vpon the fagot, & ready to ſuffer death, he cried forth : *O Solon, Solon, vera ſunt quæ dixiſti neminem ante obitum fœlicem:* *Cyrus* hearing theſe words, and enquiring the meaning of them, preſently deliuered him, anſwering : *& ea quoque mihi euenire poſſunt.* Conſidering the ſtate of mans life to be vncertaine, and that none ought to plant his hopes vpon that ſtabilitie of fortune in terrene affaires, as to promiſe himſelfe

himselfe securitie in his state, or continuance of succeffe for one victorie atchieued: seeing her wings are not clipped, that her flight should be restrained, nor to any Prince so particularly engaged, that he onely should be by her attended. In briefe, as the onely hope of the vanquished consists in the expectance of all extremitie: so is it the principall glory of the Conquerour, to moderate his fortune by a mild and temperate bearing of himselfe to the conquered. Hence also haue wee sufficient argument of reproofe, towards such as take pleasure or delight in their abundance, as *Crœsus* did, so as their minds become drowned, hauing no respect to the eternitie promised. The reason is, they repose their beatitude and felicity in things transitorie and vncertaine, not looking vp to the Author of all blisse and happinesse, who is the director and protector of all men, disposing them to the line and leuell of his blessed will, by expecting them foreslowing, inuiting them resisting, recalling them wandering, and embracing them returning: without whose aide our strength is weakenesse, without whose light our sight is blindnesse, and without whose grace our endeuours are fruitlesse. For alas, what is mans direction but distraction, what is his knowledge but imperfection, and what is the best of his resolution but confusion, wanting his gracious preuention that giueth to each worke a happy period and conclusion? Especially in this curious and intricate Labyrinth of mans life, wherein many Cymmerian windings (to wit, priuate seducements)

OF VAINEGLORIE.

ments) are framed and cunningly contriued by that fubtil-winged *Dedalus*. So as miferably are we forced to erre and ftray, vnleffe by *Ariadnes* threed, that is, the heauenly light of Gods illuminating Spirit, we be directed and conducted in this vaft Theatre of intricacy, to the *flowrie Eden* of endleffe felicitie. For without that allworking power, we are ouerwhelmed with darkneffe, not able to attaine to the comfort of our foules, to enioy the fruition of eternall confolation in the life to come.

To fhew you the worthie intendments and refolutions of the *Ancient*, would but make a flourifh without effect: as by way of illuftration examplefide in mortification, to fhew you how *Origen* made himfelfe an Eunuch, *Democritus* put out his owne eyes, *Crates* caft his monie into the fea, *Thracius* cut downe all his vines. Seeing then that to examplifie a mans writings in these daies, is but to beate the aire, vnleffe inuection or a bitter Satyre moue it, I will make hafte to runne into my former reprehenfion, fince with *Iuuenall* I may well conclude,

Spite of our teeth when vice appeares in fight,
We muft the Satyres play, and tartly write:

Where a good Poets greateft difficultie, is to reftraine himfelfe from Satyricall poefie; for impiety like a tetter vniuerfally fpreading, is fuch, as no man but he will either be a gamefter or a fpectator in gaming: either wanton or a fauourite of wantonneffe: therefore now or neuer:

—*Rumpantur*

—Rumpantur Ilia Codri,
Inuidia.

Now to our Satyre.

THE FOVRTH SATYRE.

THou happie Crœsus in thy heapes of gold,
  Erect thy selfe a God vpon thy throne,
Let it be framed of a purer mold,
Then of the Pumice, or the marble stone:
Let it be honor'd euen in Crœsus name,
Since golden Crœsus did erect the same.

Wilt thou indeed, be honour'd for a god,
And with the starres aray thy Princely head?
Be sure ere long to feele an iron rod:
To crush thee downe, and thy accursed seede.
For if thou do denie * thy God his right,
He will depriue thy power, abridge thy might.

* Qui in Deum delinquit, eum relinquit.

Art thou a crauling worme, a feeble creature,
And yet dost thinke thy selfe a god on earth?
Canst thou so easily transforme thy nature:
Chang'd to immortall, from a mortall birth?
Poore simple gull, a cockhorse for this god,
No god but * man, whose sinnes deserue Gods rod.

* Homines cum hominibus sanguinem & genius miscent.

Star-staring earthling, puff'd with insolence,
Conceipted of thy selfe without desert,
Comparing with the Deuine excellence,
For which thy follie, thou shalt feele the smart;

Do

Do not * thinke God will suffer thee to raigne,
That sleights his workes, and takes his name in vaine.

* Quicquid à vobis minor extimescet, Maior hoc vobis dominus minatur.

And as for Crœsus, if he liue for aye,
Then will I thinke he is a god indeed:
But he ere long shall haue a dying day,
And be inclosed in an earthly weede.
Therefore fond Crœsus, thinke but of thy gold,
As rusticke people of the vilest mold.

Yet thou mayst * vse it Crœsus, to thy good,
So thou repose no confidence therein,
So thou abuse it not, it is allow'd,
Abuse, not vse, is Author of the sinne.
Be not deceiu'd through any false pretence,
To hoord vp coine, and hurt thy conscience.

* The difference betwixt the poore wanting, and rich not vsing, is by these two expressed, the one carendo, the other non fruendo.

This is a simple traine, a net for fooles,
Not able to deceiue * the wiser men.
Fishes be sooner catcht, in glistring pooles,
Then in a troubled creuise, marsh or fen,
But wisest fishes, neuer will appeare,
Where they perceiue the smallest cause of feare.

* Sapiens ipse fingit fortunam sibi.

Lucan. in bell. Phar.

Thus is the forme of wisedome well explaned,
Euen in a Christall glasse most eminent,
Wherein our distinct natures are contained,
As in a Table aptly pertinent,
How that bewitch'd we are, in seeming good,
And that prooues poyson which we tooke for food.

OF CRVELTIE.

This is my Satyre, Crœsus which I send thee,
To th'end thou mayst admonish'd be of this;
I hope my Satyre will in time amend thee,
And draw thy mind from earth-opinion'd blisse,
Wherefore farewell, and if thou wilt be blessed,
Flie from this rust, by it thy mind's oppressed.

The Argument.

TRogus Pompeius relateth in his generall History, how *Astyages* dreamed that there sprong a vine forth of the wombe of his daughter *Mandanes*, whose broad-spreading branches ouershadowed all Asia, wherefore to take away the ground and foundation of his feare, hauing vnderstood by the *Magi*, that by the vine was intimated *Cyrus*, who should ouershadow all Asia with his victorious and conquering hand, he commanded *Harpagus* one of his priuie Counsell to take the babe and slay it, that whatsoeuer his dreame imported, might by this meanes be preuented: but *Harpagus* more cōpassionate then *Astiages* (though too remorcelesse) exposed it to the crueltie of sauage beasts, where (so carefull is nature of her owne) it found more pittie in the wild forrest, then in his grandfathers Pallace, being for some dayes nourished by a she-wolfe or bitch,

bitch, (whence Nurſes to this day reſerue the name of *Spacon*,) and after found by one *Fauſtulus* a ſhepheard, was deliuered to his wife to be brought vp and nurſed: which ſhe, delighted with the chearfull countenance of the child, did accordingly, till in tract of time *Cyrus* came to the vnexpected height of an Empire, and fullfilled thoſe predictions and Prophecies which were formerly ſpoken of him. This *Argument* haue I culled, to the end my Satyre, vſing the liberty of ſo materiall an *Argument*, may inueigh againſt ſuch as ſeeke by all wayes to dilate and propagate the borders and bounders of their kingdome, (not reſpecting the meanes, ſo they may attaine the end) or ſtrengthen the continuance of their vniuſt claime by ſiniſter meanes: not vnlike to *Polynices* and *Eteocles* in the Tragedie; who though they were brethren, euen the hapleſſe children of wofull *Oedipus*, yet could they not content themſelues with their peculiar ſhares feuerally limited, and mutually allotted, but muſt crie:— *Aut Cæſar, aut nullus:* wherefore they enioyed the fruites of ſeldome proſpering deuiſion, *a ſhort reigne, attended on with perpetuall infamie after death.* Wherefore that is the beſt labour or trauell, where they do *— *Proponere laborem vt cum virtute & iuſtitia coniungant.* This is the beſt ſtrife, the beſt contention, which *(in a glorious emulation)* is conuerſant about vertue, not entertaining an vniuſt practice to gaine a kingdome, but euer to conclude with *Aurelius Sextus:*— *Ex peſſimo genere ne catulum:* Man that is wicked in his proceedings, getting an Empire by bloud (with-

Heſiod. in operi: & die.

Polynices & Eteocles monomachia de regno decertantes, mutuis vulneribus concidere runt, ibid.

* *Vide Ethicorum axiomata & eorum præcipua ratiocinandi argumēta, quorum certiſſimis principijs fundamenta virtutum innixa ſunt.*

out regard of election or descent) may liue, and for a while flourish, but he shall die without an *Heyre:* therefore this Satyre is purposely directed to *such,* (with an equall reflex from superiour to inferiour) as respect not the meanes how to obtaine a kingdome, so they may haue a kingdome, agreeing with that in the Poet; *Regam, modum regnandi non quæram.* I will gouerne, though I seeke not the meanes how to gouerne well : or thus : *I will gouerne, though I regard not the meanes whereby I come to gouerne.* Thus much for a wicked *Amulius,* who will gouerne though it be by the death or deposing of his brother *Numitor,* or an impious *Pigmalion,* who will murther *Sychæus* his brother to be enioyer of his treasure, or a faith-infringing *Polymnestor,* who betrayes the trust of a Protector, in praying vpon the Orphane *Polydore.* Of these my Satyre shall intreate, and brand them with the marke of an iniurious possession.

* Polidorum obtruncat & auro vi potitur 3. *Ænead.*

THE FIFT SATYRE.

* Et fatu terra nefando.

*T*Hou hellish* brood, borne to thine owne offence,
   Thou that wilt run into a streame of bloud,
Yet cries againe; It's in mine owne defence,
Hauing no care of vow-linckt brotherhood;
Be thou thine owne destroyer, thine owne foe,
And may thy conscience fret where ere thou goe.

What doest thou get, by getting of a crowne,
Deposing him, that is the lawfull heire?

But

*But cares and feares, and sorrowes of thine owne,
With* * *gastly visions, motiues to despaire?
Lament thy raigne, dominions got by wrong,
May floure awhile, but last they cannot long.*

Though Numitor *depos'd be by his brother,
Fate hath her stroke, some* Romulus *will spring,
Or if not* Romulus, *there will some other
Depose his greatnesse, make himselfe a king.
Thus as he got his kingdome, shedding* * *bloud,
He of his bloudie purchase reapes small good.*

*Where Iurisdiction is obtain'd by might,
Without apparent right vnto the crowne,
Shall soone extinguish all her former light,
And change her forme like to the waining Moone.
For such vsurping kings as aime at all,
Shall misse their aime, and with their Scepter fall.*

And thou Pigmalion, *who art neuer fil'd,
But euer gapes for riches and for gold,
Till thou with might thy Brothers bloud hast spil'd,
Or till thy yauning mouth be stopt with mold,
Either repent thy wrong, or thou shalt heare,
A thousand* * *Furies buzzing in thine eare.*

Foolish Astyages *that meanes to raigne,
And plant thy throne on earth eternally,
I tell thee (doting King) though thou disdaine,
 *Cyrus *should raigne, he will part stakes with thee:
No, he'le haue all, thou art his subiect made,
And with his vine all Asia's shadowed.*

Though

* *As it is written of* August: *that he had broken sleepes and vsed to send for some to passe the night away in telling tales or holding him with talke.* Tit. Liu. dec 3.

* *As* Mithridates *was said to plant his kingdome on an indirect foundation, Blood.* Appian. Alexan.

De cæde fraterna vberiori modo exarata, vid. Virgil. 1. Lib. AEnead.

* A Tergo Nemesis.

Though thou do marry, and assure to wife,
Thy faire Mandanes, *to a countrey* * *squire,*
That her meane marriage might secure thy life,
A king shall spring from such an homely sire.
It is in vaine to plot, when gods resist,
Who can defeate our proiects as they list.

* *Cambyses.*

What Polynices, *wilt thou fight, with whom?*
With thine owne brother deare Eteocles;
Will you contend, since you be both as one?
**Cleon will neuer fight with* Pericles;
Then why will you, the children of one sire,
Against each other mutually conspire?

* *2 Brothers.*

Fie on you both, what sauage crueltie,
Hath thus possest you in your tender age,
Brother gainst brother most inhumanely,
To shew your selues as Men in beastly rage?
Farewell vngodly Twins, borne for debate,
When Ruine knocks, Repentance comes too late.

Farewell Astyages, *that reignes for aye,*
And thou Pigmalion, *who do'st gape for wealth,*
Amulius *too, who learning to obay,*
Perceiues how Realmes decline that's got by stealth.
Farewell, and if my tart lines chance to spite ye,
My Satyre sayes, A dead dog cannot bite me.

The

OF ADVLTERIE.

The Argument.

*C*Lytemneſtra Agamemnons wife, forſaking her owne husband Agamemnon, ran to the vnchaſt bed of Ægiſtus, where ſhe proſtituted her ſelfe, regardleſſe of her birth, and neglectfull of her honour. This Agamemnon perceiued, but through the exceeding loue he bore her, ſeemingly couered this her apparent diſhonour, labouring to reclaime her rather by clemencie then rigour: but ſhe perſiſting in her hatefull luſt and vnlawfull affection, perſwaded Ægiſtus by vrgent folliciting to continue in his former adulterie, without regard to Agamemnons loue, or the infamie of her owne life. And hauing not as yet ſpun the web of her miſchiefe, ſhe ſeconds her laſciuious attempt with a ſecret practiſe, conſpiring with her fauourite Ægiſtus her husbands death, which was afterwards effected, but not vnreuenged. This inſtance ſhall be the firſt ſubiect vnto my Satyre; wherein I meane to diſplay the impudencie of ſuch, as out of a godleſſe ſecuritie, vſually auouch and iuſtifie their wicked and ſenſuall pleaſures with Phædra in the Poet, writing to her ſonne in law Hyppolytus after this manner:

* *Vt tenuit domus vna duos, domus vna tenebit,*
  Oſcula aperta dabas, oſcula aperta dabis.

For ſuch inceſtuous Phædraes, let them diuert their eyes

* *One houſe hath held, one houſe ſhall hold vs twaine, once did we kiſſe, and we will kiſſe againe.*

eyes to the enſuing Satyre, and then anſwer me, whether they do not bluſh at their decyphered follie, which more apparent then light will ſhew it ſelfe to euery eye : for the retiredſt angle or corner cannot giue vice a couer, whoſe memorie may be darkned, but not extinguiſhed : nor can the wide wombe of the earth find her a graue wherein to interre her, being like *Paſyphaes* iſſue, * euer a ſhame to the Parent. And as *Hecubaes* ſonne, portending * deſtruction to the Troian Citie, was thought fit to be caſten forth, left the euent thereof ſhould be anſwerable to the Propheſie : ſo ſhall this accurſed iſſue, this execrable Progenie ſhew it ſelfe, and be fitter for caſting forth then preſeruing, ſince *Clytemneſtra* ſhall feele the edge of cruelty, and the ſcourge of deuine furie.

* *The Minotaure.*

* Per ſomnum ardentem facem ſe peperiſſe ſentiens.

THE SIXT SATYRE.

WHat Clytemneſtra, *com'd ſo ſoone abroad,*
Forth of Ægiſtus bed thy husband's foe !
What is the cauſe thou makeſt ſo ſhort abode,
Is it becauſe thy huſband wills thee ſo ?
No it's becauſe * *he's weary of thy ſinne,*
Which he once ſought, but now is cloyed in.

What's that thou weares about thy downie necke ?
O it's a painted heart, *a Iewell fit,*
For wanton Minions who their beauties decke,
With gariſh toyes, new Suiters to begit :
Thou haſt a painted heart for chaſtitie,
But a true heart for thy adulterie.

* Quæritur AEgiſtus quare ſit factus adulter in promptu cauſa eſt, deſidioſus erat. *Ouid.*

Speake

OF ADVLTERIE.

Speake on Adultreſſe, let me heare thy tongue,
Canſt varniſh ore thy ſin with * eloquence ?
Silence ; ſuch ſinnes ſhould make the ſinner dumbe,
And force his ſpeech to teare-ſwolne penitence ;
Do not then ſhadow thy laſciuious deeds,
For which the heart of Agamemnon *bleeds.*

* Inſipiens eloquentia, vti gladius in furentis manu, nõ obeſſe maxime non poteſt. *Mirand. in laud. Herm.*

Leaue of (foule ſtrumpet : keepe thy huſbands bed,
Thou haſt no intereſt in Ægiſtus *ſheetes :*
Infamous acts, though cloſely done are ſpred,
And will be blaz'd and rumour'd in the ſtreetes.
Flie from this ſcandall, leſt it ſoile thy name,
Which blemiſht once, is nere made good againe.

Is not thy huſband worthy of thy loue ?
Too worthy huſband of a worthleſſe whoore,
Then rather chuſe to die then to remoue :
Thy chaſt-vowd ſteps from Agamemnons *boore ?*
He's thine, thou his, O * may it then appeare,
Where ere he is, that thou art onely there.

* Vſing the words of that chaſt Romane Matron : where thou art *Caius*, I am *Caia*.

But for Hyppolitus *to be incited*
By his ſtep-mother, O inceſtuous !
And to his * fathers bed to be inuited :
What fact was euer heard more odious ?
But ſee (chaſt youth) though ſhe perſwade him to it,
Nature forbids, and he's aſhamed to do it.

* *Theſeus.*

* *The Application of the Morall.*

* *You* * *painted Monkies that will nere reſtraine,*
Your hote deſires from luſts-purſuing chaſe,
Shall be conſumed in a quenchleſſe flame,
Not reft of griefe, though you were reft of grace.

* Quis fucum in proba virgine non damnet ? Quis in veſtali non deteſtetur ? *Pic. Mirand. in Epiſt.*

Bereſt

Bereft of grace, and buried in shame,
Regardlesse of your honour, birth, or name.

I can discerne you by your wanton toyes,
  Your strutting like Dame Iuno *in her throne,*
Casting concealed fauours vnto boyes:
  These common things are into habits growne,
  And when you haue no fauours to bestow,
Lookes are the lures which draw affections bow.

Trust me I blush, to see your impudence,
Sure you no women * are, whose brazen face,
Shewes modestie ha's there no residence,
Incarnate diuels that are past all grace;
Yet sometimes wheate growes with the fruitlesse tares,
You haue fallne oft, now fall vnto your prayers.

* Si puellam viderimus moribus lepidam atq; dicaculam, laudabimus, exosculabimus: hæc in matrona damnabimus & persequemur. ibid.

The Argument.

WHosoeuer will but consider the fortune, or rather misfortune of *Tereus* for his wickednesse, shall behold as in a glasse or transparent mirror, the fruite of adulterous beds. For his licencious and inordinate lust contained within no bounds, but continuing in all prohibited desires, and now pursuing with an incestuous heate *Phylomele* his wiues sister, hath transformed himselfe into a reasonlesse creature; for now *Tereus*

OF INCEST.   31

reus in *Vpubam* changeth his former nature and condition, becoming in ſhape as odious, as his life was impious, as the Poet teſtifieth :

Vertitur in volucrem, cui ſtant pro vertice criſtæ.

Thus may adulterous want-graces looke into *Tereus* fall, and then apply his ruine to their preſent ſtate. I gather theſe Arguments out of fictions and Poeticall inuentions, yet are not theſe fables without their deuine Morals; for ſuch men as are touched with this crime or the like, ought to be aſhamed of their follie, ſince the very heathen Poets, whoſe beſt of ſacred knowledge was the light of Nature, could exclaime againſt them, and pourtray the forme of their liues in a fained inuention. For to exemplifie ſpeciall puniſhments inflicted on particular ſinnes, *Thoſe birds which   * *The Harpyes.* ſtill frequented *Phineus* armie, and annoyed him with ſuch a filthy ſent, that euen vpon ſhipboord they would come flocking to his Nauie, and bring a loathſome ſtench, whereby they vſed to infect his meate, neuer departing from him, either morne or night, but would — *Eſcopulis exire, & vniuerſam claſſem teterrimo fætore inficere.* Wherefore was this, but foraſmuch as by the perſwaſion of his ſecond wife *Idæa*, he put forth the eyes of his children had by his firſt * wife ? of which   * *Cleopatra.* in the latter part of this Satyre I meane eſpecially to inſiſt, declaring by way of aggrauation the wickednesſe of ſuch *Iniuſtæ Nouercæ*, who will tyrannife ouer their ſtepchildren, reſpectleſſe of *Phineus* puniſhment or *Idæas* vexation. And though ſome obiect, that theſe Arguments be but fruit-
                                                                leſſe

lesse inuentions hatched forth of Poets braines; yet must they of force confesse ingenuously, that their Morals conferre no lesse benefit, then if deriued from a truer subiect: for whosoeuer will not beware of *Idæas* fact, shall vndergo *Idæas* * punishment; let them therefore auoyd the fact precedent or let them expect the punishment subsequent.

* Quem fecere parem crimina, fata parem. *Ibid.*
* Par tibi culpa fuit, par tibi pena subit. *alib.* Nec culpa est leuior, nec tibi pæna minor.

THE SEVENTH SATYRE.

*H*Ow now fond Tereus, whither rid'st so fast,
To Progne or to Itis? O, it's true,
Thou goest vnto thy sister, made vnchast,
By thy enforced rape, for she nere knew
What lusts-embraces meant, till thou hadst taught her,
Which gaue her cause of sorrowing euer after.

Come backe againe, go to thy chast wiues bed,
Wrong not the honour of a spotlesse wife,
What fruite yeelds lust when thou hast surfeted,
But wretched death, drawne from a wicked life?
Returne fond lustfull man, do not dishonour
Poore Phylomele, for heauens eyes looke on her.

* Forsitan & narres quam sit tibi rustica coniux.

*It may be thou alledg'st, * rusticity*
Appeareth in the fashions of thy Deare;
Is this a cloake to liue licentiously?
No, if her breeding more vnciuill were,
These should not be occasions of thy shame,
For in discretion thou shouldst couer them.

Thou

OF INCEST.

Thou art that Rusticke, she the modest flower,
Not seeking for to grow with other plants
Then with thy selfe, though thou *for euery boore,*
Suites thy affection, yet affection wants:
She * *loues, thou lusts, thine is a borrowed name,*   Amor perennis
For shame-fast loue needs neuer blush for shame.   coniugis castæ manet. *Sen. in.* Octau.

How now Prince Phineus, *where's thy childrens eyes,*
Are they put out, who mou'd thee to offend?
Was it Idæa, *whom the gods defies?*
Whom neither heauen nor earth can well commend.
It was Idæa, *she the Step-dame cries,*
Haste, Phineus *haste, pull out thy childrens eyes.*

He'le do it for thee, there's no question why,
To faire Idæa, *chast Queene to his bed,*
He should the murdring of his foule deny,
Much lesse to cause his childrens bloud be shed;
See step-dames *see, how hatefull is your guilt,*
When to raise yours, anothers bloud is spilt!

Murder thy children, put out Orphans eyes,
God cannot salue their extreame heauinesse:
He cannot heare them when they make their cries,
Nor can he comfort them in their distresse.
Yes, he can heare and see, and though he come
With a flow pace, he will at last strike home.

Then grieue, but let not griefe driue to despaire;
Trust, but let Trust breed no securitie,
For crying sinnes when they presuming are,
Oft wound so deepe they find no remedie.

                D   Farewell

Farewell Idæa, *may my Satyre heare,*
For each bloud-drop th'aſt ſhed, thou ſhedſt a teare.

The Argument.

THe Argument of this Satyre ſhall be againſt all wicked *Iulians*, all godleſſe Apoſtates. And though in the third Satyre I haue touched this Argument briefly: yet now more amply meane I to deblazon the forlorne condition of theſe vnnaturall monſters. For to produce the Authorities & Opinions of the very heathen Phyloſophers, they haue generally concluded, not onely a God, but a Trinitie, *Three in-beings or perſons coeſſentiall.* As firſt the Platoniſts, who haue concluded a *Minder*, *Minding, and a Minded*, but the chiefe hereof the *Minder.* From the Platoniſts let vs deſcend to the Pythagorians, amongſt whom *Numenius* moſt worthie for his learning (inſomuch as *Porphyrie* a man of ripe iudgement and pregnant conceit, albeit a profeſt enemie of Chriſt, wrote many ſeuerall Commentaries vpon him) ſpeaketh thus: Touching the Indiuiduate eſſence of God, it is compact of it ſelfe in one, ſubſiſting of none, in and of himſelfe alone, not to be contained or circumſcribed within any limits or bounds, being euer during in time, before time, and without time; incomprehenſible in his works, indiuiſible,

The Pythag.
Numenius.

in

in his substance insubstantiate. The Academicks in like sort conclude the same, yeelding to an omnipotent power, working according to the diuine will of the worker; wherein they giue excellent instances and similitudes in the * Sunne, and the heate proceeding from the Sunne, drawing from thence a singular argument to proue *the diuine Trinitie*. *Zeno* the father of the Stoicks, acknowledged the *Word* to be *God*, and also the *spirit* of *Iupiter*. Thus Academicks of later times, Stoicks, Pythagorians, and Platonists, confesse this heauenly power: and shall we who are borne in the dayes of light and truth deny the same? *Hermes* can conclude, how—*Radij deuini sunt eius oporationes miræ, Radij mundani sunt naturæ & rerum similitudines variæ, Radij humani sunt artes & scientiæ.* And shall we confesse the later, but not the first, from whence the later be deriued? *Plato* in his 13. Epistle to King *Dennis* writeth thus. When I write in earnest, you shall know hereby, that I begin with one God; but when I write otherwise, then I begin with many gods. *Aristotle* likewise that serious inquisitor in the secrets of Nature, could say:—*Ens entium miserere mei*. Thus are our Atheists conuinced by Pagans; for neither *Orphuus* whose inuention gaue that opinion of pluralitie of gods first footing, nor *Diagoras* the Athenian, who denied that there was any God, were exempted from seuerest censure, the one hauing his opinions publickly refelled, the other for his contempt of the gods, expulsed. For such nouell opinions as Antiquity had not traduced vnto them,

The Academ.

* *The Sunne, beames, and heate alluding to the blessed Trinitie. Stoicks.*

Hermes his description of the diuerse workings.

13 Epist. to King Dennis. vid. Sene. in Epist. ad Lucil.

God was not made at any time, in as much as he is euerlastingly vnbegotten. Galen.

them, but seemed repugnant to what they beleeued touching their gods, were esteemed perillous, and the founders of them worthie due punishment. And how much more ought we reuerently to obserue and carefully retaine what Sacred authoritie, grounded on better warrant then Pagan Antiquitie, hath commended to vs, where euery clause, euery syllable, sentence and title are full of sententious sweetnesse, and diuine fulnesse? As for the palpable blindnesse of such as see not, or wilfull ignorance of such as see but will not, the time will come when *He*, whom they denie shall reueale himselfe in furie, and those grosse opinions which with such asseuerance they maintained, shall be testimonies against them to conuince them. And though, as *Suetonius* witnesseth, there be some, who like *Caligula* will threaten the aire, that she shall not raine vpon his publicke games or stately spectacles, shewing himselfe so peremptorie, as though he would cope with the immortall Gods, yet would he—*ad minima tonitrua, & fulgura conniuere, caput obuoluere, ad vero maiora proripere se è strato, sub lectumq condere solebat:* at the noise of thunder or lightning winke hard, couer his head, and stop his eares, to take away the occasion of his feare: yea more then this, he would leape out of his bed and hide himselfe vnder it. Thus did he contemne *him* whose works made him tremble, derogating from his power, yet astonished with the voice of his thunder: and though in his time and his predecessor *Tiberius* there flourished a * worthie Philosopher, who allbeit

Vid. Sueton. Tranq. in vit. Calig.

Phylo the Iew.

beit a Iew by nation, yet frequent amongſt the Romanes, had great iudgement in matters diuine, and ſpake profoundly of the things which belonged vnto the expectation of Nations: Notwithſtanding all this, they continued without the leaſt acknowledgement of a Deitie, and in contempt of the diuine power, threatning the heauens if they ſcouled or frowned vpon the Romane gameſters, as I haue before mentioned. Whereby it ſeemes they repoſed ſuch confidence in the height of their preſent eſtate, as they imagined ſo firme a foundation could be ſhaken by no Superiour power; for indeed worldly pompe makes men for the moſt part forgetful of their duty towards their Creator, thinking (as men in a fooles Paradiſe) that this preſent Sunſhine of their ſeeming felicitie ſhall neuer ſet. Yet no ſooner ſhall hoarie age draw neare, then—*friget æſtus honoris*, and their former chearefulneſſe enfeebled with all infirmities, ſhall with lame limmes and a queaſie voice crie out,—*Non eadem eſt ætas:* then ſhall the cureleſſe itch of honor by the brine of age be allayed, youthfull ſports abandoned, and a quiet life rather deſired then magnificence of eſtate. Concluding with *Seneca* the Phyloſopher, inueying againſt the tyrannie of *Nero* to this effect: Petitur hac cælum via.

Well did I liue, when I from enuie rid,
Was pent vp 'mongſt the Rocks of th' Corſian ſea,
Where if I ſtill had liu'd as once I did,
Well had it gone both with my ſtate and me. *In the Tragedie of Agrip.*

For whoſoeuer ſhall but ſeriouſly conſider the ſtate and courſe of mans life, which is intangled with

with so sundrie and manifold perills, shall call it with the Poet,—*mundum vitro similantem*, where life is an exile, the passage a perill, and the end doubtfull. Thus farre of those who either with successe of fortune puffed, or height of honour transported, or through a carnall libertie benummed, trust so much in the arme of flesh, as they wholly denie the power and maiestie of the onely God (or soueraigne good) preferring a momentanie delight before a celestiall reward. Now to my Satyre.

THE EIGHT SATYRE.

Now stout Caligula *that dar'st the gods,*
Saying, they must not frowne vpon thy pleasure,
Thou and immortall powers are still at odds,
Whose * *gold's thy god, whose deitie's thy treasure.*
Thou'lt feele the smart hereof, when thy estate,
Founded on frailtie shall be ruinate.

* Modo auaritiæ singulos increpans, & quod puderet eos locupletiores esse, quā se. *in vit. Calig.*

Thou wilt not feare him while thou liues on earth,
Though life and power, and all be in his hand,
Thou'lt fight with him (poore worme) that giues thee breath,
And with the breath of flesh checke Ioues *command.*
Vnhappie Prince, though thou the happiest seeme,
This reigne of thine is but a golden dreame.

And when this dreame is past, and thou awake,
From thy soule-charming slumber thou must on,

Ta-

OF BLASPHEMIE.

*Taking thy iourney to the * Stygian lake,* * Sperent te tartara regem.
Or flame exhaling quenchleſſe Phlegeton,
Where poyſoned Adders ſhall infect thy tongue,
Which did ſo impiouſly her maker wrong.

Flie from the horror of thy damned ſoule,
For ſure ere long thou ſhalt be puniſhed.
See how thy ſoule deformed is and foule,
Soiled with ſinne, with errours blemiſhed.
*O * waſh them then, ſome hope doth yet remaine,*
But now vnwaſht they'le nere be white againe!

* Chriſtus lauacrũ eſt animæ, canalis gratiæ: Lauacrum, in quo anima immergitur & lauatur, Canalis, à qua omnis gratia animæ deriuatur.

Art not aſham'd for to denie his *power,*
Who giueth life vnto each liuing thing?
To heauen, to earth, to ſea, and to each flower,
He giueth meanes, for by him all things ſpring.
Who will not then, and knowing this, account
The earth's the Lords, and he's Lord Paramount?

Doeſt thou not ſee the fabricke of this earth,
And all the plants which flouriſh in their kind,
How by his power each creature bringeth forth,
As if indeed they knew their makers mind:
Where th'very earth-worme that's endu'd with ſence,
*Is not excluded from his * prouidence?*

* The very hedghog is not excluded from his prouidence. Aug.

Then leaue this damn'd opinion, Iulian,
Be not too confident of earthly rule:
Remember ſtill thou art a mortall man,
And in his power who can the ſeas controule.
It's he can make this earths foundation ſhudder,
Whoſe Empires reach from one Sea to another.

D 4   Yet

OF BLASPHEMIE.

Yet thou Caligula *canst threat the gods,*
If they descend but in a winters showre,
And saist in scorne, Thou'lt beate them with thy rods,
If they hold on, vpon thy games to lowre.
Yet cowardize constraines thee for to flie,
At euery flash, and like a Babe to crie.

Thou'lt menace death vnto Eternitie,
If they obey not thy imperious pleasure:
Thus gods themselues must feele thy tyrannie,
Enioynd to dance attendance at thy leysure:
Yet for all this, if thou but Thunder heares,
Thou pulls thy cap downe ore thy frighted eares.

So euery false Apostate will be stout,
Before he feele the Viols of Gods wrath:
But when he tasts thereof he gins to doubt,
*And calls to mind how he * forsooke his faith.*
His fall from which, confessing with his tong,
His tongue is speaking, but his heart is dombe.

* *But see, being in the way of doing well, shame holds him from the faith from which he fell.*

Dumbe shalt thou be, for heauen will haue it so,
Since thou appliest thy tongue to wickednesse,
Abusing that, gainst him who did bestow
All that thou hast, this's thy vnthankefulnes.
Yet but relent, and doubt not to obtaine,
That heauenly grace, which else thou canst not gaine.

Gracelesse beware, and feare the power of heauen,
Who can destroy thee in a minutes space,
*He who can make, the * steepest mountaines euen,*
Whose footstoole's earth, & heauen his dwelling place,

* Excelsa humiliando & humilia exaltando.

Feare

Feare, gracelesse feare, and thou shalt liue for euer,
For feare giues life to death, health to the liuer.

Liue thou shalt neuer, if thou do not care
To shew respect to th'supreme Maiestie,
He whom we feare, who tenders our wel-fare,
And guides vs in this vale of miserie.
Pagan thou art, vnlesse thou do amend,
Whose endlesse sinnes expect a * wofull end.

Therefore as thou regardst thy sweete soules health,
Or honour of thy Maker, now reclaime
Thy breach of faith stain'd with the worlds filth,
If thou a sonne of Syon meanes to raigne.
Fare well or ill; if well thou meanes to fare,
Vnto the Temple of thy God repaire.

* *Iulian and Fælix had both miserable ends: while Iulian that impious Apostate continued in his blasphemie:* Ecce quam sumptuofis vafis filio Mariæ miniftratur! vid. *Venerab. Bed.* 3. *lib.*

The Argument.

HYppeas that worthy Grecian, who ftroue for the games in the Olympiads, wore no other apparell faue what with his owne handes (being a generall Artift) he had framed, hauing not fo much as the ring of his finger, or bracelet about his arme, but were made by him, yea & the fhooes of his feete, which with his owne skill he made likewife. This *Hyppeas* hauing gained the chiefeft prizes by meanes of his actiuitie; and now returning

ning in the triumph of a Conquerour with a Coronet of floures empaled, to receiue the proposed reward: the publicke Notarie of these games came (according to the wonted custome vsually obserued) to demaund the best raiment or choycest particular ornament the Conquerour had about him. Now this fellow, whom continuance of time had made impudent, seeing the bountie of the conquering *Hippeas,* according to the manner, receiued the best raiment the Victor wore: and scarce contented therewith, (like an infatigable suiter) begged farther his stockings, and *Hyppeas* denied him nothing. So long he continued in begging, and he in giuing, till *Hyppeas* went naked forth of the Olympiads, hauing nothing wherewith he might shew his friends any semblance of conquest or victorie, saue his naked bodie, which he presented vnto them, vsing these words vnto the Notarie:—*What I haue giuen thee, I would haue bestowed on my professedst enemy, for such motiues of vaineglory should rather moue me to loath them then loue them, leaue them, then liue with them, remembring, how*

The sage Eutrapelus *expresly bad,*
His foes should haue the choycest robes he had,
Wherein he found by proofe this speciall good,
To make himselfe more humble, them more proud.

The name of this begger was *Mynthos,* who hauing thus polled & spoiled this worthy Conqueror of all his apparell through his importunacie in demanding, presently thus answered one by whom he was sharpely taxed: *Nemo est quin aliqua in*
arte

arte præclarus eſt, ego autem in præmia & veſtimenta comparando, palmam & gloriam adeptus ſum meque diuitem ex aliorum paupertate feci. This ſhall be the Argument of this ninth Satyre, touching impudent crauers: *Theſe—Iri egentes,* of whom the Poet ſpeaketh, who make themſelues rich by their ſeruile baſeneſſe, and as Vultures feede beſt vpon the ſtinkingſt carrion, ſo they vpon others riot, prodigalitie, and diſſolution, ſucking like the *Sangui-ſugæ,* who feede themſelues with bloud till they burſt. Reaſon haue I to inuey againſt them, ſince Iſrael the elect and ſelect people of God were not to receiue them—*Let there be no begger in Iſrael.* Time was not then for Paraſites to currie fauour, when none was to haue reliefe but by his labor; ſo expreſly was euery one enioyned to apply his vocation, that * *he who would not labour ſhould not eate.* And may theſe inſatiable *Mynthes* taſte the like fare, being deriued from as baſe beginnings as they are oftimes aduanced without merit to great meanes and poſſeſſions, yea compoſed of as ignoble and degenerate minds, as they are ſprong of ingenerous bloud.

<small>Gen. 3. 19.
2. Theſ. 3. 10.
Prou. 5. 15.
1. Theſ. 4. 11.</small>

THE NINTH SATYRE.

Hyppeas, *your cloake I craue, that is my due,*
     Your ſtockings too, and ſuch like toyes as theſe,
Free to beſtow a Bountie were in you,
And yet a debt, for you to know my fee's.
But Debt to mention I do think't vnfit,
When Bountie is ſo neare to anſwer it.

                                        And

And yet I want, and yet what can I want,
When He of whom I craue's so prone to giue?
When store by Ioue is sent, there is no scant,
All famine leaue, and all in plentie liue.
See what thou wants then Minthos, and but craue it,
Hyppeus is stor'd, and thou art sure to haue it.

Belt, Beuer, Buskin, view from top to toe,
See what thou wants his Wardrope will supply,
And laugh at him when thou hast vs'd him so,
And bid him triumph in his victory.
Let him go nak'd, and boast what he hath done,
Whilest thou enioyes the Booties he hath won.

The true description of a Parate.

Yet tearme him Prince of bountie, and requite
In seeming Protestations, and in vowes,
Yet care not for him when he's out of sight;
For those thriue best who can make fairest showes:
In speaking much, but little as they meane,
And being such, but not the same they seeme.

* Satis domi talium salutatorum habeo. *Plut. in vit. Tiber.*

I would I could, thus maist * thou bring him on,
I could extend my wealth vnto my will,
I would erect to show what you haue done,
Some Time-outliuing Monument, to fill
The world with amazement, when they heare
What you haue bene, and what your actions were.

And then impart thy want, how fortunes are
Vnequally deuided, yet to such
As He whose Bountie giues to each his share,
Though much he hath, yet ha's he not too much:

And

And then with cap in hand befeech his worth,
Be good to thee, *that's borne of obfcure birth.*

Indeed thou feemes to be an obfcure Affe,
A fpacious Beggar, *begging euery where,*   Vid. Perfi. in Satyr.
Who wilt not fuffer a patcht boote to paffe,
But thou wilt beg it for thy leg that's bare.
Indeed too bare thou art, too impudent,
That with thy owne ftate canft not be content.

Pefantlike Baftard, hate thy Beggarie,
Liue on thy owne, not on anothers ftate;
Thou that defcendeft from bafe penurie,
Wilt by thy Begging *liue at higher rate?*   Vid. Iuuenal. Saty.
Numbred thou art amongft fuch men as begs,
The fmoke of Chimnies, fnuffes, and Vintners dregs.

Thou art defam'd, for all deride thy kneeling,
Thy capping, cringing, and thy temporizing,
As if thou hadft of modeftie no feeling,
But from anothers razing drew thy rifing.
Well, for thy begging *we will beg for thee,*
The Pattent of difgrace and infamie.

So with thy wallet as a beggar *fhould,*   Qualis es, talis appare.
Be not afham'd to feeme that which thou art,
Sowe patch on patch, to keepe thee from the cold,
And fhew thy want in each feame-rented part:
But do not rere thy fortunes on mens fall,
For fuch bafe Beggars *are the worft of all.*

OF BEGGARIE.

I write not to thee in a sublime stile, [Vultum verba decent. *Horat.*]
Such is vnfit thy errors to conuince;
Satyres though rough, are plaine and must reuile [A Satyres natiue Rhetoricke.]
Vice with a Cynicke bluntnesse, as long since
* Those graue iudicious Satyrists did vse, [* Eupolis, Aristobulus, Aristeas, &c.]
Who did not taxe the time, but times abuse.

And yet I wish my pen were made of steele,
And euery leafe, a leafe of lasting brasse,
Which might beare record to this Commonweale,
When this Age's past, to Ages that shall passe.
But * these as others must, shall lose their name, [Debemur morti nos nostraq;.]
And we their Authors too must die with them.

Yet well I know, I shall Characterd be,
In liuing letters, prouing what I write,
To be authenticke to posteritie,
To whom this Ages vices I recite.
Which, much I doubt, as they're successiue still,
By course of yeares, so they'le succeed in ill.

For vice nere dyes intestate, but doth leaue,
Something behind, to shew what it hath bene;
Yea canting knaues that hang on others sleeue,
Can charge their heires still to pursue the streame,
Where Iohn *a style bequeathes to* Iohn *a noke,*
His Beggars *rags, his dish, his scrip, his poke.*

With which Ile beg; *no, with my soule I scorne it,*
Ile rather carrie tankards on my backe;
Yet th' trade is thriuing, true, but I'ue forsworne it,
Nor would I beg, *though competent I lacke.*

Before

Before I should make congies to a swayne,
I would forsweare to take my legs againe.

I am but poore, and yet I scorne to beg,
To be a Bastard to my Progenie,
Yea I will rather with * Sycites *seg*,   * *Poyson.*
Receiue my death, then get me infamie.   *Sycites sig.*
I'le be a galley-slaue in Turkish ship,   *a Prouerbe.*
Rather then scrape my crums out of a scrip.

Bias *was poore, and yet his wealth increased,*
All that he had he carried still about him;
Bias *is dead, his goods by death are seised,*   Vid. dict. Cre-
Mydas *is poore, his goods were all without him.*   tensium.
Bias *and* Mydas *both agree in this,*
Earths blisse when we're in earth quite vanish'd is.

a Candaules *he was rich, yet he was poore,*   a Candaules in
Rich in his coffers rammed downe with gold,   primo libro Iu-
Yet poore *in this, his wife did proue a whoore,*   stini, Qui osten-
Showne naked vnto Gyges *to behold.*   dens eam Gigi
Collatine *poore, yet rich, his wife is chast,*   (deposita veste)
Both these agree in this, by death embra'st.   tantæ insaniæ
                                                  pœnas luit,
                                                  à Gige enim
                                                  confoditur mi-
                                                  ra virtute an-
                                                  nuli cooperto.
                                                  Vnde Poeta;
b Irus *was poore, but* Crœsus *passing rich,*   coniugis vt nu-
Irus *his scrip differs from* Crœsus *boord,*   dam speciem
Yet now compare them and I know not which,   monstrasset a-
                                                 mico:
                                                 Dilectam speci-
                                                 em perdit, ami-
                                                 cus habet.

Quasi silentium damnum pulchritudinis esset. *ibid. Vid. Cic. de off.* 3. *Lib. Plato. de leg. l.* 1.
b Irus, qui in domo Vlissis post reditum suum, ab Vlisse, pugna nimirum eius, per-
emptus est; Irus qui Scrinio suo & Obba in plateis Greciæ mendicare solebat, super-
bia quadam (aut spe suauioris lucri) affectus, in Penelopem, inter Penelopis socios,
(vt nuncius potius quam procus) accedere ausus est;—Dignum supplicium pertulit,
quia tanta animi audacia (more procacis mendici) in lares consularis dignitatis viri
procedere ausit. *Vid. Hom. Ili. interp. Calab.*

Is

Is better furnish'd or the worser stor'd :
For see their fates, they both in one agree,
Since by pale Death they both arrested be.

<small>* Demosthenes an Orator of Athens.</small>

Priscillaes *purse,* * Demosthenes *his hand,*
Do differ much, the one is alwayes shut,
The other open, for rewards doth stand ;
Yet if we measure either by his foot,
That close-shut purse, and that receiuing hand,

<small>* Virga sepulchralis. Varr.</small>

*Haue equall shares made by the * Sextons wand.*

Yet Beggar, *thou that* begs, *and hopes to gaine*
Store of rewards, for to relieue thy need.
Or surfet rather, tell me what's thy aime,

<small>* Pascentur à nobis quæ pascuntur in nobis. Vermes.</small>

*When those * thou feeds, shall on thy carkasse feed?*
For then where's the Beggar *now become,*
Whose shame's too great, to hide with shroud or tombe?

Take these rude Satyres as compos'd by him
Who loues his state farre better then thy trade,

<small>* Expos'd to shame, and infamie betraid.</small>

*For * Beggars lose more then they seeme to win,*
Since their esteeme for euer's blemished :
Liue at a lower rate, and beg the lesse.
I'le liue to write, if thou thy fault redresse.

Amicus non Mendicus.

The

The Argument.

Taurus * a rich Iustice, seemed to carrie great port and state in his countrie where he liued, though more feared then loued: *for the proud miser seldome liues to be inheritour of a friend:* but afterward his misery was most apparently known by his desolate house, as vnacquainted with hospitality as an vsurers heire with frugalitie, hauing onely a case for a man, a *blew-coate* I meane without a man, a shadow without a substance. In this Satyre next ensuing is described the miserable nature of such, as notwithstanding their outward port, glorying of more then euer their vnworthie minds could reach to, be the very pictures and *Ideas* of *misery*, as I may well call them: where desire of hauing so much ouerswayes them, as care of reputation lightly moues them. This Argument is short, for the Satyre will shew her owne meaning without any further illustration.

* Raptus abit media quod ad æthera Taurus arena, non fuit hoc artis sed pietatis opus.
Martial. in Epi. in Amphythe. Cæsa.

It is a great shame for a man to haue a poore heart and a rich purse.

THE TENTH SATYRE.

*T*Aurus * *a Iustice rich, but poore in mind,*
(Riches make rich-men poore through miserie,)
Had long time liu'd as one in hold confin'd,
With gates close-shut from hospitalitie:

* Cornua Vibrando, nescit sua cornua Taurus; *Whereto it was shrewdly answered:* Cornua dum cernit, retrahit sua cornua Taurus.

E   Meanes

Meanes without men he had him to attend,
Left what he spar'd his Retinue should spend.

One time a Traueller chanc'd to repaire
To Taurus *house, to quench his vehement thirst,*
But he poore man could find no comfort there:
Drinke could he get none, if his heart should burst;
Men he saw none, nor ought to cheare his want,
*Saue a * Blew-coate without a cognisant.*

<small>* Signa dat Hospitij, sed habentur in Hospitis vmbram.
* As quicke conceits will passions best allay.</small>

The Traueller conceited in distresse,
*Straight thus discours'd, his * passion to allay:*
This Iustice is a Seruing-man I guesse,
Who leaues his coate at home when he's away:
Therefore I was deceiu'd and did amisse,
To seeke a Iustice where a blew-coate is.

But as the Traueller went on his way,
He met the Iustice in a ragged suite,
Who in a Bench-like fashion bad him stay,
Saying—He ought a Iustice to salute:
The man at first perplex'd, and now awake,
Tooke heart of grace, and did this answer make.

Sir, if I haue forgotten my regard
Vnto your place, forgiue my ignorance,
My eye could not discerne you, till I heard
Your selfe report your owne preeminence,
Whose name is Terror, and whose awfull breath,
Is messenger of furie, and of death.

And

OF HYPOCRISIE.

And great I heare's endowments you poſſeſſe,
But worthie greater then you do enioy,
Witneſſe your open houſe, *which doth expreſſe*
The care you haue your fortunes to employ
In bounties ſeruice: your good beere doth ſhow it,
Being kept ſo well, as none can come vnto it.

Taurus *he ſtamp'd, cald his attendants knaues,*
And ſo he might, for none could be offended,
Where art thou Tom (*quoth he*) Iack, George, *out*
Faining their voyces, All ſhall be amended. *(ſlaues,*
Then anſwers he himſelfe, Let none depart,
But entertaine all with a chearefull heart.

The Traueller *though he conceiued all,*
Seem'd to admire the bountie of the place,
Till th'badge-leſſe coate that hung within the hall,
Forc'd him to laugh the Iuſtice *in the face.*
Why doeſt thou laugh (quoth he?) I laugh to note,
For want of men, what ſeruic's in a coate.

The Argument.

Claudius a Romane, for his approued honeſty
reſpected for the moſt part, gained no leſſe
good

good opinion with the Conscript fathers in the Senate-house, then popular loue in the Citie: for his grauitie was such, as none could detect him of the least imputation, hauing alwayes in the whole course of his pleading such pithie, sententious, and select discourse, that it yeelded no lesse admiration to the hearers, then a generall estimation to himselfe, at that time reputed one of the hopefullest young Orators: but most especially for his deuotion and religion to the gods, then, amongst the Romans adored and worshipped. This *Claudius* after this generall report and good liking which all had of him, vpon a solemne night appointed for the sacrifizing to * *Mars* in behalfe of a battell which was to be made against a Prince of Numidia, (in which holy rites there were appointed *Augurs* for the coniecturing of these things) seeing the opportunitie of the *Augures* absence, renewed the familiaritie which he of long time had with one of the *Augures* wiues. Now the *Augur* hauing left behind him his Oscines or Prophesing birds (a neglect of such importance as it discouered his owne shame,) came to his house where he detected *Claudius*, who had long * time counterfeited puritie.

* Et festa solennia Martis. vid. *Varr.* & *Ouid. de fast.*

* The fish *Sepia* is betrayed by a blacke colour which she casteth out to couer her, so these counterfets by the cloud of a pretended holinesse, which shall be as a cloud of witnesse against them.

THE ELEVENTH SATYRE.

Claudius *is pure, abiuring prophane things,*
Nor will he companie with wickednesse:
He hates the source whence leud affections springs,
He'le not consent with deeds of naughtinesse:
Yet

OF HYPOCRISIE.

Yet he will deale, so none do see his sinne,
Yea though heauens eyes he cares not looke on him.

He will not speake vnto a Maide in th'strecte,
Lest his repute should fall vnto decay:
Yet if they two in priuate chance to meete,
He in a pure embrace will bid her stay.
Saying: I will instruct thee prettie Nan,
How thou shalt be a formall Puritan.

Then drawes he forth to moue the Maids affection,
The forc'd description of their puritie,
How he and she be children of election,
And must be sau'd what ere the wicked be.
For vices are tearm'd vertues, where we make
Lust but an Act for Procreation *sake.*

What then are Maids, *thus* he *induceth her,*
But Virgins still that do impart their loue,
To such an * *One as is their furtherer*   * Vt prurit vrit.
In holy zeale, *and can the* spirit *moue?*
Nought lesse but more, for there's a heauie væ,
Or curse denounc'd on them that barren *be.*

Cloze *then in silence, eyes of men are shut,*
None can detect vs, *but the eyes of heauen,*
And when we act, those lights are sealed vp,
For vnto vs *more libertie is giuen*
Then vnto others, *since the very name,*
Of lust is chang'd when th'righteous *vse the same.*

E 3   *Thou*

54   OF EXCESSE.

> * Hypocrifis duplex eſt malum, ｖdiſſimulatio & peccatum.

Thou * hypocrite, whoſe counterfeited zeale,
Makes thee ſeeme godly to the worlds eye,
Yet doeſt the golden fruites of Veſta ſteale,
When thou perceiues no man thy ſins doth ſpie.
Leaue this diſſembled zeale, for thou art knowne
The wickedſt ſinner, when thy inſide's ſhowne.

The Argument.

THe Hiſtorie of *Phyloxenus* is moſt amply related in the diuerſe writings of ſundrie authenticke Authors, being infamous for his greedie deſire vnto meate and drinke, and therefore as is teſtified of him, * *Gruis collum ſibi dari optabat, vt cibum potumq́ maiori cum delectatione caperet.* This *Phyloxenus* and that rauenous Heliogabalus *ſhall be the ſubiects of this enſuing Satyre, touching or rather concluding the condition of all Epicures in theſe two.* If thou that readeſt me be touched, as tainted with this particular ſinne, bluſh, but do not ſhew thy paſſion towards the poore Satyre, for Bee-like ſhe hath no ſooner ſtung thee, then ſhe loſeth her power of being further reuenged of thee. Wage not warre againſt a dead Monument, ſince *Plinie* warnes thee: *Cum mortuis nil niſi laruas luctari.* Take therefore this Satyre in good part, and rather fret againſt thy ſelfe, in that thou haſt matter in thee fit for a Satyriſts ſubiect, then vent thy

> * *Ariſtotle mocking the Epicures, ſaid, that vpon a time they went all to a Temple together, beſeeching the gods that they would giue them necks as long as Cranes and Hernes, that the pleaſure and taſte of meate might be more long in reliſhing: complaining againſt Nature for making their necks too ſhort.*

ſplene

fplene towards him, who makes thy defects the effects of his subiect.

THE TWELFTH SATYRE.

PHyloxenus *lookes lanke with abstinence:*
Poore man I pittie him, I thinke he's sicke;
No, this his seeming is a false pretence,
The greedie Cormorant will each thing licke:
Whose drum-stretch'd case can scarce his guts containe
Since he hath got the gullet of a Crane.

Thou thinkes there is no pleasure but in feeding,
Making thy selfe, * *slaue to thy appetite;*
Yet whilest thou crams thy selfe, thy soule is bleeding,
And Turtle-like mournes, that thou shouldst delight,
In such excesse *as causeth infamie,*
Starues soule, spoiles health, and ends with beggarie.

Remember (thou besott'd) for I must talke,
And that with serious passion, thou that * *tasts*
The choycest wines, and doest to Tauernes walke,
Where thou confumes the night in late repasts.
Confusion now, drawes neare thee where thou kneeles,
Drinking deepe healthes, but no contrition feeles.

It may be, He *that teacheth may be taught,*
And * Socrates *of* Softenes *may learne,*
Euen He, *that for thy good these precepts brought,*
To publicke light, may in himselfe discerne
Something blameworthie, true, and heauen he could,
Reforme his errors rightly as He *would.*

* *Like those vnsatiable gluttons* Vitellius *and* Appius, *to which Cormorants neither land, water, nor aire might be sufficient. And* Cambletes *the gluttonous king of Lydia deuoured in a dreame his wife, while she lay sleeping together in the same bed; and finding her hand betweene his teeth when he awaked, he slue himselfe, fearing dishonour.*

* *Well described by that Motto.* Non citius edit quam excedit; pascit & poscit.
* Elpenoris vice. vid. Geor. Virg. Silenus in Antro.

* Socraticum speculum non chalibæum & materiale. vid. Brasiuo. in præfatione.

But harder is't by much for to performe,
Then to prescribe, where many seeme to vrge,
The present times abuse, but n'ere reforme
Those crimes in them which they in others scourge:
But where the Author *makes vse of his paines,*
As well as Reader, *there's a double gaines.*

And these are th'gaines which I do sue to haue,
Seeking no lesse thy benefit herein,
Then my peculiar good: where all I craue,
Is but thy prayer to purge me of my sinne.
I do not write, as I my paines would sell,
To euery Broker, vse them and farewell.

Nam inepto risu res nulla ineptior est.   *Catull.*
      Finis Satyrarum.

An end of the *Satyres* composed by the foresaid Author in the discharge of Natures Embassie: purposely penned to reclaime man, whose vicious life promising an vnhappie end, must now be taxed more sharply, since vice comes to greatest growth through impunitie.

A

A CONCLVSIVE
ADMONITION TO THE
READER.

F any man shall reade, and making vse
Of these my Satyres, grow distemperate,
By making of a good intent abuse,
In that I seeme his life to personate;
Let him content himselfe, be it good or ill,
Gall'd horses winch, and I must gall him still.

A Satyrist ought to be most secure,
Who takes exception at his cancred style,
And he that most repines, let him be sure,
That he's the man whom Satyres most reuile.
Therefore who would be free from Satyres pen,
Ought to be Mirrors in the sight of men.

These two months trauell like the Almond rod,
May bring forth more when oportunitie
Giueth fit time, wherein vice loath'd by God,
May be displaide, and curb'd more bitterly.
Till which edition, take these in good part,
Or take them ill, how-ere, they glad my heart.

HERE

HERE FOLLO-
WETH SOME EPYCEDES
or funerall Elegies, concerning sundry exquisite Mirrours of true loue.

The Argument.

Wo louely louers so deuided be,
As one to other hardly can repaire,
In *Sestos* she, and in *Abydos* he,
He swims, she waits & weeps, both drowned are:
Waues cut off *Heroes* words, the Sea-nimphs mone,
One heart in two desires, no graue but one.

I. ELEGIE.

Hero *was willing to* Leanders *suite,*
But yet Leanders *opportunitie*
Could not be so, as answers his repute :
Lust sometime weares the robe of modestie :
Silent he woes, as bashfull youths must do,
By sighs, by teares, and kissing comfits too.

But what are these where fancie seated is,
But lures to loose desires, sin-sugred baits,
That draw men onward to fooles paradice,
Whose best of promises are but deceits ?

And

And such Leanders *were, meere golden dreames,*
That leaue the waking senses in extreames.

But loue flame-like, though it restrained be,
Will still ascend, and so it far'd with him :
For now he cries, Hero *I come to thee,*
And though I cannot run, yet I will swim,
Where, while I swim, send thy sweet breath but hither,
And Zephire-like it will soone waft me thither.

Hero *remaineth on the floting shore,*
Waiting the blest arriuall of her friend,
But she (poore she) must neuer see him more,
Seeing him end before his iourney end:
In whose hard fate a double death appeares,
Drownd in the sea, and in his Heroes *teares.*

Still she laments, and teares her forlorne haire,
Exclaming 'gainst the fates, whose crueltie
Had chang'd her hope-reft fortuue to despaire,
Abridging loue, true louers libertie ;
But since its so (quoth she) the waues shall haue,
More then by right or iustice they can craue.

With that she leapt into the curled floud,
And as she leapt, she spake vnto the waue,
Remorcelesse thou (quoth she) that stain'd his bloud,
Shall now receiue two louers in one graue.
For fit it is, who liuing had one heart,
Should haue one graue, and not inter'd apart.

Yet

Yet in my death I do inuoke the Powers,
Which do frequent this wofull Riuer side,
That they adore and decke our Tombe with flowers,
Where ere our loue-expofed corps abide.
And if they aske where they shall find our graues,
Let them looke downe into these surging waues.

And I intreate my friends they do not weepe,
In that we are departed to our rest,
Sweete rest, may Hero *say, when in her sleepe*
She clips Leander *whom she loued best:*
She lou'd him best indeed, for she did craue
To be enhearsed with him in one waue.

This was no sooner spoke, but raging streames,
Cut off poore Heroes *speech, and with their force,*
Clos'd her in silence, while each Nimph complains,
And chides the Riuer for his small remorse.
Thus ended they, their ends were their content,
Since for to die in Loue, their minds were bent.

Let not fond loue so fondly thee embrace,
Lest like the Iuie or the Missselto,
It winde about thee to thy owne disgrace,
And make thee slaue to brutish passions too.
Be constant in thy loue, as chast not spotted,
Loue well and long, but not in loue besotted.

The Argument.

Louers consent finds fit place of recourse,
For Loues content chang'd into discontent,
King *Ninus* tombe their sconce or sorrows source,
To which a dreadfull Lyonesse is sent:
Which *Thisbe* spies and flies: her bloudie tyre,
Bereaues her Loue of life, and both expire.

II. ELEGIE.

WEll then we will repaire vnto that place,
 Where we shall haue fruition of our ioy,
By Ninus *tombe, farre from our parents face,*
Where mutuall Loue needs little to be coy:
Where met, we may enioy that long-sought pleasure,
Which Loue affoords, when Loue vnlocks her treasure.

Thisbe was mute, in being mute she yeelded,
Who knowes not Maides, by silence giue consent?
So on her silence her assent was builded,
Since in his loue she plac'd her sole content;
Onward he goes most forward to obtaine,
That which she wish'd, but Parents did restraine.

And coming nigh vnto king Ninus *Tombe,*
Erected neare a Christall riueling,
There as she mus'd a Lion fierce did come
Forth of the groue, whence he his prey did bring.
                                              Who

Who all embrude with *slaughter* and with *bloud*,
Came for to quench his thirst at that same floud.

Thisbe *perceiuing this enraged beast,*
Fled for her refuge to a hollow tree,
Yet she for hast, what she suspected least,
Let fall her Tire, and to her shelfe did flee ;
Where in the shade while she affrighted stood,
The Lion tinct her virgine-tire with blood.

And hauing now well drench'd his bloudie iawes,
Making returne vnto his shadie den,
Young Pyramus *for to obserue loues lawes,*
(Loues lawes must needs be kept) did thither tend,
And coming neare, her *could he not espie,*
But her vnhappie Tire di'd bloudily.

Which he no sooner with his eyes beheld,
Then he exclaim'd against his destinie,
Since Thisbe *was by his request compeld,*
To be a pray to Lions cruelty :
And taking vp the bloud-besmeared Tire,
Amintas-like his end he doth conspire.

Yet fore his end in dismall sort he cried,
Fie on the fates, that did poore Thisbe *kill,*
Fie on those ruthlesse gods that haue decreed,
Wilde sauage beasts her crimson bloud to spill ;
But why do I stand arguing with fate,
Lamenting ore her breathlesse corps too late ?

For

*For if thou lou'd her, shew thy loue in this
Lost, to regaine her presence by thy death;
Death, which hath left thee this poore Tire to kisse,
On which I'le breath and kisse, and kisse and breath:
Farewell my loue, if* Piramus *did loue thee,
He'le shew his loue, his loue shall be aboue thee.*

*Strike home (fond man) and do not feare grim death,
But meete him in the mid-way to thy graue;
For* Thisbes *loue I gladly lose my breath,
And that is all that* Thisbe *now can haue:
And with this speech, deepe griefe cut off his word,
He slue himselfe with his owne dismall sword.*

Thisbe *long trembling in her hollow Caue,
Came forth at last to meete her dearest loue.
How apt is loue the chastest to depraue,
Making a rauenous Vultur of a Doue;
Wherefore in haste she hies her to the spring,
Where she might heare a dolefull Syluane sing.*

*And to receiue the sorrow more at large,
Nigher she drew vnto that mournfull tune,
Where like a merchant in a splitted barge,
She stood amaz'd, and standing listned one.
Sorting his griefe vnto her deare friends griefe;
Whom she sought out, to yeeld her some reliefe.*

Good Siluane *say (thus spake she) hauing found him,
Did'st see a youth coast neare this darkesome way?
For much I feare, some sauage beast hath wound him,
If thou canst guide me to him, pray thee say:*
Here

*Here is the Tombe where he appointed me,
To ſtay for him, yet him I cannot ſee.*

*Virgin (quoth he) that youth you ſeeke is gone;
Whither (kind* Siluane *?) I will after him,
He ſhall not leaue me in this wood alone,
For truſt me* Siluane *I haue frighted bin,
And by a dreadfull Lion ſo beſet,
As I am hardly my owne woman yet.*

*See Ladie, ſee; with that he vaniſhed,
To waile the loſſe of* Nais *he had kept,
Who by a Centaure lately rauiſhed,
Was quite conueyd away while th'*Siluane *ſlept.
She turnes her eye, yet ſcarce will truſt her eye,
No, nor the place where ſhe doth ſee him lye.*

*Dead! why it cannot be, thus ſhe began,
Who could harme thee that nere did any harme,
No not in thought to any liuing man?
With that ſhe felt his pulſe if it were warme,
But breathleſſe he, key-cold as any ſtone,
She lookes and weepes, and bathes him looking on.*

*Yet long it was ere ſhe could ſhed a teare,
For greateſt grieues are not by teares expreſt,
Deepe-rooted ſorrowes greateſt burden beare,
Kept moſt in heart, but ſhowne in eye the leaſt.
For leſſer grieues haue eyes to bring them forth,
But greateſt ſtill are ſtrangled in their birth.*

Griefe

Griefe therefore doth rebound, and with rebound
She shakes her Piramus *and strokes his cheeke:*
Loue was all eares, for he did heare her sound,
And mou'd his head from ground, but could not speake;
Yet did he hold her hand, as if her hand
Staid Deaths arrest, and could him countermand.

And as a man who ship-wrack'd on the Sea,
Not able to endure vnto the Port,
Takes hold on wracke, which He *as constantly*
Keepes in his hand, as he did labour for't:
From which, no danger whatsoere betide him,
Nor death it selfe can any way deuide him.

Euen so did Piramus *keepe in his armes,*
The choifest body of his chastest loue,
Whereby he thinkes himselfe so free from harmes,
As die he cannot till he thence remoue:
Yet though it's death to him, since Thisbe *would,*
He is contented to let go his hold.

This seene, (sayes Thisbe*) since thy loue is such,*
That to deuide thy selfe from thine owne loue,
To thee's a second death or harder much,
And mou'd by me thy hold thou doest remoue;
Ere long will Thisbe *shew her selfe to thee,*
An equall Mirror of loues constancie.

Yet do I pray those friends who are conioyned
To vs in Bloud, to take of vs compassion,
That as our Loues, our corpes may be combined,
With funerall rites after our countrie fashion:

F   *And*

And when to ashes they our corps shall burne,
Let both our drearie ashes haue one vrne.

Let both our graues (poore graues) be ioyn'd in one,
As both our hearts were linked in one twist:
And let our corps be couer'd with one stone,
So may our bones so neerely ioyn'd be blist;
For gods this priueledge to louers giue,
When others die by death, in death they liue.

By this young Thisbes *speech was finished,*
Who was as wearie to enioy her life,
As a loose Matron of her husbands bed,
Or a young spend-thrift of his long-liu'd wife:
Euen so was Thisbe, *whom death did afford,*
Though not same hand to kill, yet selfe-same sword.

But yet some Plant *is still affectionate,*
Vnto a Louers death, whose constancie
Neuer doth alter from her wonted state,
But perseueres in stedfast certaintie:
For th' Mulberrie, seeing them Mourners lacke,
Milke-white before put on a sable blacke.

Morus *thus altred in her former hue,*
Changing her colour for the death of Loue,
Hath to this day her mourning-weed to shew;
Well might they moue vs then, when they did moue
The senselesse trees, who did so truly grieue,
As for their sake they would their colour leaue.

The

The Argument.

THe losse of *Didoes* honour and her loue,
Are both bemon'd: *Anna* but all in vaine,
Seekes to recomfort her: she seemes to proue
No faith in strangers: she dissolues her traine:
Incense is burn'd; a fire she doth deuise,
Wherein she makes her selfe the sacrifice.

III. ELEGIE.

DIdo *lamenting, that Æneas should
So soone conuert his loue to bitter hate,
The thought whereof surpast a thousand fold,
The losse of Scepter, honour, or estate:
Curseth the hap she had to entertaine,
Or giue such harbour to a thanklesse Swaine.*

*Yet do not so (quoth she,) he's generous,
Sprong from the Troian stocke and Progenie:
Curse him not Dido, it were ominous
To his proceedings and his dignitie;
He did requite thy loue, thou knowst deuoutly,
And did performe his Turnaments as stoutly.*

*Sweete was the Pleasure, though the fruite be sower,
Deare his embraces, kind his fauours too,
Witnesse that Bower (aye me) that rosie Bower,
In which heauen knowes, and few but heauen do know,*

I gag'd my heart to him, he his to me,
Which makes me ty'd in faith how ere he be.

And he protested, Simple woman, thou
To credit what a stranger had protested:
For what is he that liues, and will not do
As much or more, till he hath fully feasted
His eager Appetite, which being allaid,
He streight forgets the promise he hath made?

And so did he, respectlesse of his vow,
Or (breach of faith) which whatsoere he thinke,
Will be reueng'd by Heauen, and sharply too,
Gods do not euer sleepe when they do winke.
For though they spare, They *will at last strike home,*
And send Reuenge to th'infant in my wombe.

Poore Orphane Infant, whose iniurious birth,
As closely done, shall closely be suppressed,
And haue a double Mother, Mee and Earth,
And for thy Fathers sake a double chest:
Whose Tombe shall be my wombe, whose drerie shrowd,
Shall be my selfe, that gaue it life and food.

This as she spake, her Sister she came in,
Aduising her vnto a milder course,
Then to afflict her selfe with thought of him
Whose heart was reft of pittie and remorse;
Wherefore (said she) since sorrow is in vaine,
Forget his absence, that will salue your paine.

Will salue *my paine (quoth she!) and then she gron'd,*
                                                Cures

LOVE STAIND WITH LVST.

Cures to apply is easier then to cure:
No, no, my sorrowes may be well bemon'd,
But nere redrest: for th'eye of heau'n's too pure,
To view my sinne, my foile, my guilt, my staine,
Whose di'es so deepe 'twill nere be white againe.

Yet to preuent the scandall would ensue,
If fame should know what hath in priuate bene,
I'le lop this Branch, lest Time should say, it grew
(Adulterate Issue) from the Carthage Queene:
Which ere I do, lest I incurre heauens hate,
With Incense burn'd, their wrath I'le expiate.

Wherewith I'le purge (if such may purged be)
The fact I did, which grieues me that I did,
Staining my honour with his periurie,
Which gods do see, though it from man be hid:
For this (deare sister) build me here a fire,
To sacrifice my shame, appease heauens ire.

Anna, for so her Sister hight, doth rere
This fatall pile, preparing all things meete
For such a sacrifice, as Iuniper,
Spicknarde, and Mirrhe, to make the Incense sweete,
Vnknowne to what her Sister did intend,
Whose faire pretence came to a timelesse end.

Sister (quoth Dido*) now you may be gone,*
Sweete is Deuotion that is most retir'd,
Go you aside, and leaue me here alone,
Which Anna *did as* Dido *had requir'd:*
Who now alone with heauen-erected eyes,

Her wofull felfe fhe makes the facrifice.

Anna *retir'd, did heare her Sifter fhrike,*
With which at firft affrighted, she made hafte,
To see th'euent, the fight whereof did ftrike
Such a diftraction in her, as it paft
The bounds of Nature, where experience tries,
More forrow's in the heart then in the eyes.

At laft her eyes long fhut vnfealed were,
To eye that mournfull Obiect, now halfe turn'd
To mouldred afhes, for it did appeare,
As halfe were fcorch'd, the other halfe were burn'd:
Which feene, fhe cries, and turnes away her fight,
Black woe betide them that fuch guefts inuite.

Anna *thus left alone, yet mindfull too,*
Of Didoes *honour, reares a Princely shrine,*
The like whereof that Age could neuer fhow,
Nor any Age, till * Artemifias *time:*
On which was this engrauen : Loue was my loffe,
Rich was my Crowne, yet could not cure my croffe.

* *Wife to Maufolus king of Caria.* vid. Plutar. in Apotheg.

Thus Dido *di'd, who was not much vnlike*
Vnto the Countriman who nourifhed
The * *dead-ftaru'd Viper, that vngratefull fnake,*
Who reft him life, that it had cherifhed :
So Dido *fhe, whofe fall my Mufe recites,*
Lies flaine by him, whom fhe in loue inuites.

* Latet Anguis in herba.

Nec Hofpes ab Hofpite tutus.

AN

AN ELEGIE VPON
THESE ELEGIES.

Et fond Leander *warne thee, to remaine*
Vpon the Riuer banke in safetie:
Let Piramus *rash fact thy hand restraine,*
Too deare costs Loue, mix'd with such crueltie:
Lastly, let Dido *warne thee by her end,*
To trie that Guest thou makes thy bosome friend.

Venit amor grauius quo serius vrimur intus,
  Vrimur, & cæcum pectora vulnus habent.

THE SECOND
SECTION OF
DIVINE AND MORALL
SATYRES:
With
AN ADIVNCT VPON THE PRECEDENT; WHEREBY THE
Argument with the firſt cauſe of publiſhing
theſe Satyres, be euidently related.

Diſce & doce.

LONDON,
Printed for RICHARD WHITAKER.
1 6 2 1.

TO THE WOR-
THIE CHERISHER AND NOVRISHER OF ALL GENE-
rous ſtudies, *S. W. C.* Knight,
R. B.
His affectionate Country-man wiſheth the
increaſe of all honour, health, and
happineſſe.

IR,
When I had compos'd theſe rag-
ged lines,
Much like the Beare who brings
her young ones forth,
In no one part well featur'd, ſhe
repines,
That ſuch a lumpe of fleſh ſhould haue a birth:
Which to reforme, ſhe's ſaid to vndertake
A ſecond taske, and licks them into ſhape.

So I producing theſe vnriper ſeedes,
Scarce growne to their perfection, knew not how,
(Since different humour, different cenſure breeds)
How they ſhould come to ripeneſſe, but by you:
                                                Whoſe

Whose faire acceptance may such count'nance show,
As you may others moue to grace them too.

Nor do I doubt but these shall purchase grace,
'Mongst such as honour vertue, for how low
So'ere the style be, Subiect is not base,
But full of Diuine matter; and I know,
The Sunne giues life, as well to simple weeds,
As vnto flowers or other fruitfull seeds.

Yours in all faithfull
Obseruance,

Richard Brathwayte,
Musophylus.

Vpon the Dedicatorie.

T*Hough he (and happie he) bereft by fate,*
  To whom I meant this worke to dedicate,
This shall find shelter in his liuing name,
  He's chang'd indeed, but I am still the same.

The

The Argument.

Of Elpenor *an Epicure, liuing senfually in a Caue, respectleffe of the soules eternitie.*

Lpenor, who long time liuing (as the Dormoufe) in the caue of fenfualitie and fecuritie, refted careleffe of a future bleffing, as one rauifhed with the prefent delight of carnall libertie, became at laft reftrained by the vertuous edict of a gracious Emperour; by whom he was exiled and banifhed, not onely from the Princes Court, but from the vtmoft coafts of *Arcadia* wherein he liued. Now it chanced, that during fuch time as he remained in *Cadmos*, a Satyrift of no leffe refpect then approued grauitie, well obferuing the impietie of *Elpenor*, as alfo the deferued cenfure which his Epicureall life had incurred; endeuoured to defcribe his condigne fall, with no leffe pregnancie of wit, and maturitie of iudgement, then a fetled feuerity in reprehenfion of his godleffe opinions: which Defcription he fixed (as may be imagined) vpon the Portall gate, where he might of neceffitie fee his owne impietie as in a glaffe tranfparent, perfpicuoufly demonftrated. What difcontent he con-

conceiued in the difplaying of his owne fhame, may be coniectured by the fubiect of this Inuection, taxing him of his infamous life, the onely occafion of his obfcure end: whofe fortunes were aforetime moft eminent, now moft deiected.

Et quanta eft infœlicitas, fuiffe fœlicem, &c? Boæthius.

THE FIRST SATYRE.

ELpenor *groueling in his duskie caue,*
Secure of God or Gods high prouidence,
Nought but luxurious difhes feemes to craue,
To fatisfie the appetite of fence.
He fpurnes at heauen, contemnes all fupreme power,
Priding in that will perifh in an houre.

God is of no respect with Epicures,
Senceleffe of of heauen or minds tranquilitie,
Senceleffe of Hell, *which euermore endures,*
Glad to receiue earths ioyes fatietie:
Where rapt with Obiects of deceiuing Pleafure,
They liue to fin, but to repent at leafure.

Is not that Statue (fay Elpenor*) thine,*
With eyes-inflam'd and palfie-fhaking hand,
Vpon whofe forehead's writ, Abufe of time?
I know it is, for I do fee it ftand
Neare Baccus fhrine, where either drinkes to other,
Healths to Eryca, *their lafciuious Mother.*

Where Syren voyces fo apply the eare,
With an affected melodie, that earth

Might

Might a phantasticke Paradise appeare,
Through consort of an vniuersall mirth,
Which these inchanting harmonists did vse,
To th' wofull friends of wandring Ithacus.

But who is He *that seemes to challenge thee,*
Yet staggers in his challenge ? O I know him,
It's Hans *the Dutch-man, new arriu'd from Sea,*
Stand fast Elpenor, *if thou'lt ouerthrow him.*
But why enioyne I that thou canst not do,
Halfe of a stand were well betwixt you two.

And much I doubt, lest Cripple-like you grow,
So long it is, as it is out of mind,
Since you were seene by any man to go,
Which makes me heare your legs are hard to find :
For vse brings on Perfection, and I feare
Your dropsie-legs are out of vse to beare.

See thou vnweldy wretch, that fatall shelfe,
To which thou art declining, being growne
A heauie vselesse burthen to thy selfe,
In whom no glimpse of vertue may be showne :
A Barmie leaking vessell (which in troth)
For want of reason is fill'd vp with froth.

Aged Turpilio *grones at mispent time,*
Wishing he had his youth to passe againe :
For then He *would not vse't as thou doest thine,*
But mone the houres which He *hath spent in vaine.*
But Time runs on, and will not make returne,
When Death succeeds, whom no man can adiourne.

And

*And seeſt thou this, and wilt thou not prouide
For Deaths arreſt, whoſe ſad approch will be
So full of horror, as thou ſcarce ſhalt bide,
So grim he is, that* He *ſhould looke on thee?
And yet* He *will, for he no diffrence makes,
Twixt rich and poore, but whom* He *likes he takes.*

*Thy Prince thou seeſt, whoſe vertues are ſo pure
He cannot breath on vice, hath thee exil'd,
Forth of his royall confines, to ſecure
His Realme the more, leſt it ſhould be defil'd
By thy deprau'd example, which once ſtain'd,
(So ranke is vice) would hardly be reclaim'd.*

*Trunke of Confuſion, which deriues thy being
From no ſupernall eſſence, for with it,
Thy works, words, motions haue but ſmall agreeing,
But from ſecuritie, where thou doeſt ſit;
Feeding thy vaſt-inſatiate appetite,
With euery day new diſhes of delight.*

*O rouſe thy ſelfe from that obſcureſt vale,
And ſing a thankefull Hymne vnto thy Maker,
Creepe not vpon thy bellie like the Snaile,
But like the Larke mount vp to thy Creator;
Adorning thee with reaſon, ſenſe and forme,
All loſt in thee, through want of Grace forlorne.*

*Honour doth ill become the ſlothfull man,
Who* Zanie-*like becomes a ſlaue to pleaſure,
For* He *when vrgent cauſes moue* Him, *than
Neglects Occaſion, and reſerues that leaſure,*

Which

OF SLOTH.

Which might haue bene employd in cares of ſtate,
For his delights, bought at too high a rate.

This thy experience tells thee, whoſe eſtate
Once high, now low, made ſubiect to diſgrace,
Shewes thou art chang'd from what thou was of late,
Yet to my iudgement in a better caſe:
So thou conſider th'ſtate from whence thou came,
And leaue that vice which did procure the ſame.

But doubt I muſt, (ô that my doubts were vaine)
Such great expence is made of precious time,
As 'twill be much to do to waſh the ſtaine
Of that enormious loathſome life of thine.
Yet* Teares haue power, and they are ſoueraigne too,
And may do more then any elſe can do.

* Sicut nullus eſt locus in quo malum nō perpetratur, ita nullus fit locus in quo de malo pœnitentia non agatur.

Then comfort take, yet comfort mixe with teares,
Thou* Cadmos leaues, and it's thy natiue ſoile;
Suppoſe it be, each coaſt or clime appeares
The good-mans wiſhed Country, which bleſt ſtyle,
Exceeds all worldly comfort, which thou had,
For this is paſſing good, that paſſing bad.

* Cadmos *a hill by* Laodicea *out of which iſſueth the Riuer* Lycus, *it taketh this name from* Cadmus *ſonne to* Agenor *king of* Phænicia.

I do not ſpeake, as thoſe whoſe guilded breath,
Traines on the vicious with deceiptfull hope;
For I haue ſet before thee life and death,
And this I aim'd to make my chiefeſt ſcope:
That if reward of life could no way gaine thee,
The feare of death & vengeance might reclaime thee.

Life as a Crowne or Diadem is due,

To fuch whofe wayes are not in Error led,
Death as a guerdon doth to fuch accrue,
Whofe carnall hearts with pleafures captiued,
Thinke not on Death, till Death his flag difplay,
And now fecure fhall take their life away.

Turne then vnto the coaft of Arcadie,
From whence thou waft exil'd, and there furuey
The vertues of that Prince did banifh thee,
And weigh the caufe why there thou might not ftay:
Which done, feeke to regaine thy Princes loue,
But chiefly His, *that is thy Prince aboue.*

The Argument.

Cornelia wife to *Pompey,* furnamed the Great, after her husbands ouerthrow in *Pharfalia,* flaine within fhort time after by the procurement of *Septimius* in the kingdome of *Egypt;* became much diftreffed with the difcomfort of her loffe, and the forrowfull iffue of his death. Which is as paffionately expreffed by *Lucan* in *Pompeies* expoftulation with *Cornelia* his beloued Ladie, —*Quid perdis tempora luctu?* *Cornelia* thus depriued of all affiftants faue Teares (forrowes hereditarie treafures) for the better reliefe of her eftate (the poore remainder of her fortunes) fued out a petition vnto the Emperour *Cæfar,* whofe royall

royall clemency (as she thought) could not choose but take pittie on the wife, whose husband was become a bootie to his Conquest. But how reasonable soeuer her demands were, it skilled not, for by the corrupt and indirect dealing of *Cælius* and *Tuberculus* she was resisted. The Satyrist therefore in deploring of *Cornelia's* miserie, and inueying against the two Courtiers corruption, morally dilateth on the desolate estate of a forlorne widdow, and the sinister practises of corrupt Aduocates.

THE SECOND SATYRE.

POmpey *the* Great *no sooner was interr'd,*
  But poore Cornelia *his distressed wife,*
To her deceassed Lords estate preferr'd,
Was drawne by Consul Asper *into strife:*
And so opprest by hote pursuite of foes,
That she deuoid of friends was fraught with woes.

She, wofull she, lest she should lose her state,
Makes meanes to * Cælius *to preferre her suite,*   * *A prodigall Courtier, but in great fauour with Cæsar.*
Which he's content to do, but at such rate,
As 'twill cost deare to bring the cause about:
Yet she remedilesse, to worke her peace,
Stood not much on't, but did the Courtier please.

Cælius *possest of his iniurious fee,*
Which he consum'd in riotous expence,
Forgot the widdows cause dishonestlie,
Without remorse or touch of conscience.

For vnderhand (as Courtiers vſe to do)
He takes a priuate bribe of Aſper *too.*

Cornelia *now in hope of good ſucceſſe,*
Comes vnto Cælius *as her purchas'd friend,*
And humbly craues to know what's her redreſſe,
Or in what ſort her ſuite is like to end:
Where He *as ſtrangely anſwers her demand,*
And ſay's, her ſuite came neuer to his hand.

No ſuite! (thus did this Matron ſtreight reply)
O Rome where is thy* Iuſtice now enthron'd,
Thou that didſt vſe to heare a widdow crie,
And right her cauſe as thou her wrongs bemon'd!
But ſpare Cornelia, *what reliefe can come*
Frō corrupt Courts, where gold makes Conſuls dumbe?

* *Iuſtice may be aptly compared to the Caledonie ſtone, which retaineth her vertue no longer then it is rubbed with gold.*

If my much-honor'd Lord, whoſe Country loue
Reſt him of breath, ſhould ſee this preſent time,
How gifts can limit Iuſtice, would't not moue
His Royall ſpirit, ſeeing me and mine,
Whoſe onely comfort's this, we may repoſe,
And ioy in this, we haue no more to loſe?

Whileſt wrong'd Cornelia *ſat thus penſiuely,*
*Tuberculus *a Courtier paſt that way,*
Who in compaſſion of her miſerie,
Knowne to her ſelfe not to her grieues, did ſtay;
For generous minds are neuer more expreſt,
Then in applying comfort to th'diſtreſt.

* *One of eſpeciall eſteeme with Pompey before his ouerthrow.*

Ladie (quoth he) if I could eaſe your griefe,

The

OF CORRVPTION.

The loue I owe vnto your familie,
Me thinks might promise to your selfe reliefe,
Impart them then, what ere your sorrowes be:
Cures haue bene wrought where little was expected,
For where the mind is willing, ought's effected.

She hearing him so vertuously inclin'd,
Prone vnto pittie, sighing did declare,
How that her sonne young Pompey *was confin'd,*   Sext. Pompe.
Which was the greatest subiect of her care:
Whom if He would make meanes for to release,
The current of her sorrowes soone would ceasse.

Another suite I haue, which Asper *moues,*
To force me from my right of widdowhood,
Wherein his worser cause the better proues,
For* mightie men can hardly be withstood: * Inimicitiæ potentum violentæ *Senec.*
In these I must intreate your Lordships care,   * Like *Verconius in the time of Alexander Seuerus, who pretending familiaritie with the Emperour, tooke mens mony for preferring their suites, abused them, & did them no good at all: at last conuented before the Emperour, he was iudged to be hanged vp in a chimney, and so perish with smoke, for that he sold smoke to the people.* Lamprid. in Seu. Verco.
In lieu whereof I'le gratifie with prayer.

Tuberculus *did answer her demands,*
But he expected * *ointment, and delaying,*
To giue her further comfort, there He stands,
He for his fee, she for her cause stood praying.
Cornelia *well perceiuing what He would,*
Good gods (quoth she) is Iustice wholly sould?

How do you meane (quoth he) it is our meanes,
Could we be thus enameld euery day,
Or in such port maintaine our fauning friends,
If we receiu'd not profit by delay?
No Ladie, no, who in these dayes do liue,

And would haue Iuſtice, muſt not ſticke to giue.

Thus was Cornelia *croſt, her meanes preuented,*
No comfort now remaining ſaue despaire;
Wherefore (perforce) ſhe reſts hope-reft, contented
To loſe the ſight of her confined heire,.
Who liues reſtrain'd: Aſper *her ſtate hath got,*
And poore Cornelia *with her cauſe forgot.*

The Argument of Lucian.

LVcian a profeſſed enemy to Christ, detracting much from the deuine & ſole-healthfull Myſteries of our Redemptiõ, wherby he became odious to the all-ſeeing veritie; chanced to trauell for delight, (as one of generall obſeruation) into forraine places: where (as heauens iuſt doome would haue it) he was worried by dogs, as a iuſt reward for his impious and egregious contempt towards God; reuiling that all-ſeeing Maieſtie of Chriſt with the ſacred office of his Miniſters, and like a ſnarling or biting Curre, barking at the admirable and ineffable workes which were wrought by Gods omnipotencie: for which cauſe God accordingly puniſhed him. A remarkable ſpectacle to all enſuing ages, concluding emphatically with the Satyriſt.

Ingenioſus

OF ATHEISME.

Ingeniosus erat, superum sed acerrimus hostis,
At canis est superum tempore præda canum.

Wittie, but foe to God, who long in vaine,
   Barking at God, by barking currs was slaine.

The Satyre followeth, Morally applyed.

THE THIRD SATYRE.

INgenious Lucian, *ripe in poesie,*
Apt to compose, and pregnant to inuent,   In vit. Luci.
Well read in secrets of Phylosophie,
And in all Morall knowledge excellent;
For all these rarer parts vnto him giuen,
Ceas'd not to * *barke against the power of heauen.*   * Isti latrant non mordent, non nocent : *August.*

This snarling Curre, for he detracted God,
As profest enemie to pietie,
Chanced to trauell, where Gods irefull rod
Made him a witnesse to posteritie ;   (*power,*   * Thus as he bark'd against the
For this same * *wretch who bark'd against heauens*   God of heauen,
Did barking currs (such was heauens doome) deuoure.   To barking currs he for a prey was giuen.

Soile to his soule, and so to Christs profession,
For He *no Christ profest, but thought't a scorne*
That God made man, from God should haue cõmission,
Without mans helpe to be of Virgin borne :
Yet see his fall, who did himselfe deceiue,
Vnpitied dies, and dying ha's no graue.

What's Sions *peace (sayes* He*) there's no such place ;*   The Atheists opinions.
Earth hath her Sion, *if we ayme our care*
At any other Mansion, it's a chafe

So fruitleſſe, as if we ſhould beate the ayre,
Or plant our hope in things which cannot be,
And ſuch's our truſt in fained Deitie.

Thou vglie viſard, that with faire pretence
Of Morall diſcipline ſhadowes thy ſin,
Reclaime thy ſelfe by timely penitence,
And loath that horrid Caue thou walloweſt in:
Thy ſin's deep-dide, yet not of that deepe ſtaine,
But* Teares & Prayers may make them white againe.

* Lachrymæ verbis, ſuſpiria votis immiſceantur.

Haſt thou no * Anchor to relie vpon?
No Refuge nor no Recluſe for thy hope?
Behold thy Ieſus he's thy corner ſtone,
Make him thy ayme, thy ſuccour, ſhelter, ſcope,
And he'le receiue thee in the * Throne of bleſſe,
The boundleſſe Ocean of all happineſſe.

* Anchora cui ſpes eſt innixa, Angularis lapis in quem fundata.

*θρόνος τῆς ἡδονῆς.

Returne thou wicked Lucian, *make thy verſe*
Thy* Retractation, be not ouerbold,
Leſt when good-men ſhall view thy forlorne hearſe,
In thy reproch they cauſe this to be told
To after-ages: Here he lies interr'd,
Who * erring knew, and in his knowledge err'd.

* Vt medicus, perite tractat vulnera, Qui opera retractat perperam edita.
* Errando diſco.

Sweete and delightfull * Poems canſt thou make,
Of Hymen *rites, or* Venus *dalliance,*
And pleaſant ſeemes the labour thou doeſt take,
While to thy Pipe deluded Louers dance:
But in ſuch ſacred meaſures thou art ſlow,
As teach men how to liue, and what to know.

* Qualis ergo eſt iſta, quæ tam multa de cæteris nouit, & ſe qualiter facta ſit prorſus ignorat? *Auguſt.*

Mirrha

OF ATHEISME.

Mirrha *the wanton mother of a wanton,*
Gamesome the Mother and the Daughter too,
Giues a fit subiect for thy Muse to chant on,
Relating what a Louer ought to do;
In which lasciuious straine, fond Loue is brought
To hate what's good, but to affect what's naught.

Thou canst report how Romanes ioyned were,   Vid. Tit. Liu. in
First with the Sabines, and what strange delights   Dec. 1, & 3.
Tooke their inuention from those feasts were there,   Ouid. in fast.
Duly solemniz'd on their nuptiall nights;
Of Sphinx, Charybdis, Scilla, Ctesiphon,
With Prœtus *letters against* * Bellerophon.   * *Who slue the two monsters Chymera and Solymos in Lycia.*

These thou canst feature as Apelles, He
The Prince of painters could not better show
Their formes, then thou their natures, which may be
Portrayers of thy wit and learning too:
But what are these but shadowes, if thou moue
Thy eye to those blest obiects are aboue?

Lend but thy eare to aerie warbling Birds,
Which day by day sing pleasant madrigals;
And thou shalt heare what praise the Larke affoords,   Larke.
Whilest with sweete Hymnes she on her maker cals,   * A laudes dicendo dicitur
Where each repayes their due in their degree,   Alauda.
And much abashd do rest asham'd of thee.

The flower which hath no sense, nor hath no feeling,
Nor apprehends the difference of things,
Performes her office in delight of smelling,
Likewise the tree most fruitfull blossoms brings:

The

The Serpent, Adder, and each crauling worme,
Haue mutuall duties giuen them with their forme.

<small>* *The Pismire and Locust (of all other creatures) haue no king nor leader.* vid. AElian. & Plin. in natur. Hist.</small>

The Basiliske the * *king of Serpents is,*
The Lion of all beasts, the Cedar tree
Is chiefe of Trees, Leuiathan of fish,
And man ore these hath sole supremacie:
Thus euery Creature in her seuerall kind,
Hath seuerall Lords and limits her assign'd.

Thou Lucian *art endu'd with what these want,*
And canst distinguish betwixt good and ill,
Yet thou denies what other Creatures grant,
And which is worse, thou so continuest still:
Thou laughs at Adams *fall, and thinks't a shame,*
Man should auouch an Apple caus'd the same.

Wo worth that fruite that had so bitter taste,
Bringing Perdition to the soule of man,
That free-borne Creature, *which so farre surpast*
Mans fraile condition when it first began;
That was an Apple that too dearely cost,
Which made so many soules for euer lost.

If I should Catechise thee Lucian,
And tell the vertue of each seuerall thing;
How reason first was distribute to man,
And how the earth globe-like in aire doth hing,

<small>* Spicas creuisse cernimus, eas autem quando creuerunt non cernimus.</small>

The secret grouth of Plants which daily grow,
Yet * *how or when no humane sense can know.*

The

OF ATHEISME. 91

The * Fabrick of the heauen, whose eminence
Shewes admiration to vs that behold
Her glorious Bodies sacred influence,
Whose distinct Motion, who is't can vnfold?
None but the Author and the founder can,
For it exceeds the reach of any man.

* *That starrie Gallerie embost with gold, fretted with orbs of Christall, siluer'd ouer, with pearle pau'd, roofed with an Agget couer.*

If I should question thee, whence these deriue
Their proper Motion, it would thee behooue
To yeeld, that some to these do Motion giue,
Since what se're moues doth by another moue:
Which thou confirmes and adds, nought vnder Sunne
Is done in these, *but is by Nature done.*

So thou * referrs that wonderfull Creation,
After the Deluge to a mortall wight,
Discoursing vainly how Deucalion,
Refurnish'd earth which was vnpeopled quite;
But thou deceiued art, it's nothing so,
For it was God that gaue increase to Noe.

* *Holding with Albumazar that his leading the children of Israel ouer the Red sea, was no more but obseruing the influence of Starres, and waining season of the Moone that withdraweth the tides; and that miraculous issuing of water out of the rocke, by the stroke of a rod was no more, but noting those spring-heads, whereto the wild asses resorted to quench their thirst.*
b *Whom th' morning sees so proudly go, ere euening come may lie full low.* Senec.

We are his clay, we must confesse his power,
He is our Potter, whose deuine command
Can dash vs earthen vessels in one b *houre,*
Subiect vnto the iudgement of his hand;
For he no sooner shall withdraw his breath,
Then Man leaues to be Man, and welcomes death.

Heauens power to which no Mortall can extend,
(Not to be argued or disputed on,)
Because it's not in Man to comprehend,
The radiant Splendor of the glorious Sunne:

Much

Much leffe profounder fecrets, which were fram'd,
For admiration, not to be prophan'd.

<small>* We haue heard of diuerfe, exemplarily punifhed euen in that wherein they cōtemptuoufly profaned; as Iulian, Herodias, Balfhafar, and Thymelicus the enterlude-plaier; who dancing vpon the fcaffold in a Cope (a robe of the Church) fell downe dead. Thymelico faltatori, &c. Vid. Val. Maxi. lib. 1. cap. 2.</small>

* *Prophan'd, if nam'd without due reuerence,*
To that Supreme all-working Maieftie,
Whofe Palme containes this Earths circumference,
Whofe praife takes accent from heauens Hierarchie.
Let not, O let not him who gaue man tongue,
To yeeld him praife, for filence make it dumbe.

Thou canft compofe a fong of Shepheards liues,
Spent in a pleafant veine of Recreation,
How they fit chatting with their wanton wiues,
Tricking and toying in a Shepheards fafhion:
This thou canft do, and it's done pretily,
For it fhews wit, yet fpent vnfittingly.

O if thou would confine thy felfe in reafon,
And leaue fond Poems of a doting Louer,
Obferuing Natures tone, tune, time, and feafon,
How well would thefe feeme to that powerfull mouer;
Whofe eyes are pure, and of that piercing fight,
As they loue light, but hate fuch works are light.

But O too vaine's the current of thy vaine,
Soild with the Motiues of vntamed luft,
Which layes vpon thy Name that endleffe fhame,
As fhall furuiue, when thou return'd to duft,
Shalt much lament thofe Poems thou haft writ,
Through th'light conceit of thy licentious wit.

Nor is it gaine mou's thee to proftitute,

That

That precious talent which thou doeſt poſſeſſe ;
No, it's delight thou haſt to gaine repute,
'Mongſt men made* beaſts through their voluptuouſnes*   * Sicut Belluæ
O hate that affectation, leſt this ſhelfe,   ſunt humanæ,
Of vaine applauſe do ruinate thy ſelfe !   ita homines
                                                                                                                ſunt belluini.

For ſuch eſteeme, what honour wil't afford,
What comfort in the graue, where thou lies dead;
When thy laſciuious * works ſhall beare record,   * By thoſe ſtu-
Of what was by thee writ or publiſhed ?   dies, which
Nay 'twill preiudice thee, it cannot chuſe,   I affected, am I
Vaine's that opinion ill-men haue of vs.   condemned, by
                                                                                                                thoſe I praiſed,
                                                                                                                 am I diſpara-
                                                                                                                 ged. Aug.

Thus thou ſuſtaines the height of miſerie,
To ſee a * Cleobes and Biton grac'd,   * Two brothers,
With honour, fame, deſertfull dignitie,   ſonnes to Argia
Thy glory prun'd, thy laurell-wreath defac'd :   a Propheteſſe in
The triumphs of thy wit ſo quite forgot,   the temple of
As if (ſo fickle's fame) thou flouriſh'd not.   Iuno.

Nor can we ſay thoſe flouriſh, whoſe renowne
Conſiſts in praiſe of vice, for though they ſeeme
Vnto the worlds eye ſo fully knowne,
Yet they ſhall be as if they had not bene ;
When vice, which to aduance was their deſire,
Shall melt away as waxe before the fire.

Reſt not, but labour Lucian *to preferre*
The ſage contents of ſacred Myſteries,
Before ſuch Rithms as teach men how to erre,
Whoſe beſt inſtructions are but vanities ;
Which if thou do, wits Treaſure ſhall increaſe,

                                                                        And

And crowne thee Laureat *in the Land of peace.*

Yet reade not so, as not to vnderstand
The graue remainders of Times ancient Booke;
For what a follie is't to haue in hand
Bookes nere red ouer! This, that * *Sage forsooke,*
When in his course of reading He *did vse,*
The choycest flowers in euery worke to chuse.

* In Demo-
sthene magna
pars Demo-
sthenis abest,
cum legitur &
non auditur.

Thus Lucian *haue I warn'd thee to forbeare,*
That snarling humour, of detracting such
Whose vertues shine as Starres in highest Sphære,
Whose worthie Liues can well abide the tutch;
Defame not * *vertue, rather emulate,*
Good-mens example, that's a vertuous hate.

* Ea sola neque
datur dono ne-
que accipitur.
Salust.

The Argument of Stesichorus.

Stesichorus is fained to haue lost his eyes for dispraising *Helen* of Greece, and afterwards to have recouered the same by praising her. The Morall alludeth to such, who ouerborne with the vnbounded height of their owne conceit, distaste the opinion of a multitude, to make their owne irregular iudgement passe for current. These (as we say) vse euer to swim against the streame, affecting that least, which seemes approued by the most: scorning to guide their ship by anothers Card,

measure

measure their life by anothers line, or walke in a common path. Some other application may this Morall make, as *One* vpon this fable would haue *Stesichorus* to shadow a Malecontent, by whom things generally esteemed vse to be most disualued, delighting in nothing more then opposition. Others by way of similitude compare him to *One*, who by much gazing on the Sunne becomes dim-sighted; so *He*, by too intentiue fixing his eye vpon beautie, became blinded: the deuine application whereof I leaue to euery mans peculiar conceite, not louing to presse *these* further, then their owne natiue sence will beare. The subiect whereof this Satyre intreateth, more particularly applyed, may chance to glance at some whose singularitie gaines them Opinion aboue reason; but silence is their best salue, labouring rather to redeeme the time, then reueale their owne shame. Let them be of more humble nature, and I will spare to prosecute any further. *Nihil tam volucre est quàm maledictum*, the poyson whereof is as strong as the passage swift; the vnworthinesse of which condition as I haue euer loathed, so a milde and temperate reproofe for vertues sake haue I euer loued: not ignorant, how some vices (as other sores) are better cured by lenitiues then corasiues, lest the Patient crie out — *Grauiora sunt, haud feram.* Iudge of the Satyre.

THE

THE FOVRTH SATYRE.

[*] *A lyrick Poet, famous for his sweete and pleasing veine.*

Stesichorus * *like* Zeuxes *cannot paint,*
Nor like Lysippus *can delineate;*
For then He *would giue that accomplishment*
To Hellens *beautie, as might propagate*
Her fame to following times, when Ages passe,
Which by Record might shew what Hellen *was.*

Blind Byard now, see how thy iudgement err'd,
By gazing long on beautie thou art blind,
Recanting all too late what thou auerr'd,
So diffrent is th'opinion of that mind,
Where onely selfe-conceit drawes men to shew
Their priuate iudgement, giuen they care not how.

Was she not faire that made all Troy *to burne,*
That made Prince Paris *wander to and fro,*
That made Queene Hecuba *so sore to mourne,*
Both for her selfe and for her Issue too?
Yes she was faire, how ere thy eye esteeme her,
Nor can conceit of one make beauty meaner.

What made stout Menelaus *passe the Sea?*
What Telamon *to rig his well-mann'd ship,*
What Aiax, *what* Achylles? *It was she,*
Whose sweete ambrosiacke breath and cherri-lip,
Relish'd of Nectar, *and infus'd a spirit,*
In Cowards breasts, to gaine true fame by merit.

Old subtill Sinon *can prepare assault,*

Against

OF SINGVLARITIE.

Againſt the ſtrongeſt battlements of Troy,
Whileſt armed Grecians in that ribbed vault,
Preſt for encounter, purpos'd to deſtroy,
Iſſue from Pallas horſe, so aptly * made,   * *It was made by Phereclus, who was after ſlaine by Merion in the ſiege of Troy.*
As Troy had cauſe to curſe the cunning Iade.

Art thou perſwaded yet to praiſe her beautie,
Sith Nature hath ſurpaſt Her ſelfe *in skill,*
As one ingag'd in ſome reſpect of dutie,
Vnto her ſex, to make them honor'd ſtill?
O be perſwaded, to her ſhrine repaire,
For howſoere thou ſaies, thou thinks Her *faire!*

Faire in proportion, motiue in her pace,
An eye as chearefull as the morning-Sunne,
Her haire, her ſmile, her well-beſeeming grace,
By which ſo many Troians were vndone:
In briefe, examine Her *from top to toe,*
And then admire each part accompliſh'd ſo.

Such admiration as like Linceus *eyes,*
Tranſparent Brightneſſe ſeemes to penetrate:
For if Apollo *ſeeing* Daphnes *thighes,*
Wau'd by the Eaſterne winde, forgot his ſtate,
Himſelfe and all, Proportion well may moue,
Since gods themſelues were toſt by guſts of loue.

Did not faire Phyllis *dote vpon a Swaine,*
She paſſing faire, and he a witherd lad,
Whence we may reaſon, none can loue reſtraine,
Nor ſet it limits which it neuer had:
For when we haue done all that we can do,

H   It

It will haue th'courſe and readie paſſage too.

Yet Loue's ſo pure it can endure no ſtaine,
Stain'd Loue is luſt, which is not in her breſt:
Spotleſſe content ſhe ſeekes, which if ſhe gaine,
She freely liues, and fairely takes her reſt:
But barr'd of this, without repoſe ſhe lies,
And dying liues, and liuing loathed dies.

* Nærus erat veneri ſpecies, Helenæq; cicatrix gloria, quæ Paridem fecit amore parem.

It is not Venus * *mole nor* Hellens *ſcarre,*
Adds fuell to affection, for though theſe
Gaue beautie ſummons to commence Loues warre,
Yet outward graces do but onely pleaſe,
As Obiects do the eye; where Loues beſt part
Conſiſts not in the eye, but in the Heart.

But now to thee, *who did diſpraiſe that faire,*
Whoſe beautie ruin'd Cities, now diſclaime
Thy purblind iudgement, and withall compare
Hellen *with* Hero, *or ſome choicer Dame:*

* Lumine qui ſemper proditur ipſe ſuo.

And then it may be * Cupid *will reſtore*
Thine eyes to thee, which He *put out before.*

The Argument of Pigmalion.

P*Igmalion*, whom no ſurpaſſing beautie in all *Cyprus* could captiuate, at last hauing made a curious Image or *Picture* of an amiable woman,

was

OF DOTAGE.

was so rauished with the accomplished proportion of his owne worke, that enamoured therewith, *He* intreated *Venus* to put life in his Image, which with such Artfull delineature he had composed. *Venus* taking commiseration vpon his prayers and teares, infused life in his Picture, whereof *He* begat a beautifull daughter called *Papho*, from whom (or from *Mount Paphos*) *Venus* is said to haue taken her name, styled sometimes by the Poets *Eryca*, sometimes *Paphia*: whose feasts with all ceremoniall rites vsually performed in the honour of an immortall goddesse, were originally solemnized and celebrated onely by the Shepheards of those Mountaines, but afterwards more generally obserued. The Morall includeth the vaine and foolish *Loues* of such as are besotted on euery idle picture or painted Image, whose selfe-conceited vanitie makes beauty their Idoll, becoming Creatures of their owne making, as if they dis-esteemed the creation of their Maker. The Satyre though compendious, compriseth much matter. Reade it, and make vse of the sequele.

Note this you painted faces, whose natiue Countrey (once white Albion) is become reddish, with blushing at your vanities.

THE FIFT SATYRE.

PIgmalion *rare, in rare Proportions making,*
  Yet not in quickning that which He *had framed,*
So exquisite in artfull curious shaping,
In nought (if Zeuxes *iudged) could he be blamed:*
Yet skillfull though He *were in formes contriuing,*
Yet not so skilfull in those formes reuiuing.

            Reuiu'd

Reuiu'd! I wrote amiſſe, they neuer liued:
Improper then to ſay, they were reuiued.

He builds him * Temples for his Image-gods,
And much beſotted with their faire aſpect,
In admiration of his worke, He nods,
And ſhakes his Head, and tenders them reſpect;
I cannot tell (quoth He) what paſſion moues me,
But ſure I am (quoth He) faire Saint I loue thee,
Thou art my handie-worke, I wiſh my wife,
If to thy faire Proportion thou hadſt life.

* Like thoſe Puluinaria erected by the heathen for their Pagan images.

Canſt thou Pigmalion dote ſo on ſhrines,
On liueleſſe Pictures, that was neuer rapt
With any beautie Cyprus Ile confines?
Theſe (fooliſh man) be for thy Loue vnapt;
They cannot anſwer Loue for Loue againe,
Then fond Pigmalion do thy Loue reſtraine;
Such ſenſeleſſe creatures as haue onely being,
Haue with embraces but an harſh agreeing.

They haue no moyſture in their key-cold lips,
No pleaſure in their ſmile, their colour ſtands;
Whileſt youthfull Ladies on the pauement trips,
They ſtand as Pictures * ſhould, with ſapleſſe hands;
And well thou knowes, if Paſſiue be not mouing,
The Actiue part can yeeld ſmall fruits of louing:
Why art thou ſo beſotted ſtill with woing,
Since there's no comfort when it comes to doing?

* Quid agunt in corpore caſto ceruſſa & minium, centumq; venena colorū? Victor. ad Salmonem.

Can any idle Idoll without breath,
Giue thee a gracefull anſwer to thy ſuite?

Nay

OF DOTAGE.

Nay rather like dead corps surpriz'd by death,
It answers silence when thou speakes vnto't.
Desist then (fond Pigmalion*) and restraine*
To loue that Creature cannot loue againe;
What will it pleasure thee a shrine to wed,
That can afford no pleasure in thy bed?

Thou art not so * bewitcht with any beautie,*
How faire soere within thy Natiue Ile,
No Nimph can moue thy Loue, or force thy dutie,
As doth this Picture, *whose art-forcing smile*
Can giue thee small content, and wherefore then
Should painted Statues so entangle men?
It's loue thou sayest, Pigmalion, *that doth moue thee,*
But thou loues such as cannot say they loue thee.

* —Sine coniuge Cælebs Viuebat, thalamique diu consorte carebat. Metam. 10 lib.

Turne thee vnto leud Pasyphaes *lust,*
Wife to a braue and valiant * Champion,*
Who on a Bull (see how affection must
Passe Reasons limit) fondly dotes vpon;
* *Ioue on a Heifer,* Danae *of a shower,*
Such is the vertue of loues-working power:
No time, place, obiect, subiect, circumstance,
Can still Loues pipe, when Cupid *leades the dance.*

* Minos king of Crete.

* Non frustra dictus Bos ouis Imber Olor, Whence our English Poet as properly annexed this Disticke, imitating the former in matter and manner:
In vaine Ioue was not stil'd right sure I am, From th'shape he tooke of Bull, sheepe, shower, and swan. vid. Ouid. in Metamorph.

Then who will aske the reason of thy Loue, (sun,
Which shewes most strength when she can shew least rea-
And cannot Proteus-*like with each blast moue,*
Nor free her selfe from foule-deluding treason!
She like the Moone is not each month in waine,
For th'obiect of her loue is of that straine,
Nor land, nor sea, nor tempests though they thwart her

Can

Can from her Sphere by oppoſition part her.

Do but torment Her *with the ſight of woe,*
Vexe her with anguiſh and with diſcontent,
She will not make her friend in heart, her foe;
No, if ſhe were with depth of ſorrowes ſpent;
Yet * *like* Anthæus, *when ſhe's moſt caſt downe,*
She gathers ſtrength, and is not ouerthrowne:
She cannot breake her vow, her legall oath,
But meanes (if life permit) to keepe them both.

* *Which is elegantly expreſſed by our moderne Poet. Whoſe fall (Anthæus-like) prouok'd him more, And made him ſtronger then he was before.*

Then (honour'd Picture) let me thee embrace;
With that He *hugd it in his luſtfull armes,*
And now and then He *ſmeer'd the Pictures face,*
Praying the gods to keepe it from all harmes:
And prayed (a ſensleſſe prayer) Ioue *to defend,*
His Picture from diſeaſes to the end;
So to enioy her dalliance with more pleaſure,
Whoſe preſence He *eſteem'd the precious't Treaſure.*

Each euen *he vs'd to dreſſe it for his bed,*
For in a gowne of Tiſſue was it clothed,
And put a night-tyre on it's iuorie head,
Aud when night came He *made it be vnclothed;*
Where, leſt He *ſhould his luſtfull fauours hide,*
He vs'd to lay the Picture by his ſide,
Where He *drew to it as* He *ſaw it lie,*
But when it would not be, He *wiſh'd to die.*

Vngratefull Creature (would Pigmalion *ſay)*
That neuer doeſt afford one ſmile on me,
That dallies thus with thee, each night, each day;
                                                    Faire

OF DOTAGE.

Faire Saint, what needes this curiositie?
While with a* kisse He oft his speech would breake,   * Oscula dat,
By threats or faire intreats to make it speake: reddit; petit,
And when He had his fruitlesse pratling done,   loquiturque te-
He would in rage call it an Idoll dumbe.   netque. *Meta.*
                                              10 lib.

But angrie with himselfe, He streight would blame
His too rash furie, crauing pardon too,
That he should stile it with so harsh a Name,
And wish'd him powre to die, or it to do,
Swearing by heauen, if sheete did chance to moue,
It was the nimble action of his Loue.
Coy-toying Girle (quoth He) what meaneth this,
Is it your modestie, you will not kisse?

Naught though it answer'd, he would prosecute
His wooing taske, as if it stood denying,
And thus would vrge it; Deare accept my suite,
Be not so fearefull, feare thou not espying,
I haue excuses store, then listen me;
For I will vow I was enam'ling thee:
Then sport thee wench, securely frolick it,
That I on thee a Niobe *may get.*

Thus whilest He vainely pratled to his Shrine,
Aurora *with her radiant beames appeared,*
And blushing red, as if she tax'd the time,
For such licentious motions, slilie peered
In at a chinke, whereby she did discouer
An idoll courted by an idle Louer:
And scarce Aurora *now had time to show her,*
But fond Pigmalion *made this speech vnto her.*

What haue I done (thou iealous light) said He,
That I should thus depriued be of louing!
What couldst thou do, to adde more miserie,
Then in thy speedie rising, hastie mouing?
Thou might haue spar'd one day, and hid thy light,
Enioyning Earth to haue a * *double night,*
Where ghastly furies in obliuion sit,
For darke misdeeds for darknesse be most fit.

* Vt geminata duos nox inclyta iungat amores.

But He *cut off his speech with many grone,*
Hastning to rise, yet went to bed againe,
And as He *goes,* He *sees the darknesse gone,*
And Phæbus *coursers galloping amaine:*
Which seene, at last He *rose with much adoe,*
And being vp, began afresh to woe;
Yet hauing so much sense as to perceiue,
How he had err'd, He *ceasseth now to craue.*

For He *intends to worke another way,*
By Inuocation on some heauenly power,
The onely meanes his passion to allay;
Which to performe, retiring to his bower,
He made these Orisons: Venus *faire Queene,*
Then whom in heauen or earth nere like was seene,
Be thou propitious to my prayers, my teares,
Which at thy Throne and Pedestall appeares.

I whom nor Swaine nor Nimph could ere inchant,
Am now besotted with a senselesse creature,
Whom though I do possesse, yet do I want,
Wanting life breathing in her comely feature,
Which by infusing life if thou supplie,

Ile

Ile liue to * *honour thee, if not, I die;*
For what is life where difcontent doth raigne,
But fuch a farme as we would faine difclaime?

* *By offring facrifice to Venus in the Ile of Cyprus.*

Venus *much mou'd with his obfequious prayers,*
And liquid teares, his fuite did fatisfie,
Infufing breath into her fenfleffe veines,
Now full of iuyce, life, and agilitie;
Which being done, the Picture *mou'd, not miffing*
To lure Pigmalion *to her lips with kiffing,*
Reaping great ioy and comfort in their toying,
Depriu'd before of bliffe, bleft now enioying.

Bleft in enioying and poffeffing that,
Which doth include true Loues felicitie,
Where two are made ioynt owners of one ftate,
And though diftinct, made one by vnitie;
Happie then I, (Pigmalion *did reply,)*
That haue poffeffion of this Deitie,
No humane creature but a Parragon,
Whofe liueleffe formè once Nimphs admired on.

This faid, fhe ftreight retires vnto the place,
Where fhe her moulding had, by whom fhe now
(I meane Pigmalion*) obtain'd fuch grace,*
As He *her maker and her hufband too,*
Tooke fuch content in his now-breathing wife,
As they fcarce differ'd once in all their life,
But this was then: Let this fuffice for praife,
Few wiues be of her temper now adaies.

The faire and fruitfull daughter He *begat,*

De fobole Pigmalionis.

Of

Of this same liuely Image *had to name,*
Papho the faire, *a wench of Princely state,*
From whence * *Ile* Paphos *appellation came,*
Consecrate vnto Venus, *beauties Queene,*
By whose aspect that Ile is euer greene;
Wherein there is a pleasant Mirtle-groue,
Where a shrine stands to shew Pigmalions *loue.*

* Illa Paphum genuit, de quo tenet insula nomen. *Ibidem.*

The Argument of Pytheas.

PYtheas *an Athenian Orator much delighted with good cloaths, and proud of his owne tongue: when law began to grow out of request (for the Athenians endeuoured to bring in* Platoes *commonweale) whereby the Court of the A-reopagitæ became much weakened, and the frequencie of Clyents discontinued;* Acolytus *a bitter Satyrist, chancing to meete with* Pytheas *this spruce Lawyer in rent clothes, at a bare Ordinarie, liuing vpon* Pythagoras *diet, viz. rootes; obserued this vnexpected mutation, and with* Democritus *readie to laugh at others miserie, compiled this short Satyre, to adde new fuell to* Pytheas *discontent.*

THE SIXT SATYRE.

PYtheas *a Laywer of no small respect,*
Garded, regarded, *dips his tongue in gold,*

And

OF PARTIALITIE. 107

And culls his phrase, the better to effect
What He and his penurious Client would;
Vpon his backe for all his anticke showes,
More clothes He weares then how to pay He knowes.

And what's the reason; he hath Law at will,
Making a good face of an euill matter,
And euery day his thirstie purse can fill;
With gold thou liest; with nought but wind and water:
Ile tell thee why, Platoes *new Commonweale,*
Makes Pytheas *leaue off pleading, and go * steale.*

* Siste latrare foris, & promoue cœpta latronis.

What Pytheas, *steale? is't possible, that He*
That had a Pomander still at his nose,
That was perfum'd with balls so fragrantly,
Should now another trade of liuing choose?
He must and will, nor dare He show his face
Halfe casement-wide, that open'd many a case.

The other day but walking on the streete,
I saw his veluet gerkin layd to pawne
His graue Gregorian, for his head more meete,
Then Brokers shop, and his best pleading gowne;
Nay which was more, marke Pytheas *conscience,*
There lay to pawne his Clients euidence.

Sic toga, sic crines, pignora iuris erant.

But it's no maruell, Pride must haue a fall, (streame,
Who was on Cockhorse borne through Fortunes
*Is now cashier'd from th'*Areopagites Hall,
And on each bulke becomes a common theame:
O blest vacation, may thou neuer cease,
But still haue power to silence such as these!

Well

OF INGRATITVDE.

Well farewll Law if Lawyers can be poore,
For I esteem'd them onely blest in this,
That Danaes *lap with gold-distilling shower,*
Had made them line all heires to earthly blisse:
But since these conscript fathers we adore,
Feele want of wealth, we'le worship them no more.

The Argument of Periander.

PEriander that wise Prince of Corinth, elected one of the *Sages* of Greece, fell in his old age to pouertie; whereby, though his Axiomes were no lesse esteemed, his deuine Aphorismes no lesse regarded, (as held for the very * Oracles of some superiour power) yet the respect which former time had of him grew lessened, through the decrease of his friends and fortunes: which was no sooner perceiued, then the *distressed Sage* lamenting the worlds blindnesse, that vseth to be taken sooner with a vaine shadow then any solid substance, wrote this Satyricall Elegie in a pensiue moode, inueying against the vncertaine and inconstant affections of *men*, who measure happinesse not by the inward but outward possessing. Whereby *He* inferreth, that howsoeuer the wiseman may seeme miserable, *He* is not so, but is more rich in possessing nothing, then the couetous

* Vid. Laer. de vit. Phylofo.

tous foole in enioying all things: for his eſtimation is without him, whereas the other hath his within *Him*, which is to be more preferred, (I meane *the minds treaſure*, before the rubbiſh of this world,) then light before darkneſſe, the radiant beames of the Sunne before thicke and duskie clouds, or pure and temporate aire before foggie and contagious vapors.

THE SEVENTH SATYRE.

VNgrateful Greece, *that ſcornes a man made poore*
Reſpecting not the treaſure of his mind,
Whoſe want of wealth muſt ſhut him out of doore;
The world's no friend to him that cannot find   Virtus poſt
A maſſe of gold within their mouldred cell,   nummos.
No matter how they get it, ill or well.

This I experienc'd *of, may well perceiue,*
Euen *Periander *I, of late a* Sage   * *Whoſe fathers*
Of ſtately Greece, whom now ſhe'le not receiue,   *was Cypſelus,*
Becauſe oppreſt with want, ſurpriz'd with age;   *deſcending from*
Euen I, that of the * Ephori *was one,*   *the Heraclyd fa-*
One of the chief'ſt, but now retires alone.   *milie.*
   * *Ephorus was*
   among the Lace-
   demonians as
   Tribunus among
   the Romans.

Yet not alone, *though none reſort to me,*
For wiſedome will haue ſociats to frequent her:
And though proud Greece frō hence ſhould baniſh thee,
Friends *thou haſt ſtore, will knocke and knocking enter:*   * Amicis & fæ-
And firme * *friends* too, *whoſe vertues are so pure,*   licibus & infæ-
Vice may aſſay, but cannot them *allure.*   licibus eundem
   re prebe.
   Laert. in ſenten.
   With Periand.

With what respect was I once grac'd by you,
You gorgeous outsides, Fortunes painted wall,
When rich; but poore, you bid my rags adue,
Which did at first my troubled mind appall;
But noting well the * worlds inconstant course,
I thought her scorne could make me little worse.

<small>* Be not afraid (saith Petrarch) though the house (the bodie) be shaken so the soule, (the guest of the body) fare well. Petrarch. de Remed. vtriusque fortunæ.</small>

Remorcelesse Greece, wert thou of marble made,
Thou might shed teares to see thy Sage dismaide,
By whose direction thou hast oft bene stayd,
When both thy hope decreast, and fame decaid;
Both which restor'd by Him, got that report,
To Him and his, as thou admir'd him for't.

Yet canst thou not discerne, twixt wisedomes straine,
And those discording tones of vanitie,
For all thy ayme is benefite and gaine,
And these are they thou makes thy Deitie;
To second which, this caution thou doest giue,
Who know not to dissemble cannot liue.

<small>Demadis saying was, that Dracoes lawes were written with bloud and not with inke.</small>

I know thy follies, and will brute them too,
For thou hast mou'd my splene, and I must speake,
Since thou applies no salue to cure my woe,
I must complaine perforce, or heart-strings breake;
Iustice is turn'd to wormewood in your land,
And corrupt dealing gets the vpper hand.

You itch (and out of measure) with desire
Of hearing nouelties, and strange deuices,
And scorch'd with heate of lusts-enraged fire,
Set marks of Loue, make sale of Venus prizes,

Broad

OF INGRATITVDE.

Broad-spreading vice, how deare so'ere it cost,
To purchase it, you'le vye with who bids most.

You Hydra-*headed monsters full of poyson,*   Plin. in nat. hist.
Infecting euery place with stinking breath,   Alcyat. in Emblem.
What ere proceeds from you is very noysome,
And like the Basiliske procuring death:
I care not for your hatred, if your loue
Like Tritons *ball, with such inconstance moue.*

These fleering flies which flicker to and fro,
And beate the vaine *ayre with their rusling wings,*
Be their owne foes, and they professe them so,
When they their wings with flames of furie cinge;   * *Ixions wheele,*
For they whose hate pursues a guiltlesse one,   *Tantalus apples,*
With * Sysiphus *do role his restlesse stone.*   *and Sysiphus stone: peculiar punishments inflicted on these persons for their lust, auarice, & crueltie, as the Poets saine.*

You cannot grieue me with your enmitie,
Nor much offend me with your hatefull breath,
For ill-mens loue and hate, are equally
Priz'd by the good, whose chiefest aime is death,
And how to die: for much it doth not skill,
What ill-men speake of vs, or good or ill.

What golden promises did I receiue,
Yet see their issue; base contempt and scorne
Ore my deiected state triumphed haue:
So as proud Greece vnmindfull to performe
What merit craues, and what she's bound to do,
Neglects my want, and glories in it too.

Bias *my Brother-sage I now remember,*
                        Shipwrack'd

Shipwrack'd in Priene Ile, *whose wofull case*
Seemes to resemble fate-crost Periander,
Like Ianus *statue, shewing face to face ;*
Let's then, since equall fortune frownes on either,
(Kind Bias*) sound our wofull plaints together.*

Let Priene Ile *relate* thy *hard mischance,*
Let * *Greece bewaile my fall, my ruin'd state,*
Thou while on Sea thy exil'd ship doth lance,
Thou lightly weighes th'inconstancie of fate:
Rouze Periander *then, that't may be said,*
Thy * *patience hath thy fortune conquered.*

* *Or Corinth in Greece.*

* Infælicem dicebat, qui ferre nequiret infælicitatem. *in vit. Bi.*

Get thee to Schooles, where pure Phylosophie
In publicke places is sincerely taught,
And thou shalt heare, there's no calamitie,
Can dant a spirit resolu'd to droupe with nought
That want or woe can menace, for though woe,
Make * *good-men wretched seeme, they are not so.*

* Omnia aduersa exercitationes accidentibus bonis esse putat. *vid. Boæt. in lib. de malis.* Potest dici miser, non potest esse. *ibid.*

Well may misfortunes fall on our estate,
Yet they're no blemish to our inward worth,
For these are but the gifts of purblind fate,
That domineers sole soueraignesse on earth ;
But we are placed in an higher seate,
Then to lie prostrate at Dame Fortunes feete.

Her palsie hand wherewith she holds her ball,
Moues with each blast of mutabilitie,
And in whose lap she lists, she lets it fall,
Thus mocks she man with her inconstancie ;
Then who is he (if wise) esteemes her treasure,

OF INGRATITVDE.

No sooner giuen, then tane when we displease her.

She faunes, she frownes, she lasts not out a Moone,
But waines each month, and waining doth decrease:
Those whom she did aduance, she now throwes downe,
And those which lik'd Her once, do now displease:
Thou reeling wheele, that moues so oft a day,
*That weaues thy * weft, and takes thy web away.*

* Sic licium texit, sic telæ stamina soluit.

Titus *that Prince so much admir'd by men,*
Stiled Mans Darling *for his curtuous mind,*
Did thinke all powers by fate *to haue their raigne,*
As if she had no limits Her *assign'd,*
But (though deuinely-learn'd) did erre in this,
*For fates be rul'd by supreme * Deities.*

Sueton. Tranq. in vit. Tit.

* Quicquid boni egeris in Deos refer. Laert. in vit. Phil.

Then why should I (fond man) so much depend,
Vpon a Creature, which hath her existing
In a Superiour power, and doth extend
No further then heauens please? for her subsisting,
Essence, power, Empire, soueraigne command,
Hath her direction from Iehouahs hand.

Rest thee then Periander, *and despise*
Vulgar opinion swaide by multitude,
Thou was esteemed once for to be wise,
Shew it in publicke; let liues enterlude
**Acted by thee vpon this worlds stage,*
Contemne that Greece which scornes distressed age.

* Vniuersus mundus exercet Histrionem.

I   The

The Historicall Argument of Terpnus *Musician vnto* Nero; *with a Satyre annexed to it as followeth.*

*Erpnus* a Romane Lyrick, or as some will haue him, a cōmon Cytharede, with whom *Nero*, yᵗ president to Tyrants vsed to consort, and with whose admirable skill he was exceedingly delighted: in processe of time fell into *Neroes* disgrace, for playing to him at *Agrippina* his mothers funerals: where he sung the dismall and incestuous bed of *Orestes*, the crueltie of *Sphinx*, reuiling at their tyrannie; which so greatly displeased *Nero*, that he banished him his Court and royall Pallace, inioyning him withall neuer to frequent the *Muses Temple.*

The Morall importeth *Such*, as laying aside *Time-obseruing*, do not few pillowes to their Princes elbowes, but with bold and resolued spirit, will with *Calistenes* tell *Alexander* of his drunkennesse, with *Canius* tell *Tyberius* of his crueltie, with *Brutus* tell *Cæsar* of his vsurping, with *Cato Censorius* will reprehend the Commonweale for her

OF FLATTERIE.

her ryoting. And true it is, that a Commonwealth is better gouerned (if of neceffitie it muft be gouerned by either) by *Cynickes* then *Epicures*; more offences for moft part arifing by alluring and inducing men to fenfuall pleafures, then by *Spartas Damafymbrotos*, his reftraining of youth. The *Laconians* neuer liued fo fecurely, as when they liued barely; nor euer did Romes Commonwealth dilate her bounders more then by the practife of legall aufteritie, nor decreafe more then by introduction of lawleffe libertie. And yet I find it more rare to heare any admonitions but *Placentia* in the Courts prefence, then to fee a graue and demure *feeming*, couer an hypocrites ranke diffembling. We haue more * *Seiani* (which I wifh had *Seians* fall) then *Vticani* to prouide for a Commonweals fafetie. There were many could greete *Cæfar* with an *Aue*, but there were few would put him in mind of his *Memento mori*. Many could perfwade *Phaeton* that he could guide the *Sunnes chariot* in better order then his gray-hair'd father, but by affenting to their perfwafions, he was like to make a flame of the world. Nothing more dangerous to the ftate of a well-gouerned Commonweale, then *Parafites, the tame beafts of the Citie* (as *Diogenes* calls them). If the perfwading fycophancie of Times-obferuancie had not befotted *Candaules* with his wiues beautie, he had preuented that miferable euent which by his owne *Gyges* was practifed and performed. *Dicit Varius, negat Scaurus vtri creditis?* *Varius* affirmes it, *Scaurus* denies it, whether beleeue you? The one fincerely voyd

* *Ayming no leffe at priuie glozers and deluders, then at afpiring plotters, and fatc-intruders.*

of dissembling flatterie: the other glosingly voyde of truth and veritie. By the one we are subiect to the ruine of our state: by the other aduanced to a firmer constancy then such as may be any way subiect to mutabilitie. *Nero* in the * beginning of his time banished al the *Spintriæ, Inuentors of beastly pleasures* out of his kingdome; I would he had banished time-obseruing flatterers, and that he had retained such as *Terpnus*, that would reprehend him in his enormities. *Iulius Cæsar* was too much addicted to his Parasites, but his successour *Augustus* was—*ad accipiendas amicitias rarissimus ad retinendas vero constantissimus.* It was long ere he would entertaine a friend, but being retained, he was most constant in his fauour towards him. The old approbation of friendship comes into my mind, to eate a bushell of salt ere we be acquainted. We may trie our friends as *Pilades* did his *Orestes, Damon* his *Pythias, Æneas* his *Achates*, but it will be long I feare me, ere any of vs possesse such impregnable Assistants, such Presidents of true friendship. The skilfull Painter when he depictures an vnthankfull man, becaufe he cannot well delineate him in his colours, without some proper Motto better to explaine him, representeth him in the Picture of a Viper, that killeth her feeder. There be many such Vipers, which appeare in externall shew as true hearted as Turtles, I feare them more then the open force of mine enemie: for these sugred kisses bring destruction to the receiuer. *Boæthius* defining a good man, saith: *He may be* thus defined: *he is a good man—cui nullum bonum*

* Quinquenniū Nero.

bonum malumue fit nifi bonus malufue animus: to whom nothing is efteemed either good or euill, but a good or an euill mind; and what effectually maketh this euill mind, but either an inbred euill difpofition, which arifeth from the crookedneffe of his nature, or frō the euill perfwafions of depraued time-obferuers: for the beft natures be (for the moft part) fooneft peruerted & feduced. Then how neceffarie is it to roote out fo noyfome and peftilent a weede as *flatterie,* which corrupteth the affections of the worthieft and moft pregnant wits, as daily example hath well inftructed vs? How hatefull was it to that worthie *Thebane* Prince, *Agefilaus,* that memorable mirror of iuftice (& no leffe hatefull to our renowned Prince, whofe exquifite endowments make him as eminent abroad, as vs bleffed at home) to fee a *flatterer* in his Pallace? nay fo much contemning popular applaufe, that he would not fuffer his Statue to be erected, left thereby the vaine and profane *adorations* of his fubiects fhould grieue the gods, difdaining that *veneration* of any mundane power, fhould be confufedly mixed with *adoration* and worfhip of the gods immortall: well remembring *Hefiods* caueat— μέδε αὐτοῦ, we muft not mixe prophane worfhips with deuine. That Court-gate in Rome called *Quadrigemina,* I would haue it demolifhed in Troinouant, left her eftate fecond Roms flauery. *Cicero* thinks that no vice can be more pernicious then *affentation,* the verie helper and furtherer of all vices. She can giue life and being to the afpiring thoughts of man, when *He* foares too ambi-

The Parafite-gate.

tioufly to the pearch of preferment, honour, or the like. That wicked *Catiline* who confpired againft Rome, and afpired to the Diadem, feeking to reduce the Empire from a gouernment Ariftocraticke, to a *Catilines* Monarchie; was egged & inftigated thereto by complices fit for that purpofe, and well forting with fuch an agent, fuch a cruell practitioner — *Incredibilia, immoderata & nimis alta femper cupiendo*, in defiring things incredible, immoderate, and too high aboue ordinary reach. The like befell vpon *Carba*, and thofe who fought to diffolue the Romane Monarchie, & to make it an Oligarchie or fome other gouernment, which was vncertaine, becaufe their intendments neuer came to their accomplifhed ends. Thefe things thus confidered in their natures, I haue here defcribed *Terpnus* finceritie in reprehending *Neroes* crueltie, concluding with *Flaccus* Dyftich.

—*Hic murus ahæneus efto,*
Nil confcire fibi, nulla pallefcere culpa.
What hard mifchance fo ere to thee befall,
Let thy pure confcience be the brazen wall.

The Satyre enfueth, which moft efpecially aymeth at Time-obferuers, fome whereof in particular I haue inftanced, as *Seianus, Perennius, Sycites;* the difmall euents whereof with their Tragicke ends, I haue amply defcribed.

THE

OF FLATTERIE.

THE EIGHTH SATYRE.

TErpnus * *Mufician to a tyrant Prince,*
Nero *by name, did in the funeralls*
Which were *folemniz'd on his mothers hearfe,*
Sing on his Lute thefe wofull tragicalls :
Where *euery ftraine he ftrooke vpon his ftring,*
Did vexe the confcience of the tyrant king.

> * Terpnum citharædum v-gentem tunc præter alios accerfijt. *in Vit.* Nero.

Inceftuous * Oedipus *who flue his father,*
Married his mother, and did violate
The law of nature, which aduis'd him rather
Single to liue, then take to fuch a ftate,
Becomes a fubiect fit, for this fad hearfe,
Where inke giues place to bloud to write her verfe.

> * Inter cætera cantauit Canacem parturientem, Oreftem matricidam, Oedipodem excæcatum, Herculem infanum, &c. *Suet in vit. Ner.*

Cruell Oreftes *bath'd his ruthleffe fword,*
Eftrang'd from ftrangers, in his mothers blood,
So little pittie did the child afford
To Her, *that was the parent of the brood ;*
Yet fome excufe for this Oreftes *had,*
Mad men exemption haue, and He *was mad.*

Sphinx *fubtile Giant, who did riddles put*
Vnto each paffenger He *met withall,*
Which, who could not refolue He *peece-meale cut,*
Throwing them frō fteepe rocks whence they fhould fall,
Whereby their members broke and crufh'd in peeces,
Remain'd as food in Sea to fillie fifhes.

Yet this he did vpon mature aduice,

For who so'ere He *were assoil'd this question,*
Was not opprest by him *in any wise,*
But might with safest conduct trauell on;
Where thou *foule* Matricide *doest infants vex,*
Without respect of person, state, or sex.

There is no sex which may exempted be,
From thy insatiate hand embrew'd in blood,
But waxing proud in others miserie,
Doest tyrannize vpon poore womanhood:
Blood-thirsty Tyrant there's prepar'd a doome,
To startle thee *that rip'd thy mothers wombe.*

Rauing Orestes *heard a furious crie,*
Which did attend his phrensie to his graue,
And did disturbe his restlesse sleepe thereby,
So as saue troubled dreames He *nought could haue:*
With many broken sleepes, to shew his guilt,
Of his deare mothers bloud, which He *had spilt.*

Which poore Orestes *had no sooner heard,*
Then to his pillow in a dismall sort,
Streight He *retir'd, and being much afeard,*
Lest hell and horror should conuent him for't,
With hands lift vp to heauen and hideous crie,
He oft would curse himselfe, and wish to die.

Turne me (ye gods) quoth he, to some wild beast,
Some sauage Lion, or some Tyger fierce,
Since I delight so much in bloud to feast,
For who can with remorse my deeds rehearse?
Which if time should with her obliuion smother,
          Bloud

—Ciuis gaudet Roma cruore. *Sen.*

Fugit ab agro ad ciuitatem, à publico ad domum, à domo in cubiculum. *August. in enar. Sup. 45. Psal.*

Orestes imprecation.

Bloud cries reuenge, reuenge me cries my mother.

Worfe then the beafts thou art, they cherifh them,
And bring their parents food when they grow old:
Who then can daigne to looke on thee for fhame,
That haft defac'd that forme that gaue thee mold?
The tender * Storke *that fees her parents lack,*   Bafilius hom.
Will bring them food, and beare them on her back.   8. 9.

But thou a mirrour of impietie,
Depriues thy parent of her vitall breath,
And makes her fubiect to thy cruelty,
Thus fhe that gaue thee life, thou giues her death:
A fweete reward; O then afhamed be,
Thou ftaine of Greece, that Greece fhould harbor thee.

Thus would Oreftes *frame his fad difcourfe,*
With words as vile as were his actions foule,
To moue his phrenticke paffions to remorfe,
Which long (too long) had triumpht ore his foule;
Nor could he find vnto his woes reliefe,   * He was fo
Till * *death did end his life, and cure his griefe.*   vexed with fu-
　　　　　　　　　　　　　　　　　　　　　　　　　ries (the reuen-
　　　　　　　　　　　　　　　　　　　　　　　　　gers of his mo-
　　　　　　　　　　　　　　　　　　　　　　　　　thers bloud) that
　　　　　　　　　　　　　　　　　　　　　　　　　he wandered
If all his teares and ruthfull miferies,   mad up and
Could neuer expiate his mothers death,   downe till he
To what extent fhall thy calamities   came to Taurica,
　　　　　　　　　　　　　　　　　　　　where he found
Grow to in time, that ftops thy mothers breath,   an end of his
Euen Agrippinaes *breath, whofe curfed birth,*   troubles.
Maks her to curfe the wombe that brought thee forth?   ὑγίαινε πατερ
　　　　　　　　　　　　　　　　　　　　　　　　　ὑγίαινε ματερ

This Nero *notes, and noting fhewes his ire,*
By outward paffions, yet concealeth it,

　　　　　　　　　　　　　　　　Refolu'd

Resolu'd ere long to pay the minstrels hire,
When time and opportunitie should fit;
For tyrants haue this propertie 'boue other,
They meane reuenge, yet their reuenge cā smother.

And so did Nero, *whose perplexed mind,*
Guilty of what was ill, seem'd to admire
His Art in Musicke, rather then to find
Any distast, lest He *should shew the fire,*
Which lay rak'd vp in ashes, and display
What time might sleight, but could not take away.

Yet he began to scoule and shake the head,
With eyes as fierie-red as Ætnaes *hill,*
Willing him streight to other acts proceed,
And silence them that parents-bloud did spill:
Sing to thy Lute (quoth he) straines of delight,
To cheare th' attendants of this wofull * *sight.*

* *Agrippinaes funerale.*

* Terpnus *did passe vnto another theame,*
Yet still relates He *in the end of all,*
The facts of Oedipus, Orestes *shame,*
How and by what effects succeed'd their fall;
Whereby (as well it was by all perceiued)
Nero *the tyrant inwardly was grieued.*

Terpnus *continu'd in his Lyricke ode,*
So long as Nero *in his throne remained,*
But now impatient longer of abode,
Wearied with audience (for so he feined)
Terpnus *left off from prosecuting further,*
The sad relation of this cruell * *murther.*

* *For which no law amongst the Pagans was enacted: imagining, none could be so brutish as commit such vnnaturall cruelty.*

But

OF FLATTERIE.

But see the Tyrant, who before delighted
More with the musicke of good Terpnus *lyre,*
Then anything which ere his soule affected,
Neuer more straines of Terpnus *did require;*
For being grieu'd, each day his grieues increased,
Till Terpnus *exile made his grieues appeased.*

Yet not* appeased, for each day each night,
He heard the hideous cries of Furies shriking:
Oft would He *turne himselfe before day-light,*
But got no rest, his bodie out of liking,
Yet tyranniz'd in spilling bloud apace,
Act vpon act as one bereft of grace.

* For hauing slaine his mother, he saw in his sleepe a ship, the rudder whereof was wrested frõ him guiding it, whence he was haled by Octau. to most hideous darknesse. ibid.

Sometimes He *saw his mother haling him,*
With wombe new-rip'd; there* Sporus *whõ* He *sought,*
To make of man a woman drag him in;
Here sundrie Matrons whom he forc'd to nought,
And flue defil'd, which fix'd on Him *their eye,*
Which seene, He *fled, but flying, could not flie.*

* In vit. Ner.

Like the vision appeared to Tiberius crying out —Redde Germanicum.

O conscience, what a witnesses thou brings,
'Gainst Him *that iniures thee, where no content*
Can giue houres-respite to the state of kings,
Thou of thy selfe art sole-sufficient,
To hale or heale, to hale from life to death,
Or heale the wound of which he languisheth?

Behold here Terpnus *courage, to correct*
The great abuses of his Princes mind,
Whose pompe, port, power, He *lightly doth respect,*
To taxe those crimes to which He *is inclin'd:*
                                   He's

He's no Court-Adder that will winde him in,
To Princes grace by praising of his sinne.

O I could wish we had such Terpni many,
Who would not sooth nor flatter, but auouch,
Blacke to be blacke: but there's I feare not any,
Too few at least, I doubt me rightly such;
And yet me thinks such Phœnix's might build here,
Within this Ile, as well as other where.

<small>Vid. Cornel. Tacit. & Suetu. Tranq. in vit. Tib.</small>

Seianus, *let him bloome in other coasts,*
And purchase honour with his flatterie,
Let his aspiring thoughts make priuate boasts,
To raise his Fortunes *to a monarchie,*
He *cannot prosper here, for why, we know,*
State-ruine from Court-parasites may grow.

So Seian *thought (what haue not Traitors thought)*
To currie fauour with the Senators,
The better to atchieue what He *had wrought,*
By secret plots with his conspirators;
Faire-tong'd, false-heart, whose deepe-cõtriuing braine
Gaue way to ruine, where He *thought to raigne.*

But He's *well gone, Rome is dispatch'd of one*
That would haue made combustion in the state,
Whose death made Hers *reioyce, but* His *to mone,*
Who on his fall built their vnhappie fate;
For Treason like a linked chaine doth show,
Which broke in one, doth breake in others too.

Next whom Perennius, *whose affected grace,*
Italian-

Italian-*like, feem'd as compos'd by art,*
May for his fmoothing humour take the place,
Who sole-poffeffor of a Princes heart,
The youthfull Commodus, *did so allure him,*
As his aduice feemes onely to fecure him.

Faire Prince (quoth he) if any worldly wight,   *A Parafite pandor.*
May folace those faire corps fram'd curioufly,
Expreffe Her *onely when fhe comes in fight,*
And I your pleafure foone will fatisfie;
Your Vnckle he's too ftrict, he's too feuere,   —Exeat aula
To coupe you vp in filence alwaies here.   Qui vult effe pius. *Lucan. 8. li.*

What priuiledge haue Princes more then we,
If they depriued be of open aire?
What comfort reape they in their Empirie,
If Neftor-*like, they ftill fit in their chaire?*
No, no, deare Prince, you know a Prince is borne
To be his fubiects terror, not their fcorne.

No Theater rear'd in your royall Court,
Turney, Iuft, Barrier, fhould folemniz'd be,
To which a Romane Prince fhould not refort,
Amazing Ladies with his maieftie;
O then it is a fhame for your eftate,
To feeme in ought for to degenerate!

How gorgeoufly did Rome demeane her then,
When young Vitellius *did *. banket it,*   * *Banketting euer three times,*
Seruing at table miriads of men,   *and now and then foure times*
With luftie Ladies which did reuell it?   *a day,* in vit. Vitell.
Yet you more high in ftate, more ripe in wit,

Muft

Muſt Hermit-like in cell retired ſit.

Shake off theſe Sages which do now attend you,
For they like fetters do reſtraine your pace;
Giue luſtfull youth in euery part his due,
Let ſprightly gallants take the Sages place,
By which enthron'd ſecure, you may command,
As Ioue erſt did, with Io in his hand,

<small>Nec fuge me
(fugiebat enim)
iam ̃pafcua
Lernæ, &c.
Lib. 1. Meta.</small>

This did Perennius moue, and tooke effect,
Greene thoughts receiue too aptly wanton ſeede,
Remaining with the Prince in chiefe reſpect,
As they are wont, who Princes humours feed;
Till He conſpiring to vſurpe the crowne,
Amidſt his honours was caſt headlong downe.

<small>Vid. Aurel. Sex.
in epit.
Herod. in vit.
Commod.</small>

Where he receiu'd a doome that ſeru'd for all,
(Like doome ſtill breath on ſuch infectious breath)
For ſoring thoughts muſt haue as low a fall,
Whoſe fauning liues play prologue to their death:
For well I know no bane on earth can be
Worſe to the State then ruſt of* flatterie.

<small>* Vid. Cicero-
nem in Lælio
prope finem,
&c.</small>

Then ſhould theſe laſt-enſuing times beware,
Leſt they commit offences of like kind,
Which in the common wealth procure that iarre,
As by their proiects we ſubuerſion find:
For they depraue the vertues of the beſt,
And in the higheſt Cedars build their neſt.

Sycites, he whoſe ſycophants pretence,
Made wofull hauocke of his Common weale,

Abuſing

Abufing much his Princes innocence,
At laſt by time (as time will all reueale)
Became difpleafde, who, as He *was a fo*
Vnto the ſtate, the ſtate adiudg'd him fo.

AN ADMONITION.

BE *thou a* Terpnus *to reſtraine abufe,*
Sin-training pleafures fraught with vanitie;
Be thou no Seian, *no* Perennius,
To humour vice to gaine a Monarchie;
Be not Sycites, *let examples moue thee,*
And thou wilt caufe the Commonweale to loue thee.

The Argument of Epicurus, *as in the firſt Satyre familiarly expreſſed, ſo now in his miſerable end with liuely colours deſcribed.*

EPicurus, who firſt inuented that ſect of *Epicuriſme*, delighting in nothing ſaue voluptuous pleaſures and delights, in the end being grieuouſly vexed with the ſtopping of his vrine, and an intollerable paine and extremitie of his bellie exulcerated, became mightilie tormented; yet beſotted with the fruition of his former pleaſure, (ſo violent are cuſtomarie delights) thus concluded:

ded: *O quàm fælici exitu finem expectatum vitæ meæ impofui?* With how happie an end do I limit the courfe and progreffe of my life? The *morall* includes fuch, as haue liued in fecuritie, and carelefneffe, refpectleffe of God or his iudgement; and euen now readie to make an end of fo hapleffe & fruitleffe a race, clofe vp the date of their life as fecurely as they liued carnally. The fecond *Satyre* in the former *Section* comprehends the like fubiect, though the one feeme more generall vnder the name of *Pandora*, implying a gouerneffe and directreffe in all pleafures, or exhibitreffe of all gifts: The other more particular, containing one priuate and peculiar Sect, euen the *Epicures*, who thought that the *chiefe good* confifted in a voluptuous and fenfuall life, expecting no future doome after the tearme and end of this life.

Here confider the momentanie and fraile courfe of this short and vnconftant life, toffed and turmoiled with many turbulent billows, expofed to fundrie fhelfs of perillous affaults, many homebred and forreine commotions; in which it behoueth vs (like expert Pilots) to be circumfpect in fo dangerous a voyage, left failing betwixt *Scylla* and *Charybdis*, prefumption and defpaire, by encountring either we reft fhipwracked: where if any (which is rare to find) paffe on vntroubled, yet muft *He* of neceffitie conclude with *Seneca; Non tempeftate vexor, fed naufea.* So flow is euery one to proceede graduate in vertues *Academie; —ita vt non facile eft reputare, vtrum inhoneftioribus corporis partibus rem qæufierit, an amiferit:* as

Cicero

OF EPICVRISME.

Cicero well obserueth in his Declamation againſt *Saluſt*. For who is he of ſo pure and equall temper, whoſe man-like reſolution holds him from being drawne and allured by the vaine baits and deceits of worldly ſuggeſtions? where there be more of *Penelopes* companions in euery ſtew, in euery brothell of ſinne and wantonneſſe, then euer in any age before. Euery one *vt Lutulentus ſus*—as a hogge wallowing in the mire of their vaine conceits, roue from the marke of pietie and ſobrietie, into the broad ſea of intemperance and ſenſualitie: but none more of any Seƈt then *Epicuriſme*, which like a noiſome and ſpreading Canker, eats into the bodie and ſoule of the profeſſor, making them both proſtitute to pleaſure, and a very ſinke of ſinne. The *Satyre* will explane their defeƈts more exaƈtly, which followeth.

THE NINTH SATYRE.

*T*Hat Epicurus *who of late remained*
  Subieƈt to euery fowle impietie,
Now with diſtempers and night-ſurfets pained,
Bids mirth adue, his ſole felicitie:
His vrine ſtopt wants paſſage from his vaines,
Which giues increaſe to his inceſſant paines.

Yet feeles He *not his ſoules-affliƈted woe,*
Vnmindfull (wretched man) of her diſtreſſe,
But pampers that which is his greateſt foe,
And firſt procur'd his ſoules vnhappineſſe:
He *cannot weepe,* He *cannot ſhed a teare,*

But dying laughs, as when He *liued here.*

His Bon-companions drinking healths in wine,
Carousing flagons to his health receiuing,
Whose sparkling noses taper-like do shine,
Offer him drinke whose * *thirstie mind is crauing:*
For though He *cannot drinke, yet his desire*
Is to see others wallow in the mire.

* *Resembling our Elderton, on whom this inscription was writ: here lieth drunken Elderton, in earth now thrust: what said I thrust? nay rather here lies thirst.*
In Rem. of a greater worke.

Turne him to heauen He *cannot, for* He *knowes not*
Where heauens blest mansion hath her situation:
Tell him of heauens fruition, and he shewes not
The least desire to such a contemplation:
His sphere inferiour is, whose vanitie
Will suite no court so well as * Tartarie.

* Orcus vobis ducit. pedes.

He hath no comfort while He *liueth here,*
For He's *orewhelmed with a sea of griefe,*
And in his death as little ioy appeares,
For death will yeeld him small or no reliefe:
He *thought no pleasure after life was ended,*
Which past, his fading comforts be extended.

Horror appeares euen in his ghastly face,
And summons (wofull summons) troups of diuels,
Whilst He *benumn'd with sinne reiecteth grace,*
The best receit to cure soule-wounding euils:
Forlorne He *liues, and liues because* He *breaths,*
But in his death sustaines a thousand deaths.

Vngratefull viper, borne of vipers brood,
That hates thy parent, braues ore thy Protector,

Whose

Whoſe ſeruile life did neuer any good,
But hugging vice, *and ſpurne* Him *did correct her;*
See how each plant renewes and giues increaſe,
By him, whom ſtones would praiſe, if man ſhould ceaſſe.

Nor plant, nor worme, nor any ſenſleſſe creature,
Will derogate from Gods high Maieſtie,
Since they from him, as from the ſupreme Nature,
Receiue their vigour, grouth, maturitie,
Subſtance, ſubſiſtence, eſſence, all in one,
From Angels forme vnto the ſenſleſſe ſtone.

But time hath hardn'd thy depraued thoughts,
Cuſtome of ſin hath made thy ſin, no ſin;
Thus haſt thou reap'd the fruite thy labours ſought,
And dig'd a caue in which thou walloweſt in;   The *Epicures* Caue.
The Porter of which caue, 's reproch and ſhame,
Which layes a laſting ſcandall on thy name.

A ſwine in mind, though Angell-like in forme,
Prepoſterous end to ſuch a faire beginning,
That Thou, *whom ſuch a feature doth adorne*
As Gods owne Image, ſhould be ſoild with ſinning;
Who well may ſay of it thus drown'd in pleaſures,
This Superſcription is not mine but Cæſars.

Thou wanteſt grace, and wanting, neuer calleſt,
Neſſled in miſchiefe and in diſcontent;
Thou who from light to darkneſſe headlong falleſt,
Hauing the platforme of thy life miſpent,
Rouſe thee Thou *canſt not, for ſecuritie*
Hath brought thy long ſleepe to a Lethargie.

OF EPICVRISME.

Dull Dormouſe, ſleeping all the winter time,
Cannot endure the breath of aire or winde,
But euer loues to make the Sunne to ſhine
Vpon her rurall Cabbin; that ſame mind
Art Thou *endew'd withall,* All winter keeping
Thy drunken cell, ſpends halfe thy life in ſleeping.

<small>Sic faciunt hyemem decipiendo, glires.</small>

Thou when thou read'ſt in ſtories of the Ant,
The painfull Be, the early-mounting Larke,
Thou cals them fooles, for Thou *hadſt rather want,*
Pine, droupe, and die in pouertie, then carke :
Thou thinks there is no * *pleaſure, but to dwell*
In that vaſt Tophet Epicurean cell.

<small>* According to that of the Poet.—No pleaſure but to ſwill, And full, to emptie, and being emptie, fill.</small>

Art thou ſo ſotted with earths worldly wealth,
That thou expects no life when this is ended?
Do'ſt thou conceiue no happineſſe in health,
If health in healths *be not profanely ſpended ?*
Well there's ſmall hope of thee, and thou ſhalt find,
Sinne goes before, but vengeance dogs behind.

Thou canſt not tell by thy Philoſophie,
Where th' glorious Synod of the Angels ſit,
Nor canſt thou thinke ſoules immortalitie,
Should any mortall creature well befit :
Vnfit thou art for ſuch a prize as this,   *(wiſh.*
Which Saints haue wiſh'd to gaine, and gain'd their

Thou ſings ſtrange Hymnes of loue of ſhepeard-ſwains,
How Amarillis *and* Pelargus *woed,*
Where in loue meaſures thou employes ſome paines,
To make thy works by wanton eares allow'd;
                                    For

For loues encounter loose wits can expresse it,
But for diuine power they will scarce confesse it.

Thus should each sinne of thine vnmasked be,
Each crime deblazon'd in her natiue colour :
There would appeare such a deformitie,
As th' Greeke Thersites *shape was neuer fowler ;*   Homer, in Iliad: & alibi.
Which if compar'd to th' powerfull works of grace,
Would looke agast, asham'd to show their face.

If I should moue thee, rectifie thy cares,
I know twere fruitlesse, all thy care's to sinne,
Whose barren haruest intersowne with tares,
Endeth farre worse then when it did begin ;
A ranke indurate vlcerous hard'ned ill,
Can ill be bett'red till it haue her fill.

And yet when as this phrenticke mood shall leaue thee,   Ad pœnas tardus Deus est, ad præmia velox.
There is some hope of gaine-recouerie,
When thy offensiue life mispent shall grieue thee ;
Thy wound's not mortall, looke for remedie ;
But if like Epicure *thou still doest lie,*
As thou liues ill, so doubt I thou must die.

The Argument of Diagoras
Orator of Athens.

Diagoras a corrupt Orator vsing to receiue bribes, was exiled, and this Satyre to gall him the more, engrauen vpon his shipboord: As followeth.

THE TENTH SATYRE.

Diagoras *was once to pleade a cause,*
Which th' aduerse partie hauing well obserued,
Claps me a guilded goblet in his clawes,
Which He *as priuately (forsooth) reserued;*
Speake (quoth this client) either nought at all,
Or else absent you from the sessions *hall.*

Absent He *would not be, and yet as good,*
For his mute tongue was absent in the cause,
Saying, the cause he had not vnderstood,
And therefore wish'd that he a while might pause;
But hauing paus'd too long, through his delay
The Court dismist, the Senat went away.

Seeing the Senate gone, good gods (quoth he)
Can we not haue our causes heard, whose truth
Is manifest as light? ô thus we see
Our Clients wrong'd, whose wrongs afford much ruth:

I

OF BRIBERIE.

I would not answer this before Ioues *throne,*
If I thereby might make the world mine owne.

Nought to a conscience pure and void of blame,
*Which (*Ioue *be prais'd) is in this spotlesse brest,*
For no foule act could blemish ere my name,
No corrupt bribe did ere enrich my chest;
Yes one (the Clyent *answer'd) you know when:*
It's true indeed (my friend) *and nere but then.*

Yes once you know (another *answer'd) more,*
When you protested the Angina *pain'd you,*
For which corruption, you had gold in store,
That silent speech of yours abundance gain'd you :
It's true indeed, yet there's none can conuict me,
That ere my conscience for these *did afflict me.*

Nay that Ile sweare (quoth one) I neuer knew
Remorce of conscience or relenting teare:
That heart of yours did nere repentance shew,
But could take more, if that you did not feare
You should detected be, and your offence,
As *iustice craues, should giue you recompence.

Thus as they talk'd, thus as they did discourse,
In came a Senatour, which did reueale,
His corrupt dealings, for He *did enforce*
Himselfe to publish what He *did conceale :*
Whose crimes diuulg'd, He *presently was led*
To Coos *hauen, whence* He *was banished.*

Thus was a corrupt Orator conuicted,

* *There were certaine images of Iudges (by report) set vp at Athens, hauing neither hands nor eyes: implying that Rulers and Magistrates should neither be infected with bribes, nor any other way drawne from that which was lawfull and right. But most happie were those dayes wherein Basil the Emperour of Constantinople liued, that whensoeuer he came to his iudgment seate, he found neither partie to accuse, nor defendant to answer.*

Pressing

136   *OF INVENTION.*

Preſſing himſelfe with his owne obloquie,
Whoſe ſelfe-detection made his ſtate afflicted,
His hands the weauers of his tragedie;
Which I could wiſh to all of like deſert,
Whoſe good profeſſion's made a guilefull art.

The Argument.

TRiptolemus is reported to haue inuented *Tillage* the firſt of any, and to haue taught the art of ſowing corne: whereupon the gratefull huſbandman, to repay the thankfulneſſe of his well-willing mind, rendreth this *Elegie*, as in part of payment for ſo rare inuention: Satyrically withall inueying againſt ſuch, who eate the fruite of others labours, liue on the ſweat of others browes, and muzling the mouth of the oxe that treads out the corne, reape what they neuer ſowed, drinke of the vine they neuer planted, and eate at the Altar of which they neuer partaked.

THE ELEVENTH SATYRE ELEGIACK.

A*Ged* Triptolemus *father of our field,*
  That teacheth vs thy children *rare effects;*
We do vnto thy ſacred Temple yeeld
The fruits we reape, and tender all reſpects
                                        To

To thee, *that haſt this rare* * *inuention found,*   * Dona fero
And gaue firſt light of tillage to our ground.   Cereris—Met.
    lib. 5.

Deſcribe we cannot in exact diſcourſe,
Thoſe rarer ſecrets which proceed from thee,
For poliſh'd words with vs haue little force,
That are inured to Ruſticitie ;
But what we can we'le do, and to that end,
To thee (as Patron) we our fields commend.

By thee *we till the wilde vntempered ſoile,*
Make riſing hillocks champion and plaine ;
Where though with early labour we do toile,
Yet labour's light where there is * *hope of gaine ;*   * Spes alet a-
We thinke no hurt, but trauell all the day,   gricolas.
And take our reſt, our trauels to allay.

No proiect we intend againſt the State,
But cuts the boſome of our Mother earth ;
We giue no way to paſſion or debate ;
By labour we preuent our Countries dearth :
Yet this aſcribe we not to our owne part,
But vnto thee, *that did inuent this art.*

Thoſe glorious Trophies *which* Menander *ſet,*
In honour of the ſacred Deities,
Would be too long a ſubiect to repeate,
Rear'd in ſuch ſtate with ſuch ſolemnities ;
Yet theſe *to ours, inferiour be in worth,*
Thoſe were of earth, theſe *tell vs vſe of earth.*

We ope the cloſet of our mothers breaſt,

                                And

And till the sedgie ground with crooked plough,
And in the euening take our quiet rest,
When we the heate of day haue passed through:
Thus do we sow, thus reape, and reaping we
Do consecrate our first-fruites vnto thee.

And with our fruites our wonted Orisons,
With solemne vowes to thy obsequious shrine,
Whose * dedication merits heauenly songs,
Will we protest what's ours is euer thine;
For what we haue came from thy deuine wit,
Or from His power *that first infused it*.

* *Of the dedication of Pagan Temples*, vid. Var. de Ant. & Macrob.

By thee we plant the * Vine and Oliue tree,
Contriue coole harbors to repose and lie:
By thee our * Vine sends grapes forth fruitfully,
The Almond, Chestnut, and the Mulberrie;
Thus Saturns *golden age approcheth neare*,
And (Flora-*like*) *makes spring-time all the yeare.*

*— Ex nitido sit rusticus, atque Sulcos & vineta crepat mera, preparatvlmos. *Hor.*
* *Vina generosissima, Massica, Cecuba, Falerna. Hipp. de coll.*
* *As in some parts of Egypt, which (though elsewhere exceeding fruitfull) through extremitie of heate become to the people inhabitable.*
b *As in Scythia, which region in most places is so cold, as fruites can come to no ripenesse.*

The pleasant banks of faire Parnassus mount,
With trees rank-set and branchie armes broad-spred,
The Mirtle-trees hard by Castalias fount,
With flowrie wreaths thy shrine haue honoured;
'Mongst which, no Iland's more oblig'd to thee,
Then this same Ile of famous Britannie.

* Others intemporate through parching heate,
Haue their fruites blasted ere they come to light,
b Others are planted in a colder seate,

For as the Astrologers are of opinion, there is a certaine breadth in the heauen, on earth *from North to South, bounded out by some of the principall Circles, of the which are 5. in all: one fierie betweene the two Tropicks which is called Zona Torrida: two extreme cold, betweene the Polare circles and the Poles of the wold: and two temperate betweene either of the Polare circles and his next Tropicke.*

Whereby

Whereby the Sun-beames feldome shew their might ;
But we (and therein blest) inhabite one,
Which as it's fruitfull, it's a temp'rate Zone.

How can we then if we do ought, do lesse
Then labour to requite as we receiue ?
For such a burning wind's *vnthankefulnesse,*
As by it we do lose that which we haue :
Let each then in his ranke obserue his measure,
And giue Him *thanks that gaue* Him *such a treasure.*

How many regions haue their fruites deuoured,
By th' Caterpiller, Canker, Palmerworme ?
Whil'st by thy grace so richly on vs powred,
Our fields reioyce, and yeeld increase of corne ;
O then admire we this great worke of thine,
Whereby all * regions at our state repine !

* Barbarus inuidit—*Met. l.* 5.

Repine they may, for we surpasse their state,
In power, in riches, sinewes of sharpe warre ;
They led in blindnesse attribute to fate,
What ere befall, we to the morning *starre,*
By which we are directed euery day,
Or else like wandring sheepe might loose our way.

Hesiod *relates seuen fortunate reposes,*
Ilands, which Fortune *fauors for their seate,*
Adorn'd with fruitfull plants sent-chafing roses ;
Where there breaths euer a soile-cherishing heate,
By which the plants receiue their budding power,
And needs no other dew, no other shower.

Canariæ—fortunatæ insulæ.
vid Hesiod. in
li. de oper : &
die. pag. 15.
Ἐν μακάρων
κέσοισι *in beatorum insulis.*

These

These fruitfull Ilands which this Poet shewes, (*Iles in the ocean foure hundred miles frō Spaine*)
Were seated farre within the Ocean,
And neuer warr'd as other Ilands vse,
Being in peacefull league with euery man:
Confer now these *together, and then see*
If this blest Iland be not Brittannie.

Blest were those Ilanders that did possesse
The fertile borders of those healthfull Iles,
And we as blest haue no lesse happinesse,
In this our Ile, not stretch'd to many miles;
Though when those * *streames of* Hellicon *appeares,* (* *The two vniuersities.*)
It doubles fruites in doubling of her yeares.

Thames *full as pleasant as* Euphrates *flood,*
Though she containe not in her precious nauell,
The * *golden oare of* Ganges, *yet as good* (* *Tagus, Ganges, and Pactolus three riuers famous for their golden oare or grauell,*)
As any gold or any golden grauell,
Transporting hence, and bringing here againe,
Gaine *to the Citie by their fraught of graine.*

Thus water, ayre, and earth, and all vnite
Their powers in one, to benefit our state,
So as conferring profit with delight,
Well may we tearme this Iland fortunate;
For we more blest then other Iles haue bin,
Enioy both peace without and peace within.

Vnto his altar *let vs then repaire,*
That hath conferd these blessings on our land,
And sure we are to find him present there,
Apt to accept this offring *at our hand;*

Where

Where, *as* He *hath remembred vs in peace,*
We'le *yeeld him* fruites *of foules and foiles increase.*

To thee *then (blessed Deitie) is meant,*   *The true expla-*
This votall sacrifice, *how ere we speake,*   *nation of this*
Of old Triptolemus *thy instrument;*   *Elegie.*
For midst inuentions we will euer seeke
To raise thy praise, who hast thy Throne aboue vs.
And daily shewes that thou doest dearely loue vs.

The Argument.

MElonomus a shepheard of Arcadia, who hauing frequented the plaines there long time, with great husbandrie vsed to exercise his pastures, receiuing no small profite from his fruitfull flocke: in the end fell in loue with *Cynthia* Queene of the forrest adioyning: whom hauing woed with many loue-inducing tokens, and shepheards madrigals, and spent the profit of his flock in gifts (with too lauish a bountie bestowed vpon her) and yet could no way preuaile, being posted off with many trifling delayes; in the end wrote this short *Satyre* in a Cynick mood, reuiling at the couetousnesse and insatiable desire of women, who will prostitute their fauour for lucre sake vnto the meanest swaine, till *they* haue consumed the fruite

fruite of his ſtocke, and then will turne him ouer ſhipboord.

THE TWELFTH SATYRE.

MElonomus *a worthie ſhepheard ſwaine,*
Beſotted with faire Cynthia's *amorous face,*
Beſeeched Her *to loue for loue againe,*
And take compaſſion on his wofull caſe ;
Which ſhe halfe-yeelding to, diſſembling too,
Did moue the ſwaine more eagerly to woo.

<small>* Non ſumus ingratæ, poſcunt pulcherrima pulchræ ; Munera ſi referas, oſcula grata feres.</small>

And that with * *gifts moſt powerfull to enſnare*
The minds of maids, whoſe curious appetite,
Deſires as they be faire to haue things faire,
To adde freſh fuell vnto loues delight ;
Which to effect, each morne a flowrie wreath,
Compos'd the ſwaine, to breath on Cynthia's *breath.*

<small>* Rupibus extractum Calibæis mittit electrum, &c. Whence it is ſaid cometh the pureſt Amber.</small>

Fine comely bracelets of refined * *Amber.*
Vſed this Shepheard ſwaine to tender her,
And euery morne reſorting to her chamber,
Would there appeare ere Phœbus *could appeare,*
Where telling tales as ſhepheards vſe to tell,
She forc'd a ſmile, as though ſhe *lik'd* Him *well.*

<small>* Thus at Loues barre this Client, doubtfull ſtands, And weepes, & wipes, & wrings and wreathes his hands.</small>

Thus poore Melonomus *continued long,*
* *Hoping for reſolution at her hands,*
Whileſt with delayes He *mixed gifts among,*
Which (as He *thought) were* fancies *ſtrongeſt bands;*
And ſtill He *craues diſpatch of his requeſt,*
And to performe what ſhe *in ſhow profeſt.*

But

OF DISDAINE.

But she, from day to day puts off, replying,
She scarce resolued was to marrie yet:
But when his * gifts surceast, she flat denying,*
Answer'd, A swaine was for a Queene vnfit;
He rurall, homely, bred of meane descent,
She royall-borne, of purer Element.

* Inſtat amans, tamen odit amans, sic munera quærit, Queis tamen acceptis. nefcit amare magis.

Melonomus *thus answer'd, wisely fram'd*
This graue reply: And is it so indeed?
Be all those gifts I gaue (all which He *nam'd)*
To no effect? why then returne and feed
Thy wanton flocke, surceasse thy bootlesse suite,
Since she consum'd thy flocke with all their fruite.

A sudden resolution requiting her sudden disdaine.

Aged Alcmænon *who my father was,*
And as I guesse knew well the shepheards guise,
Thought scorne to set his loue on euery lasse,
Aye me vnhappie, of a sire so wise;
But this disdaine *that lowres on beauties brow,*
Shall teach me, *swaines with swaines know best to do.*

I canot trull it I, nor fancie all I see, if she be faire, wife and an heire, that girle liketh me.

The skipping Rams that butt with ragged hornes,
And brouze vpon each banke with sweete repast,
Shall not my iealous head with wreathes adorne,
(But heauen forgiue my follie that is past;)
I will not fancie Cynthia, *since* she
In my distresse scornes to conuerse with me.

The

The Argument of Protagoras.

PRotagoras adored the ſtones of the *altar*, conceiuing them to be happie, as the Phyloſopher *Ariſtotle* witneſſeth: *Lapides, ex quibus aræ ſtruebantur, fælices eſſe putabat, quod honorentur.* He thought the very ſtones themſelues to be happie, of which the altars were builded, becauſe (ſaith *he*) they might be honoured. In this *Argument*, be ſuch men ſhadowed, as moſt impiouſly worſhip the creature for the Creator, the worke for the worker. Therefore haue I ſubinſerted this *Satyre*, to inueigh againſt the ſenſleſſe Gentiles and Painims, who in the fooliſhneſſe of their hearts, vſed to adore ſtockes, ſtones, plants, and ſenſleſſe creatures, *Nunc deorum cauſam agam;* I will now pleade the cauſe of God, ſo iniuriouſly dealt withall by his owne workmanſhip. *Alexander* himſelfe being but a mortall man as we our ſelues be, commanded *Calliſtenes* his Scholemaiſter to be ſlaine, becauſe *He* would not worſhip *Him* for a god: much more aboue compariſon, may God who is immortall and onely to be feared, puniſh yea and deſtroy *them* that in contempt of his infinite power and all-working maieſtie, adore the Sunne, Moone, and Starres, *Iſis* and *Oſyris*, with many other vaine, idolatrous, and profane venerations, derogating from the power and incomprehenſible

Cic. de nat. deor.

Alan. de conqueſt. nat.

henfible effence of God. When a King beholds his fubiects to referue their allegiance to any Monarch faue himfelfe, *He* makes *them* to be proclaimed Traitors to his Crowne and perfon: Euen fo the King of heauen, when *He* feeth any fubiect of his (as we be all and happie if fo we be, and not flaues to the captiuitie and thraldome of finne,) prefently profcribeth *him*, or will punifh *him* with death, left others by his impunitie fhould attempt the like. Wherefore then fhould any profane man, fo ouerfhadowed with the duskie clouds of error and impietie, tranfgreffe the deuine precepts, Lawes, and Ordinances of the Almightie; thofe eternall decrees eftablifhed and enacted in the glorious Synod of heauen, by relinquifhing the fweet promifes of God, and communicating the worfhip of the Creator with the creature, as if there were a diftribution to be made vnto either? But I will referre them to this following Satyre.

THE THIRTEENTH SATYRE.

PRotagoras *both wicked and profane,*
Wicked in life, profane in worfhipping,
Adored ftones: *(fee Pagans, fee your fhame)*
And thought them *worthie too of reuerencing;*
For if the gods be honoured, faid He,
Needs muft the ftones *whereof their Temples be.*

The like conceit He *had of* altars *too,*
And of the ftones *whereof they were erected,*
To which He *oft would folemne worfhip doe,*

And taxe such men by whom they were neglected;
Wishing sometime He were an altar stone,
That to himselfe like honour might be done.

<small>A iust reproofe to all Idolaters.</small>

Thou senseless man depriu'd of reasons lore,
What grace art thou (forlorne) endewd withall,
That thou shouldst shrines and senseless stones adore,
That haue no eares to heare when thou doest call?
Thou deemes these relikes happie, when god wot,
If they were happie, yet they know it not.

The Altar is the shrine thou offrest to,
Thy incense, sacrifice, and fat of beasts,
Which on the altar thou art wont to do,
Not to the altar where thou makes request;
For it's enioynd thee by expresse command,
To kneele to nothing fashion'd by mans hand.

<small>* Ingentes lapidū strues erigit, nec tam curat quo erigit quā curiose disponere quod arte conficit, &c.</small>

The Manuall artist sets vp* heapes of stones,
Erecting curious Statues to adore,
But what are these, can they attend our mones?
No, they haue eares to heare, but heare no more
Then rubbish, clay, or stone, whereof they'r said,
(And such were Pagan Idols) to be made.

<small>Stadium solis.</small>

Turne thee vnto the East, from whence the Sunne
Hath his arising, whence He doth proceed,
As Bridegroome from his chamber, and doth run
His spacious course with such a passing speed,
As twentie foure houres He doth onely borrow,
To post the world from end to end quite thorow.

Each

Each plant on earth, each creature in the sea,
From whence haue they their grouth, I pray thee say?
Do they deriue't from stones or imagerie?
Nay, I must tell thee, thou art by the way,
It's no inferiour power brings this to passe,
But his, who is, shall be, and euer was.

And he it is who notes thy errors past,
And can reuenge, though He the time adiourne,
Whose loue vnto his sheepe doth euer last,   Deus cū maxi-
And still expects and waits for thy returne;   me iratus, non
   iratus, cum ira-
But how can He to thee in kindnesse shew him,   tus propitius,
That giues thee hands, yet will not lift them to him?   &c.
   Qui fecit te fi-
   ne te, non sal-
   uabit te sine te.
   August.

Vngratefull thou to haue that ill conceit,
Of his all-being and all-seeing power,
Whose blest tuition guards vs and our state,
Whose surest hold is like a fading flower,
That springs and dies, such is the pompe of man,
As there He ends in earth where He began.

Horror of men, contempt to thy beginning,
Shame to the world, wherein thou doest suruiue,
Whose best religion is an act of sinning,   Exorto tremo-
   re, erubescet
In which thou meanes to die, and loues to liue;   conscientia, ob-
   stupescet con-
What shall these shrines affoord thee after death,   scia mentis sci-
The breath of life? no, for they haue no breath.   entia, & dicen-
   di facultates
   penitus amit-
Then here Ile leaue thee, yet with sorrow too,   tent organa,
Thy Image *moues compassion, though't may be,*   &c.
Thou'lt aske the reason why I should do so,
Since sorrowes sourse hath lost her course in thee:

To which I may in reason thus reply,
My eyes are wet, because thy eyes are dry.

*Yet will I to the altar, not t' adore it,
But offer incense to assoile thy sin;
Where full of teares I'le weepe, and weeping ore it,
Wish thy returne, that thou may honour him,
Whose worship thou prophan'd (as was vnfit)
Entitling any creature vnto it.

Numen si diuidis, perdis.

Three other Satyres composed by the same Author, treating of these three distinct subiects.

1. *Tyrannie, personated in* Eurystheus.
2. *Securitie, in* Alcibiades.
3. *Reuenge, in* Perillus.

With an Embleme of Mortalitie, in Agathocles.

The Argument.

EVrystheus a potent and puissant Prince of Greece, by the instigation of *Iuno* imposed *Hercules* most difficult labours, to the end to haue him dispatched. But of such inuincible patience was *Hercules* in suffering, and of such resolution in performing, as to his succeeding glory he purchased

OF TYRANNIE.

chafed himfelfe honour through their hate, gaining to himfelfe renowne, where his foe intended ineuitable reuenge. Whence we may collect two remarkable things, no leffe fruitfull in obferuing, then delightfull in perufing. The one is, to note how prompt and prepared men of depraued or vicious difpofition are, to put in execution the pleafure of great ones, how indirect or vnlawfull foeuer their pleafures be : directing and addreffing their employments to the bent of their command, be it wrong or right. And thefe are fuch who account it good fauing policie, to keepe euer correfpondence with greatneffe, efteeming no fupportance firmer, no protection fafer, then to hold one courfe with thofe high-mounting *Cedars*, from whofe grouth the lower *fhrubs* receiue fhadow and fhelter. The fecond which I note, is to obferue what glorious and profperous fucceffe many haue, who purfued and iniurioufly perfecuted (like *Zenocrates* Sparrow) either find fome compaffionate bofome to cheare & receiue them, or by the affiftance of an vnconfined power, attaine a noble iffue in midft of all occurrences. To infift on inftances, were to enlarge an Argument aboue his bounds : few or none there are who haue not or may not, haue inftance in the one, as well as perfonall experience in the other. Efpecially when we recal to mind how many inftant & imminent dangers haue bene threatned vs, & how many gracious and glorious deliuerances tendred vs. Some other excellent obferuations might be culled or felected from the flowrie border of this subiect, but my purpose is rather to shadow at some, then amply to dilate on all. For I haue euer obserued, how Arguments of this nature are to most profit composed, when they are not so amply as aptly compiled: Long and tedious discourses being like long seruices, tending more to surfet then solace; whereas the pleasure of varietie, draweth on a new appetite in midst of satietie. Now to our proposed taske: where you shall see how harmelesse innocencie shuffels out of the hands of boundlesse crueltie.

THE SATYRE.

Hoe Euristheus, *I am hither sent,*
From Iunoes *Princely pallace to thy Court,*
To tell thee, thou must be her instrument,
(And to that purpose she hath chus'd thee for't)
To chastise Hercules, *growne eminent*
By his renowned conquests: do not show
Thy selfe remisse, Iuno *will haue it so.*

And Iuno *shall; I will such taskes impose,*
That earth shall wonder how they were inuented,
So as his life he shall be sure to lose,
What do I care, so Iuno *be contented,*
Darknesse shall not my secresies disclose?
Her will is my command, nor must I aske
Whence's her distaff; come yong man *heare your taske*

* Hesperidum horti in custodes, peruigiles retinent forores.

A fruitfull * *garden, full of choyce delights,*
Enricht with sprayes of gold and apples too,
Which by three sisters watch'd both dayes and nights,
                                                    Yeeld

OF TYRANNIE.

Yeeld no accesse vnto th'inuading foe,
Is thy first progresse ; where with doubtfull fight,
Thou must performe thy taske : this is the first,
Which if it proue too easie, next is worst.

For in this first thou art to deale with women,
And reape a glorious prize when thou hast done ;
And such an enterprize (I know) is common,
Crowning vs great by th'triumph we haue wonne :
* *Gold is so strange a baite, as there is no man,*
But he will hazard life to gaine that prize,
Which makes men fooles that are supposed wise.

* Aurifera nemora teretem ferentia corticem, aureumq; pomum.

But next taske shall be of another kind,
No golden apples pluckt from Hesperie :
For in this worke thou nought but dong shalt find,
**Augean stables must thy labour be,*
Which if thou cleare not, as I haue assign'd,
Death shall attend thee : tis in vaine to come,
By prayers or teares to change my fatall doome.

* Augei stabuli, &c.

The third, that hideous Hydra, *which doth breed*
Increase of heads, for one being cut away,
Another springs vp streight way in her stead :
Hence then away, and make me no delay,
Delay breeds danger, do what I haue said,
Which done thou liues, which vnperform'd thou dies,
This said ; Alcydes *to his labour hies.*

* Abscisso capite, caput renascitur alterum.

He coucheth all his labours (infinite in number and nature) in these three.

Alas (poore man) how well it may be said,
So many are the perils he must passe,
That he with dangers is inuironed ?

So hopelesse and so haplesse is his case,
As he by death is so encompassed,
That howsoere his power he meanes to trie,
Poore is his power, he must be forc'd to die.

Imperious tyrant, couldst thou wreake thy rage
On none but such whose valour hath bene showne,
As a victorious Mirror to this age,
And hath bene blaz'd where thou wer't neuer knowne?
Must thou his person to such taskes engage,
As flesh and bloud did neuer yet sustaine?
Well, he must trie, although he trie in vaine.

Yes, he will trie, and act what he doth try,
He'le tug and tew, and striue and stoope to ought,
Yea* die, if so with honour he may die,
Yet know, that those who haue his life thus sought,
Are but insulting types of * tyrannie,   (shelues,
Whose boundlesse splene, when He hath past these
Will be disgorg'd, and fall vpon themselues.

For see, thou cruell sauage, whose desire
Extends to bloud, how this aduentr'ous Knight,
Gaines him renowne, and scorneth to retire,
Till he hath got a conquest by his fight:
So high heroick thoughts vse to aspire,
As when extremest dangers do enclose them,
They sleight those foes that labour to oppose them.

Here see those taskes which thy imperious power,
Impos'd this Noble champion, finished;
The Serpent, * Hydra, which of heads had store,

Now

---

* Non terret mors sapientem.
* Thales milesius interroganti quid difficile; senem (inquit) videre tyrannum.

* Pro telo gerit quæ fudit, armatus venit Leone & Hydra. *Senec.*

Now headleffe lies by valour conquered,
The ftables purg'd from th'filth they had before,
The golden Apples Trophies of his glorie,
Dilate their ends vnto an endleffe ftorie.

Here fee th'euent where vertue is the aime,
Here fee the iffue of a glorious mind,
Here fee how martiall honour makes her claime,
Here fee the crowne to diligence affign'd,
Here fee what all may fee, a fouldiers fame,
Not tipt with fruitleffe titles, but made great,
More by true worth, then by a glorious feate.

For fuch, whofe natiue merit hath attain'd
Renowne 'mongft men, should *aduerfe gufts affaile them   * Si fola nobis
In fuch an Orbe reft their refolues contain'd,   adfunt profpe-
As well they may inuade but not appall them,   ra, foluimer: ad
For from efteeme of earth they'r wholly wain'd,   virtutem vero
Planting their mounting thoughts vpon that fphere,   melius per ad-
Which frees fuch minds as are infranchis'd there.   uerfa folidamur
   Greg.

Hence learne ye Great-ones, who efteeme it good
Sufficient to be great, and thinke't well done,
Be't right or wrong, what's done in heate of blood,
Hence learne your ftate, left ye decline too foone,
For few ere firmely ftood, that proudly ftood.
But fpecially ye men that are in * place,   * Locum virtus
Iudge others as your felues were in fame cafe.   habet. *Sen.*

Here haue you had a mirror to direct
Your wayes, and forme your actions all the better,
Which prefident if careleffe, ye neglect,

                         And

And walke not by this line, liue by this letter,
Hows'ere the world may tender you respect,
Ye are but gorgeous paintings daubed ouer,
Clothing your vice with some more precious couer.

Hence likewise learne ye whom the frowne of fate,
Hath so deprest, as not one beame doth shine
Vpon the forlorne mansion of your state,
To beare with patience and giue way to time,
So shall ye vie with Fortune in her hate;
And prize all earths contents as bitter-sweete,
Which armes you 'gainst all fortunes ye can meete.

This great Alcydes *did, who did with ease*
(For what's vneasie to a mind prepard)
Discomfit * *th' Hydra and th' Stymphalides,*
With whom he cop'd, encountred long and warr'd,
And gain'd him glory by such acts as these.
Obserue this Morall (for right sure I am)
The imitation shewes a perfect man.

* Has Hydra sensit, his iacent Stymphalides. *Ibid.*

The last not least, which may obserued be,
Is to suppresse splene or conceiued hate,
Which in perfidious * Nessus *you may see,*
Fully portraid, who meerely through deceit,
Practis'd Alcydes *wofull Tragedy:*
For of all passions, there's no one that hath
More soueraignty ore man, then boundlesse wrath.

—Nessus hos struxit dolos. Ictus sagittis qui tuis vitam expulit. Cruore tincta est Palla semiferi, pater. Nessusque nunc has exigit pœnas sibi. *in Herc. Oet.*

Which to restraine, (for wherein may man show
Himselfe more manly, then in this restraint)
That there is nought more generous, you should know,
                                                    Then

Then true* compaſſion to the indigent, *Flete Hercu-*
Which euen humanitie faith, that we owe *leos numina*
One to another, while we vſe to tender *casus. ibid.*
Loue to our Maker, *in him to each* member.

Thus if ye do, how low ſoere ye be,
Your actions make you noble, and ſhall liue
After your ſummons of Mortalitie,
And from your aſhes ſuch a perfume giue,
As ſhall eternize your bleſt memorie:
If otherwiſe ye liue, ye are at beſt
But guilded gulls, and by opinion *bleſt.*

The Argument.

A *Lcibiades* a noble Athenian, whoſe glorious & renowned actions gained him due eſteeme in his Country: at laſt by retiring himſelfe frõ armes, gaue his mind to fenſuality; which ſo effeminated his once imparallel'd ſpirit, as he became no leſſe remarkable for ſenſuall libertie, then he was before memorable for ennobled exploits of martiall chiualrie. From hence the *Satyre* deriues his ſubject, inueying againſt the remiſneſſe of *ſuch* as waine their affections from employment, expoſing their minds (thoſe glorious or reſplendent images of their *Maker*) to *ſecuritie,* rightly termed *the diuels opportunitie.* How perillous vacancie from affaires

Others are of opinion that he was drawne frõ ſenſuall affectiõs to the practiſe of vertue, by the graue inſtruction of Socrates: but it appeares otherwiſe by his much frequenting Timandraes companie. Vid. Plut. in vit. Alcib.

OF SECVRITIE.

faires hath euer bene, may appeare by ancient and moderne examples, whofe *Tragicall cataftrophe* wold craue teares immix'd with lines. Let this fuffice, there is no one motiue more effectually mouing, no Rhetoricke more mouingly perfwading, no Oratorie more perfwafiuely inducing, then what we daily feele or apprehend in our felues. Where euery * houre not well employed, begets fome argument or other to moue our corrupt natures to be depraued. Let vs then admit of no vacation, faue onely vacation from vice. Our liues are too fhort to be fruitlefly employed, or remifly paffed. O then how well fpent is that oyle which confumes it felfe in actions of *vertue*

Whofe precious felfe's a glory to her felfe!

May nothing fo much be eftranged frō vs as *vice*, which, of all others, moft disfigures *vs;* Though *our feete be on earth, may our minds be in heauen*: where we fhall find more true glory then *earth* can affoord vs, or the light promifes of fruitleffe vanity affure vs. Expect then what may merit your attention; a rough-hew'd *Satyre* fhall fpeake his mind boldly without partiality, taxing *fuch* who retire from *action*, wherein *vertue* confifteth, and lye fleeping in *fecuritie*, whereby the fpirit, or inward motion of the foule wofully droupeth.

* Quot horæ (fi male expenfæ) tot iræ.
Quot horæ, tot vmbræ.

THE SATYRE.

Wake, thou noble Greeke! how fhould defire,
Of fenfuall fhame (foules flaine) fo dull thy wit,
Or

Or cloud thofe glorious thoughts which did afpire,
Once to exploits which greatneffe might befit?
Where now the beamlins of that facred fire,
Lie rak't in afhes, and of late do feeme
(So ranke is vice) as if they had not bene.

Can a faith-breaking leering *Curtizan,   * Illa pictura vi-
Whofe face is glaz'd with frontleffe impudence,   tij eft. *Ambrol*
Depreffe the fpirit of a Noble man,   Hexam.l.6.c.8.
And make him lofe his reafon for his fence?
O fpan thy life (for life is but a fpan)
And thou fhalt find the scantling is fo fmall,
For vaine delights there is no *time at all!   * Sicut capillus
non peribit de
capite, ita nec
momentum de
Shall azur'd breaft, fleeke skin, or painted cheeke,   tempore. *Bern.*
*Gorgeous attire, locks braided, wandring eye,   * *All gorgeous*
Gaine thee delight, when thou delights fhould feeke   *attire is the at-*
In a more glorious obiect? O relie   *tire of finne.*
On a more firme foundation, left thou breake,
Credit with Him who long hath giuen thee truft,
Which thou muft pay be fure, for he is iuft.

O do not then admire, what thy defire
Should moft contemne, if reafon were thy guide;
Let thy erected thoughts extend farre higher,
Then to thefe wormelins that like *fhadowes glide,
Whofe borrowed beautie melts with heate of fire.   * Sunt ifta poe-
Their fhape from * fhop is bought and brought; ô art   matis vmbræ.
What canft thou promife to a knowing heart!   * Quarum vni-
cum eft officiũ,
ab officina eli-
A knowing heart, which plants her choiceft bliffe   cere formam.
In what it fees not, but doth comprehend   Lecythum ha-
bet in malis.
vid. vict. ad Sal.

By

OF SECVRITIE.

By eye of faith / not what terreſtriall is,
But what affoordeth * comfort without end,
Where we enioy whats euer we did wiſh ;
Who then, if he partake but common ſence,
Will ere reioyce, till he depart from hence ?

* Ea vita beata eſt, quando quod optimum eſt, amatur & habetur. Sola eius viſio, vera mentis noſtræ refectio eſt. *Greg. in Mor. Expo. in Iob.*

Yet ſee the blindneſſe of diſtracted man,
How he prefers one moment of delight,
(Which cheares not much when it does all it can)
Before delights in nature infinite,
Whoſe iuyce (yeelds perfect fullneſſe, ſure I am :)
O times / when men loue that they ſhould neglect,
Diſualuing that which they ſhould moſt reſpect.

For note how many haue aduentured
Their liues (and happy they if that were all)
And for a * painted trunke haue periſhed ;
O England, I thy ſelfe to witneſſe call,
For many hopefull plants haue withered
Within thy boſome, cauſe whereof did ſpring,
Mearely from luſt, and from no other thing /

* Quanta amē-tia eſt effigiem mutare naturæ, picturam quæ-rere ? *Cypri de diſcip. & hab. virg.*

How many promiſing youths, whoſe precious bloud
Shed by too reſolute hazard, might haue done
Their gracious Prince and natiue Countrie good,
In heate of bloud haue to their ruine gone,
While they on termes of reputation ſtood,
Preferring titles (ſee the heate of ſtrife)
Before the loue and ſafetie of their life ?

* Inanis gloriæ fuccum proprie ſaluti præpo-nentes.

O Gentlemen, know that thoſe eyes of yours,
Which ſhould be piercing like the * Eagles eyes,

* Cunctarum quippe auium

Are

OF SECVRITIE.

Are not to view thefe Dalilahs *of ours,*
But to eye heauen and fullen earth *defpife,*
And fo increafe in honours *as in* houres,
O ye fhould find more happineffe in this,
Then fpend the day in courting for a kiffe!

Were time as eafie purchas'd as is land,
Ye better might difpenfe with loffe of time;
Or 'twere in you to make the Sunne to ftand,
So many points t'afcend or to decline,
I'de fay ye had the world at command:
But as time * paft, is none of yours, once gone,
So that time is not yours, which is to come.

Addreffe your felues then to that glorious place,
Where there's no time, no limit to confine,
No alteration: but where fuch a grace,
Or perfect luftre beautifies the clime,
Where ye'r to liue, as th'choifeft chearefullft face,
Ye ere beheld on earth, were't nere * fo faire,
Shall feeme deformitie to beautie there.

But this fhall ferue for you! now in a word,
Heare me * Timandra *(for I muft be heard;)*
Thou whofe light fhop *all vanities affoord,*
Reclaime thy fenfuall life, which hath appear'd
As odious and offenfiue to thy Lord,
As thofe lafciuious robes (robes fuiting night)
Are in difgrace, when good men are in fight.

More to enlarge my felfe were not fo good,
Perhaps this litle's more then thou wilt reade:

But

vifum acies a-
quilæ fuperat:
ita vt folis ra-
dios fixos in fe
cius oculos nul-
la lucis fuæ co-
rufcatione re-
uerberans,
claudat. *Greg.
in Mor. Expof.
in Iob.*

* Quicquid de
illo præteritum
eft, iam non eft:
quicquid ne il-
lo futurum eft,
nondum eft.
Aug.

* Videndo pul
chra, cogita
hæc omnia, &
pulchriora, effe
in cœlo: viden
do horribilia,
cogita hæc om-
nia, & horribi-
liora, effe in
inferno. *Lanf-
perg.*
* In Timandræ
gremio paululū
recumbens, pe-
rimitur. *Plut. in
vit. Alcib.*

But if thou reade, I wiſh't may ſtirre thy blood,
And moue thee henceforth to take better heed,
Then to tranſgreſſe the bounds of womanhood:
Whoſe chiefeſt eſſence in theſe foure appeare,
In gate, looke, ſpeech, *and in the robes you weare.*

The Argument.

PErillus an excellent Artificer (being then famous for excellent inuentions) to ſatisfie the inhumane diſpoſition of the tyrant *Phalaris,* alſo in hope to be highly rewarded for his ingenious deuice: made a *bull* of *braſſe* for a new kind of torment, preſenting it to *Phalaris,* who made triall thereof by tormenting *Perillus* firſt therein. From this Argument or ſubiect of *reuenge,* we may obſerue two ſpeciall motiues of Morall inſtruction or humane Caution. The firſt is, to deterre vs from humoring or ſoothing ſuch, on whom we haue dependence, in irregular or ſiniſter reſpects. For the vertuous, *whoſe comfort is the teſtimonie of a good conſcience,* ſcorne to hold correſpondence with vicious men, whoſe commands euer tend to depraued and enormious ends. The ſecond is, a notable example of *reuenge* in *Perillus* ſuffering, & in *Phalaris* inflicting. Much was it that this curious Artizan expected, but with equall & deſerued cenſure was he rewarded: for inglorious
aimes

seconded by like ends. Hence the Satyre displayeth such in their natiue colours, who rather then they will lose the least esteeme with men of high ranke or qualitie, vse to dispence with faith, friend, and all, to plant them firmer in the affection of their Patron. But obserue the conclusion, as their meanes were indirect, so their ends sorted euer with the meanes. They seldome extend their temporizing houres to an accomplished age, but haue their hopes euer blasted, ere they be well bloomed: their iniurious aimes discouered, ere they be rightly leuelled: and their wishes to a tragicall period exposed, as their desires were to all goodnesse opposed. May all proiectors or stateforragers sustaine like censure, hauing their natures so reluctant or opposite to all correspondence with honour. Longer I will not dilate on this subiect, but recollect my spirits, to adde more spirit to my ouer-tyred *Satyre*, who hath bene so long employed in the *Embassie of Nature*, and wearied in dancing the *Wilde mans measure*, that after *Perillus* censure she must repose ere she proceede any further; and take some breath ere I dance any longer.

THE SATYRE.

B*Raue* Engineer, *you whose more curious hand*
Hath fram'd a Bull of brasse *by choycest art,*
That as a Trophie it might euer stand,
And be an Embleme of thy cruell heart:
Hearke what's thy tyrant Phalaris *command,*
     M   *Whose*

Whose will's a law ; and hauing heard it well,
Thy censure to succeeding ages tell.

Thou must (as it is iust) be first presented
A sacrifice vnto the brazen Bull,
And feele that torture which thy art inuented,
That thou maist be rewarded to the full ;
No remedy, it cannot be preuented.
Thus, thus reuenge *appeares which long did smother,*
He must be catcht, that aimes to catch another.

Iust was thy iudgement, Princely Phalaris,
Thy censure most impartiall ; that he
Whose artfull hand that first contriued this,
To torture others, and to humour thee,
Should in himselfe feele what this torture is.
Which great or small, he must be forc'd to go,
*May such * tame-beasts be euer vsed so.*

<small>* *For so Dioge-*
nes the Cynicke
tearmes all hu-
mering Timists
or temporizing
sycophants. La-
ert.
* *Who built Pal-*
las horse, and
after perished in
the siege of
Troy Homer, in
Iliad</small>

*Like fate befell vnhappie * Phereclus,*
Who first contriu'd by cunning more then force,
To make once glorious Troy as ruinous
As spoile could make it : therefore rear'd a Horse,
Framed by Pallas *art, as curious,*
As art could forme, or cunning could inuent,
To weaue his end, which art could not preuent.

See ye braue state-proiectors, what's the gaine
Ye reape by courses that are indirect :
See these, who first contriu'd, and first were slaine,
May mirrors *be of what ye most affect !*
These labour'd much, yet labour'd they in vaine ;

For

OF REVENGE.

For there's no wit how quicke soere can do it,
If powers diuine shall make ᵃ *resistance to it.*

And can ye thinke that heauen, whose glorious eye
Surueyes this Vniuerse, will daigne to view
Men that are giuen to all impietie?
You say, he will; *he will indeed, it's true;*
But this is to your further misery.
For that same eye which viewes what you commit,
Hath sight to see, and power to ᵇ *punish it.*

To punish it, if hoording sin on sin,
Ye loath Repentance, and bestow your labour,
Onely to gaine esteeme, or else to win
By your pernicious plots some great mans fauour;
O I do see the state that you are in,
Which cannot be redeem'd, vnlesse betime
With ᶜ *sighs for sins, you wipe away your crime!*

For shew me one, (if one to shew you haue)
Who built his fortunes on this sandie ground,
That euer went gray-headed to his graue,
Or neare his end was not distressed found,
Or put not trust in that which did deceiue!
Sure few there be, if any such there be,
But shew me one, and it sufficeth me.

I grant indeed, that for a time these *may*
Flourish like to a Bay tree, *and increase,*
Like Oliue branches, *but this lasts not aye,*
Their ᵈ Halcyon *dayes shall in a moment ceasse,*

---

a *Witnesse that matchlesse* Powder plot, *no lesse miraculously reuealed, then mischieuously contriued, no lesse happily preuented, then hatefully practised. Of which cruell Agents (being his owne subiects) our gracious Soueraigne might iustly take vp the complaint of that Princely Prophet Dauid.* My familiar friends, whō I trusted, which did eate of my bread, haue lifted vp their heeles against me. *Psal.* 51. and 55.
Si non parcet, perdet.
b Vbi non est per gratiam, adest per vindictam. *Aug.*
c Qui non gemit peregrinus, non gaudebit eiuis. *Aug.*

d Halcyonei dies ab Halcyonijs auibus dicti: neque boni maliue ominis aues hos esse arbitror; quantum tamen à Propheta dicitur, tantum à me afferendum afferendumque esse puto. Etiam Ciconiain cœlo nouit stata tempora sua, & Turtur, grusque, & Hirundo obseruant tempus aduentus sui. *Ierem.* 8. 7.

When night (sad night) shall take their soules away.
Then will they tune their strings to this sad song,
Short was our sun-shine, but our night-shade long.

Ye then, I say, whose youth-deceiuing prime,
Promise successe, beleeue't from me, that this,
When time shall come (as what more swift then time)
Shall be conuerted to a painted blisse,
Whose gilded outside beautifide your crime;
Which once displaide, cleare shall it shew as light,
Your Sommer-day's *become a* winter night.

Beware then ye, who practise and inuent,
To humour greatnesse; for there's one more great,
Who hath pronounc'd, like *sinne, like punishment;
Whom at that day ye hardly may intreat,
When death and horror shall be eminent:
Then will ye say vnto the Mountaines thus,
And shadie groues, Come downe and couer vs.

But were ye great as earthly pompe could make ye,
Weake is the arme of flesh, or *mightinesse,
For all these feeble hopes shall then forsake ye,
With the false flourish of your happinesse,
When ye vnto your field-bed must betake ye;
Where ye for all your shapes and glozed formes,
Might deceiue men, but cannot deceiue wormes.

* Pari culpa, pari poena.

* The priuiledge of greatnesse, must be no subterfuge for guiltinesse.

The Statue of *Agathocles*.

The Argument.

*A**Gathocles* a tyrant of Syracufa, caufed his *Sta-tue* to be compofed in this manner. *The *head of gold, armes of iuory, and other of the liniments of pureft braffe, but the feete of earth:* intimating of what weake and infirme fubfiftence this *little-world, Man,* was builded. Whence we may col-lect, what diuine confiderations the *Pagans* them-felues obferued and vfually applied to rectifie their morall life: where inftructions of nature directed them, not onely in the courfe of humane focie-tie, but euen in principles aboue the reach and pitch of *Nature,* as may appeare in many Philofo-phicall Axioms, and diuinely inferted fentences in the Workes of *Plato, Plutarch, Socrates;* and amongft the Latines in the inimitable labours of *Seneca, Boæthius, Tacitus,* and *Plinius Secundus.* Vpon the Morall of this *Statue* of *Agathocles* in-fifts the Author in this *Poeme,* concluding with this vndoubted pofition: *That as foundations on fand are by euery tempeft fhaken, fo man ftanding on feete of earth, hath no firmer foundation then mutabi-litie to ground on.*

* Caput de au-ro innuendo re-gis dignitatem brachia de ebo-re intimando eius venufta-tem, cætera li-nimenta de ære denotãdo ftre-nuitatem, pe-des vero de terra, indican-do eius fragili-tatem. *vid. Plut. Apotheg.*

THE EMBLEME.

AGathocles, *me thinkes I might compare thee,*
(So rare thou art) to some choice statuarie,
Who doth portray *with* Pencile *he doth take,*
Himselfe to th'image which he's wont to make;
How artfull thou, *and gracefull too by birth,*
A King, *yet shewes that thou art made of* earth,
Not glorying in thy greatnesse, *but would seeme,*
Made of the same mould other men haue bene!
A head of gold, *as thou art chiefe of men,*
So chiefe of mettalls makes thy Diadem;
Victorious *armes of purest* iuorie,
Which intimates the persons puritie;
The other liniments *compos'd of* brasse,
Imply th'vndaunted strength of which thou was;
But feete *of* earth, *shew th'ground whereon we stand,*
That we're cast downe in turning of a hand.
Of which, that we might make the better vse,
Me thinkes I could dilate the Morall *thus.*
Man *made of* earth, *no surer footing can*
Presume vpon, then earth *from whence he came,*
Where firmenesse is infirmenesse, and the stay
On which he builds his strongest hopes, is clay.
And yet how strangely confident he growes,
In heauen-confronting boldnesse and in showes,
Bearing a Giants spirit, when in length,
Height, breadth, and pitch he is of Pigmeis *strength.*
Yea I haue knowne a very Dwarfe *in sight,*
Conceit himselfe a Pyramis *in height,*
Ietting so stately, as't were in his power

To

To mount aloft vnto the airie tower.
But when Man's *proud, I should esteemè't more meete*
Not to presume on's strength, *but looke on's feete:*
Which nature (we obserue) hath taught the* Swan,
And ought in reason to be done in Man.
Weake are foundations *that are rer'd on sand,*
And on as weake grounds may we seeme to stand,
Both subiect to be ruin'd, split and raz't,
One billow shakes the first, *one griefe the* last.
Whence then or how subsists this earthly frame,
That merits in it selfe no other name,
Then *shell of base corruption ! *it's not* brasse,
Marble, *or* iuory, *which when times passe,*
And our expired fates surceasse to be,
Reserue in them our liuing memorie.
No, no, this mettall *is not of that proofe,*
We liue as those vnder a shaking roofe,
Where euery moment *makes apparent show,*
For want of props of finall ouerthrow.
Thus then, me thinkes you may (if so you please)
Apply this Statue *of* Agathocles ;
As he compos'd his royall Head *of* gold,
The pur'st of mettals, you are thereby told,
*That th'*Head *whence reason and right iudgement*
Should not be pesterd with inferior things; (*springs,*
And as his actiue sinnewes, armes *are said,*
To shew their purenesse, to be iuored,
Like Pelops *milke-white shoulders; we are giuen*
To vnderstand, our armes should be to heauen,
As to their proper orbe enlarg'd, that we
Might there be made the Saints of puritie ;
*By rest of th'*parts *which were compos'd of* brasse,
(*Being*

* In euius atricres pedes lumé non citius figitur, quam in seipso statim deijcitur. *Vid. Plin. in nat. Hist. Ælian. ibid. Sambuc. in Emblem. Alciat. ibid.*

* O quam contempta res est homo, nisi supra, humana se erexerit !

(Being of bigger bone *then others was)*
We may collect, men made of selfe-same clay,
May in their strength do more then others may,
Lastly on earth, *as men subsistence* haue,
Their earthly *feete *do hasten to their graue.*

* Pes in terris, mens sit in cœlis.

A short Satyre of a corrupt Lawyer.

THE XIIII. SATYRE.

Naso Iuridicus.

NAso *is sicke of late, but how canst tell?*
    He hath a swelling in his throate *I feare;*
I iudg'd as much, me thought He *spake not well,*
In his poore clients cause : nay more I heare,
His tumour's growne so dang'rous, as some *say,*
He was absolued *but the t'other day.*

And what confest He ? *not a sinne I trow,*
Those He *referu'd within a leatherne bag,*
And that's his conscience; *did* He *mercy show*
Vnto the poore? not one old rotten rag
Would he affoord them, or with teares bemone them,
Saying, that—forma pauperis *had vndone them.*

Did He *not wish to be dissolu'd from hence?*
No, when you talk'd of finall Dissolution,

He

He *with a sea of teares his face would drench,*
Wishing He *might but make another* motion,
And He *would be* diffolu'd *when* He *had done:*
But His *forg'd* motion *each tearme day begun.*

Had He *some matter laid vpon his heart?*
Abundance of corruption, foule infection.
Did He *no secret treasure there impart?*
Nought but a boxe containing his complexion.   Oleum gratiæ
What was it Sir, some precious oyle of grace?   ἔλαιον.
No, but an oyle to smeere his brazen face.

I haue heard much of his attractiue nose
How He *could draw white Riols with his breath;*
It's true indeed, and therefore did He choose   Aurū palpabile
To drinke Aurum potabile *at his death,*   & aurum pota-
Nor car'd He *greatly if* He *were to lose*   bile; Aurum ob-
His soule, *so that* He *might enioy his* nose.   rizum & aurum
   adulterinum.

It was a wonder in his greatest paine,
How He *should haue* remorse; *for well I know,*
In his successiue fortunes nought could straine
His hardned conscience, which He *would not do*
For hope of gaine, so as in time no sinne
So great, but grew familiar with him.

O Sir, the many fees He *had receiu'd,*   (him,
And hood-winck'd bribes which at his death opprest
The forged deeds *his wicked braine contriu'd*
And that blacke buckram bag which did arrest him,
Commencing suite in one, surcharg'd Him *so,*
That He *was plung'd into a gulph of wo.*

                 O

O what a smoke of powder there appeared
At the dissoluing of his vglie soule;
All *that were present there to see* Him *feared*,
His case vncas'd did show so grim, so foule:
Yet there were some had hope He *would do well*,
Make but one motion, and come out of hell.

But others fear'd that motion *would be long*,
If it should answer motions He *made here:*
Besides, that place of motions *is so throng*,
That one will scarce haue end a thousand yeare.
Then Naso *fare thee well, for I do see,*
Earth sends to hell thy mittimus with thee.

Two short moderne Satyres.

In Ambulantem. } Pseudophilia.
Hypocritam.

A *Walking* Hypocrite *there was, whose pace,*
Trunkhose, small ruffe, deminutiue in forme,
Shew'd to each man He *was the* child of grace,
Such were the vertues *did his life adorne;*
Nought could He *heare that did of* lightnesse *come,*
But He *would stop his eares, or leaue the roome.*

Discourse (thus would He *say) of things deuine,*
Soyle *not your soules with such lasciuiousnesse,*

Your

PSEVDOPHILIA.

Your veſſels *ſhould with precious vertues ſhine,*
As lamps *of grace and* lights *of godlineſſe;*
But laſſe for wo, ſin's ſuch a fruitfull weed,
Still as one dies another doth ſucceed.

Here *one doth beate his braine 'bout praĉtiſes,*
There *is another plotting wickedneſſe;*
O how long Lord wilt thou blindfold their eyes,
In ſuffering them to worke vnrighteouſneſſe?
Well, I will pray for them, *and Syons peace,*
The prayers of Saints can no way chuſe but pleaſe.

Thus did this mirror of deuotion walke,
Inſpir'd it ſeem'd with ſome Angelicke gift,
So holy was his life, ſo pure his talke,
As if the ſpirit of zeale had Ely *left,*
And lodg'd within his breaſt, it could not be,
Fuller of godly feruor then was He.

But ſee what end theſe *falſe pretences haue,*
Where zeale is made a cloke to couer ſinne,
This whited wall *to th'eye ſo ſeeming graue,*
Like varniſh'd tombes had nought but filth within,
For though of zeale He *made a formall ſhow,*
In Fortune Alley *was his Rendeuow.*

There He *repos'd, there* He *his ſolace tooke,*
Shrin'd neare his Saint, his female-puritan,
In place ſo priuate as no eye could looke,
To what they *did, to manifeſt their ſhame;*
But ſee heauens will, thoſe eyes they leaſt ſuſpeĉted,
Firſt ey'd their ſhame, whereby they were deteĉted.

Thus

*Thus did his speech and practise disagree
In one* examplar, *formall, regular,
In th'other* loose *through carnall libertie,
Which two when they do meete, so different are,
As there's no discord worse in any song,
Then twixt a* hollow heart and holy tongue.

For He *that doth pretend, and think't enough,
To make a* shew *of what* He *least intends,
Shall ere the period of his dayes run through,
Beshrew himselfe for his mischieuous ends;*
For he that is not good, but would be thought,
Is worse by odds then this plaine dealing nought.

In Drusum meretri-} Poligonia.
cium Adiutorem.

D Rufus, *what makes* thee *take no trade in hand,
But like* Hermaphrodite, *halfe man, halfe womā
Pandors thy selfe, and stands at whoores command,
To play the bolt for euery Haxter common?
Spend not thy houres with whoores, lest thou confesse,*
There is no life to thy obduratenesse.

*Obdurate villaine hard'ned in ill,
That takes delight in seeing Nature naked,
Whose pleasure drawne from selfe-licentious will,
Makes thee of God, of men, and* all forsaked;
         Shame

Shame is thy chaine, thy fetters linkes of sinne,
Whence to escape is hard, being once lock'd in.

What newes from Babell, *where that purple whoore,*
With seared marrow charmes deluded man,
So lull'd asleepe, as He *forgets heauens power,*
And serues that hireling-Neapolitan?
I'le tell thee Drusus, *sad and heauie newes,*
Death *vnto* Drusus *while he hants the stewes.*

An Admonition to the Reader vpon the precedent Satyres.

WHo *will not be reprou'd, it's to be fear'd,*
  Scornes to amend, or to redeeme the time;
For spotlesse Vertue *neuer there appear'd,*
Where true Humility, *that fruitfull* vine
Hath no plantation, for it cannot be,
Grace should haue growth but by Humilitie.

Let each man then into his errors *looke,*
And with a free acknowledgement confesse;
That there are more Errataes *in his booke,*
Then th'crabbedst Satyre *can in lines expresse:*
For this will better Him, *and make* Him *grow*
In grace with Vertue, *whom* He *knowes not now.*
                                    These

These my vnpolish'd Satyres *I commend,*
To thy protection, not that I do feare
Thy censure otherwise then as a friend,
For I am secure of censure I may sweare,
But for forme sake : *if shou't accept them do,*
If not, I care not how the world go.

     Thine if thine owne,

    Musophilus.

    Silentio culpa crescit.

THE
SHEPHEARDS
TALES.

Too true poore shepheards *do this Prouerbe find,*
No sooner out of sight then out of mind.

LONDON,
Printed for Richard Whitaker.
1621.

TO MY WORTHIE
AND AFFECTIONATE
KINSMAN Richard Hvtton
Efquire, Sonne and Heire to the much honou-
red and fincere difpenfer of judgement,
Sir Richard Hvtton Sergeant at
Law, and one of the *Iudges* of the
Common Pleas:

The fruition of his selectdest wishes.

TO fit fecure and in a safe repofe,
To view the croffe occurrences of those
Who are on Sea; or in a filent fhade,
To eye the ftate of such as are decay'd;
Or neere some filuer Rill or Beechy Groue,
To reade how Starre-croft louers loft their loue,
Is beft *of humane blefsings, and this beft*
Is in your worthy felfe (Deere Cuz) *expreft,*
Who by your fathers *vertues and your owne*
Are truly lou'd, wherefeuer you are knowne:
In State *fecure, rich in a faithfull* make, [mate
And rich in all *that may fecure your State.*
Now in thefe dayes of yours, thefe Halcion *daies,*
Where you enioy all ioy, perufe thefe layes,

The Epistle Dedicatorie.

That you who liu'd to loue, liue where you loue,
May reade what you nere felt, nor ere did proue;
Poore Swainlins *croſt where they affected moſt,*
And croſt in that which made them euer croſt.
Receiue this Poem, Sir, for as I liue,
Had I ought better, I would better giue.

RICH: BRATHVVAIT.

THE SHEPHEARDS TALES.

THE FIRST PART.

The Argument.

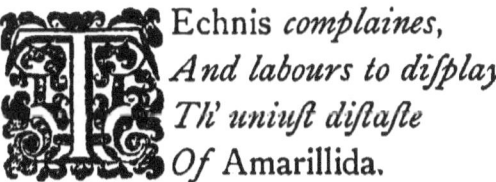

Echnis *complaines*,
And labours to display
Th' uniust distaste
Of Amarillida.

The second Argument.

Ere relates this forlorne Swaine
How he woo'd, but woo'd in vaine,
Her whose beautie did surpasse
Shape of any Country Lasse,
Made more to delight the bed,
Than to see her Lambkins fed;
Yet poore Shepheard see his fate,
Loue shee vow'd, is chang'd to hate:

For being iealous of his loue,
Shee her fancie doth remoue,
Planting it vpon a Groome,
Who by *Cupids* blindeſt doome
Is preferd vnto thoſe ioyes,
Which were nere ordain'd for Boyes:
On whoſe face nere yet appear'd
Downie ſhew of manly beard.
Hauing thus drunke ſorrows cup,
Firſt, he ſhewes his bringing vp,
What thoſe *Arts* were he profeſt,
Which in homely ſtyle expreſt,
He deſcends vnto the Swaine
Whom he ſought by loue to gaine;
But preuented of his ayme,
Her he ſhowes, but hides her ſhame.

THE SHEPHEARDS TALES.

The ſhepheards.

Technis. Dymnus. Dorycles.
Corydon. Sapphus. Linus.

THE FIRST EGLOGVE.

Technis tale.

*Hy now I ſee theſe Plaines ſome good afford,*
When Shpherds will be maſters of their word.

Dory. *Yes,* Technis *yes, we ſee it now & then*
That they'le keep touch as wel as greater men,
Who can proteſt and take a ſolemn vow
To doe farre more then they intend to doe.

Dym.

Dym. *Stay* Dorycles, *me thinkes thou goeſt too farre,*
Lets talke of Shepheards, as we Shepheards are:
For why ſhould we theſe Great mens *errors note,*
But learne vnto our Cloth *to cut our coat.*
Sapp. Dymnus, *'tis true; we came not to diſplay*
Great mens abuſes, but to paſſe away
The time in Tales, *wherein we may relate*
By one and one our bleſt or wretched ſtate.
Cor. *Indeed friend* Dymnus *therfore came we hither,*
To ſhew our Fortune and diſtreſſe together,
Lin. *Proceede then* Technis, *you'r the eldeſt Swaine*
That now feeds Flocks vpon this fruitfull Plaine:
So as your age, whatſeuer we alledge,
Doth well deſerue that proper priuiledge.
Tech. *As to begin;*
Lin. *So* Technis *doe I meane.*
Tech. *Thanks Shepherds heartily, that you will daine*
A hapleſſe Swaine ſuch grace; which to requite,
Ile mix my dolefull Storie with delight,
That while yee weepe for griefe, I may allay
Your diſcontent, and wipe your teares away.
Dory. *On* Technis *on, and weele attention lend,*
And wiſh thy loue may haue a happie end.
Dym. *Which ſhowne, each ſhall reply, and make expreſt*
When all is done, whoſe fate's the heauieſt.
Tech. *Attend then Shepheards, now I doe begin,*
Shewing you firſt where I had nurturing,
Which to vnfold the better, I will chuſe
No other words then home-ſpun Heardſmen vſe.
Firſt then, becauſe ſome Shepheards may ſuppoſe
By meere conjecture, I am one of thoſe
Who had my breeding on this flowrie Plaine,

I must confesse that they are much mista'ne,
For if I would, I could strange stories tell
Of Platoes *and of* Aristotles *Well,*
From whence I drain'd such drops of diuine wit,
As all our Swaines could hardly diue to it :.
Dor. *Indeed I'ue heard much of thee in thy youth.*
Tech. *Yes Dorycles, I say no more than truth.*
A Prentiship did I in Athens *liue,*
Not without hope but I might after giue
Content and comfort where I should remaine,
And little thought I then to be a Swaine :
For I may say to you, I then did seeme
One of no small or popular esteeme,
But of consort with such, whose height of place
Aduanced me, because I had their grace :
Though now, since I my Lambkins gan to feede,
Clad in my russet coat and countrey weede,
Those broad-spred Cedars *scarce afford a nest*
Vpon their shadie Boughes, where I may rest.
Sapp. *It seemes they're great men* Technis.
Tech. *So they are,*
And for inferiour groundlins, little care.
But may they flourish : thus much I am sure,
Though Shrubs *be not so high, they're more secure.*
Lin. *High states indeed are subiect to decline.*
Tech. *Yes* Linus *yes, in this corrupted time*
We may obserue by due experience
That where a Person has preeminence,
He so transported growes, as he will checke
Ioue *in his Throne, till Pride has broke his necke,*
Whereas so vertuous were precedent times,
As they were free not only from the crimes

To

To which this age's expofed, but did liue
As men which fcorn'd Ambition.
Dymn. *Now I diue*
Into thy meaning Technis; *thou do'ft grieue*
That thofe *who once endeer'd thee, now fhould leaue*
Thy fellowfhip.
Tech. *Nay* Dymnus *I proteft*
I neuer credited what they profeft;
For fhould I grieue to fee a furly Lout,
Who for obferuance cafts his eye about;
In nothing meriting, faue only He
Is rich in acres, to difvalue me?
Dory. *No* Technis *no, th'art of a higher fpirit*
Than thefe inferiour Gnats, *whofe only merit*
Confifts in what they haue, not what they are.
Tech. *No* Dorycles, *for thefe I little care,*
Nor euer did: though fome *there be that feede*
On fuch mens breath.
Dymn. *Good* Technis *now proceed.*
Tech. *Hauing thus long continued, as I faid,*
And by my long continuance Graduate *made,*
I tooke more true delight in being there,
Than euer fince in Court or Country ayre.
Sapph. *Indeed minds freedome beft contenteth men.*
Tech. *And fuch a freedome I enjoyed then,*
As in thofe Beechie fhades of Hefperie.
I planted then my fole felicitie.
So as howfere fome of our rurall Swaines
Prerogatiue aboue all others claimes, (ought,
That they haue nought, want nought, *nor* care for
Becaufe their minde vnfurnifht is of nought
That may accomplifh man: I could averre,
(Howfere

(Howsere I doubt these *in opinion erre)*
That in my breast was treasured more blesse,
Then euer sensuall man could yet possesse.
For my delights were princely, and not vaine,
Where height of knowledge was my only ayme,
Whose happy purchase might enrich me more,
Then all this trash which worldly men adore.
So as if Pan *were not the same he is,*
He'de wish himselfe but to enioy my blisse,
Whose choice content afford me so great power,
As I might vye with greatest Emperour.
Coryd. *It seemes thy state was happie ;*
Tech. *So it was,*
And did my present state so farre surpasse,
As th' high top'd Cedar *cannot beare more show*
Aboue the lowest Mushrom *that doth grow,*
Or more exceed in glory, than that time
Outstripp'd this present happinesse of mine.
For tell me Shepheards, what's esteem'd 'mongst men
The greatest ioy, which I enioy'd not then !
For is there comfort in retired life ?
I did possesse a life exempt from strife,
Free from litigious clamour, or report
Sprung from commencement of a tedious Court.
Is contemplation sweete, or conference,
Or ripe conceits ? why there's an influence,
Drawne from Minerua's *braine, where euery wit*
Transcends conceit, and seemes to rauish it.
Is it delightfull Shepheards to repose,
And all-alone to reade of others woes ?
Why there in Tragick Stories might we spend
Whole houres in choice discourses to a friend.

And

And reason of Occurrents to and fro,
And why this thing or that did happen so,
Might it content man, to allay the loade
Of a distemperd minde to walke abroad,
That he might moderate the thought of care
By choice acquaintance, or by change of ayre?
What noble consorts might you quickly finde
To share in sorrow with a troubled minde?
What cheerfull Groues, what silent murmuring springs,
Delicious walkes, and ayrie warblings,
Fresh flowrie Pastures, Gardens which might please
The senses *more then did th'* Hesperides,
Greene shadie Arbours, curled streames which flow,
On whose pure Margins shadie Beeches grow,
Myrtle-perfumed Plaines, on whose rer'd tops
The merry Thrush and Black-bird nimbly hops
And carols sings, so as the passers by
Would deeme the Birds infus'd with poesie?
Sapp. *Sure* Technis *this was earthly Paradise.*
Tech. Sapphus *it was; for what can Swaine deuise*
To tender all delight to eye *or* eare,
Taste, Smell, *or* Touch *which was not frequent there?*
Besides;
Lin. *What could be more, pray* Technis *say?*
Tech. *We had more ioyes to passe the time away.*
Dory. *What might they be good* Technis*?*
Tech. *'Las I know*
They'r such as Shepheards cannot reach vnto.
Dym. *Yet let vs heare them.*
Tech. *So I meane you shall,*
And they were such as we internall *call.*
Cor. *Infernall,* Technis, *what is meant by that?*
                                              Tech.

Tech. Infernall, no; thou speakst thou knowst not what:
I meane internall gifts which farre surmount
All these externall bounties in account:
For by these blessings we shall euer finde
Rich Treasures stored in a knowing minde,
Whose glorious inside is a thousand fold
more precious than her Case *though cloath'd in gold*
And all Habilliments: for by this light
Of Vnderstanding, we discerne whats right
From crooked error, and are truly said
To vnderstand by this, why we were made.
Sapp. Why, we nere thought of this.
Lin. Nay, I may sweare
I haue liu'd on this Downe, *this twentie yeare,*
And that was my least care.
Corid. Linus, I vow
To feed our Sheepe, was all that we need doe
I euer thought.
Dory. So Coridon *did I.*
Dymn. The cause of this, good Technis, *now descrie.*
Tech. Heardsmen I will; with purpose to relate,
Lest my Discourse should be too intricate,
In briefe, (for length makes Memorie to faile)
The substance of your wishes in a Tale.
Within that pitchie and Cymmerian *clyme,*
Certaine Inhabitants dwelt on a time,
Who long had in those shadie Mountaines won,
Yet neuer saw a glimpse of Sunne or Moon.
·Yet see what custome is, though they were pent
From sight of Sunne or Moone they were content,
Sporting themselues in vaults and arched caues,
Not so like dwelling Houses, as like graues.

Nor

Nor were these men seene ere so farre to roame
At any time as halfe a mile from home;
For if they had, as th' Historie doth say,
They had beene sure right soone to lose their way:
For darke and mistie were those drerie caues
Where they repos'd, so that the wretchedst slaues
Could not exposed be to more restraint,
Than these poore snakes in th' ragged Mountaines pent;
And thus they liu'd.
Lin. But never lou'd.
Tech. *To tell*
Their loues I will not: but it thus befell,
That a great Prince, *who to encrease his fame*
Had conquer'd many Countries, thither came.
Sapp. *For what good* Technis?
Tech. *Only to suruey it.*
Corid. *Why sure he had some Torch-light to display it,*
For th' Coast you say was darke.
Tech. *And so it was;*
But yet attend me how it came to passe:
By meanes he vs'd, hauing this coast suruei'd,
With all perswasiue reasons he assaid,
Partly by faire meanes to induce them to it,
Sometimes by threats, when he was forc't vnto it,
That they would leaue that forlorne place, and giue
Way to perswasion, and resolue to liue
Neere some more cheerefull Border, which in time
They gaue consent to, and forsooke their Clime.
But see the strength of Habit, when they came
To see the light *they hid themselues for shame,*
Their eyes grew dazled, and they did not know,
Where to retire or to what place to goe:

Yet

Yet was the Region *pleasant, full of groues,*
Where th' airy Quiristers *expresse their loues*
One to another, and with Melodie
Cheer'd and refresh'd Siluanus *Emperie.*
The warbling Goldfinch *on the dangling spray,*
Sent out harmonious Musicke euery day;
The prettie speckled Violet *on the Banke*
With Pinke *and* Rose-bud *placed in their ranke;*
Where chafed Violets *did so fresh appeare,*
As they foretold the Spring-time now drew neare;
Whose borders were with various colours dy'd,
And Prim-rose *bankes with odours beautifi'd;*
Where Cornell *trees were planted in great store,*
Whose checkerd berries beautifi'd the shore.
Besides, such gorgeous buildings as no eye
Could take a view of fuller Maiestie;
Whose curious pillers made of Porphyrite
Smooth to the touch, and specious to the sight,
Sent from their hollow Cell a crispling breath,
Arched aboue and vaulted vnderneath.
Yet could not all these choyce varieties
(Which might haue giuen content to choicer eyes)
Satisfie these Cimmerians, *for their ayme*
Was to returne vnto their Caues againe,
And so they did: for when the Prince *perceiu'd*
How hard it was from error to be reau'd,
Where ignorance discerns not what is good,
Because it is not rightly vnderstood;
Hee sent them home againe, where they remain'd
From comfort of Societie restrain'd.
Dym. *Apply this* Tale, *my* Technis;
Tech. *Heare me then.*

You

You may be well compar'd vnto thefe men,
Who ignorant of knowledge, doe efteeme
More of your Flocks, *how they may fruitfull feeme,*
Then of that part, *whereby you may be fed*
From fauage beafts to be diftinguifhed.
Dory. Technis *you are too bitter ;*
Tech. *Not a whit,*
Shepheards fhould tell a Shepheard what is fit:
Though I confeffe that Heardfmen merit praife,
When they take care vpon the Flockes they graze.
Yet to recount thofe Swaines *of elder time,*
How fome were rapt with Sciences diuine,
Others adorn'd with Art of Poefie,
Others to reafon of Aftrologie ;
Swaines *of this time might think't a very fhame,*
To be fo bold as to retaine the name
Of iolly Heardfmen, when they waut the worth (forth.
Of thofe braue Swaines which former times brought
Corid. *Why, what could they ?*
Tech. *Endorfe their Names in trees,*
And write fuch amorous Poems as might pleafe
Their deereft loues.
Dym. *Why* Technis *what was this,*
Can we not pleafe our loues more with a kiffe ?
Dory. *Yes* Dymnus, *thou know'ft that ;*
Dym. *Perchance I doe,*
For Dymnus *knowes no other way to wooe.*
But pray thee Technis *let vs fay no more,*
But hie thee now to where thou left before.
Tech. *I'me eafily entreated ; draw then neere,*
And as I lend a tongue, lend you an eare.
Hauing long liued in Minerua's *Groue,*
My life became an Embleme *of pure loue.*

Dym. Of Loue my Technis, *pray thee say to whom!*
Tech. As thou mean'st Dymnus, *I did fancie none:*
No; my affection soared higher farre,
Than on such toyes as now affected are:
I doated not on Beautie, nor did take
My aime at faire, *but did obseruance make,*
How humane things be shar'd by diuine power,
Where fickle faith scarce constant rests one houre;
How highest states were subiect'st to decline;
How nought on Earth but subiect vnto Time;
How vice though clad in purple was but vice;
How vertue clad in rags was still in price;
How Common-weales in peace should make for warre;
How Honour crownes such as deseruing are.
Dory. And yet we see such as deserued most,
What ere the cause be, are the oftest crost.
Tech. Ile not denie it (Swaine) and yet attend,
For all their crosse occurrents, but their end,
And thou shalt see the fawning Sycophant
Die in disgrace, and leaue his Heire in want:
While th' honest and deseruing Statesman *giues*
Life to his Name and in his dying liues.
This I obseru'd and many things beside,
Whilst I in famous Athens *did abide;*
But 'lasse whilst I secure from thought of care,
With choifest conforts did delight me there,
Free from the tongue of rumor or of strife,
I was to take me to another life.
Lin. To what good Technis?
Tech. To haue Harpies *clawes;*
To take my fee and then neglect the cause.
Sapp. A Lawier Technis!

                                           Tech.

Tech. *So my father said,*
Who as he had commanded, I obey'd.
But iudge now Shepheards, could I chuse to grieue,
When I must leaue, what I was forc'd to leaue,
Those sweet delightfull Arts, *with which my youth*
Was first inform'd, and now attain'd such growth,
As I did reape more happy comfort thence
In one short houre than many Twelue-months since?
Corid. *This was a hard command.*
Tech. *Yet was it fit*
I should respect his *loue imposed it.*
For ne're had Father showne vnto his sonne
More tender loue than he *to me had done:*
So as his will was still to me a law,
Which I obserued more for loue *than* awe,
For in that childe few seeds of grace appeare,
Whom loue *doth lesse induce than thought of* feare.
Hauing now tane my leaue of all the Muses,
I made me fit as other Students vses,
To waine my minde, and to withdraw my sight
From all such studies gaue me once delight:
And to inure me better to discerne
Such rudiments as I desir'd to learne,
I went to Iohn a Styles, *and* Iohn an Okes,
And many other Law-baptized folkes,
Whereby I set the practise of the Law
At as light count as turning of a straw,
For straight I found how Iohn a Styles *did state it,*
But I was ouer Style *ere I came at it;*
For hauing thought (so easie was the way)
That one might be a Lawyer *the first day:*
I after found the further that I went,

The

*The further was I from my Element:
Yet forasmuch as I esteem'd it vaine,
To purchase law still from anothers braine,
I stroue to get some law at any rate,
At least so much as might concerne my state.*
Lin. *I am more sorie for it.*
Tech. Linus *why?*
Lin.. *Becaufe I feare me thou wilt haue an eye
More to thy priuate profit, than deuife
How to attone fuch quarrels as arife.*
Dym. Technis *is none of those.*
Tech. *No, credit me,
Though I'me resolued many such there be
Who can difpence with* fees *on either part,
Which I haue euer scorned with my heart;
For this shall be my practice, to assay
Without a fee to doe you th' good I may.*
Corid. Technis *enough.*
Tech. *Hauing thus long applide
The streame of Law, my aged father dide,
Whose vertues to relate I shall not neede,
For you all knew him;*
Doric. *So we did indeed:
A Patron of all Iustice, doe him right.*
Sap. *Nor was there* Art *wherein he had no sight.*
Dym. *Yet was he humble.*
Lin. *And in that more blest.*
Corid. *He liues though seeming dead;*
Tech. *So let him rest.
Hauing lost him whose life supported me,
You may imagine Shepheards, what might be
My hard succeeding fate: downe must I goe*

To

To know if this report were true or no.
Which I did finde too true, for he was dead,
And had enioyn'd me Guardians *in his ſtead*
To ſway my vntraind youth.
Dym. *And what were they?*
Tech. *Such men as I had reaſon to obey:*
For their aduice was euer for my good,
If my greene yeeres ſo much had vnderſtood:
But I puft vp with thought of my demaines,
Gaue way to Folly, and did ſlacke my raines
Of long reſtraint;
Dory. *'Las* Technis, *then I ſee*
What in the end was like to fall on thee.
Tech. *O* Dorycles *if thou hadſt knowne my ſtate,*
Thou wouldſt haue pitied it!
Corid. *Nay rather hate*
Thy youthfull riot.
Tech. *Thou ſpeakes well vnto't,*
For the Blacke Oxe *had nere trod on my foot:*
I had my former ſtudies in deſpight,
And in the vaineſt conſorts tooke delight.
Which much incens'd ſuch as affection bare
To my eſteeme: but little did I care
For the inſtruction of my graue Protectors
Who neuer left me, but like wiſe directors
Conſulted how to rectifie my ſtate,
And ſome aduiſed this, and others that,
For neuer any could more faithfull be
In ſincere truſt, than they were vnto me.
At laſt, one to compoſe and end the ſtrife,
Thought it the fitt'ſt that I ſhould take a wife.
Corid. *Yea, now it workes.*

O Lim.

Lin. *Stay till he come vnto't;*
Sap. *And then I know he will goe roundly to't.*
Tech. *Nay ieſt not on me, but awhile forbeare,*
And you the iſſue of my loue ſhall heare.
Hauing at laſt concluded, as I ſaid,
 With ioynt conſent I ſhould be married,
One 'mongſt the reſt did freely vndertake
This priuate motion to my ſelfe to make ;
Which I gaue eare to : wiſhing too that he
Would me informe where this my Wife *ſhould be.*
Dym. *As it was fit.*
Cor. *Who was it thou ſhouldſt ha ?*
Tech. *Ile tell thee Boy, 'twas* Amarillida.
Cor. Lycas *faire daughter ?*
Tech. *Yes, the very ſame.*
Dory. *She was a wench indeed of worthie fame;*
Tech. *As ere fed Lambkins on this flowrie Downe :*
Whom many ſought and ſude to make their owne,
But ſhe affected ſo a virgin life,
As ſhe did ſcorne to be Amyntas *wife.*
Dym. *Is't poſſible ?*
Tech. *Yes* Dymnus *I doe know*
Some tokens of affection twixt them two,
Which if thou heard, right ſoone wouldſt thou confeſſe,
More vnfaind loue no Heardſman could expreſſe :
But to omit the reſt, I meane to ſhow
The time and tide when I began to woo.
Vpon that * Day (ſad day and heauy fate)
When euery Bird is ſaid to chuſe her mate,
Did I repaire vnto that faireſt faire,
That euer lou'd, or liu'd, or breath'd on aire.
And her I woo'd, but ſhe was ſo demure,

* *S. Valentines* day; on which *Birds* are said to chuse their *Mates*, with whom they repose and partake in mutuall ioyes.

So

So modeſt baſhfull, and ſo maiden pure,
As at the firſt, nor at the ſecond time
She would no eare to ſound of loue incline.
Cor. *But this (I'm ſure) would be no meanes to draw*
Thy loues aſſault from Amarillida.
Tech. *No* Coridon, *for then I ſhould not ſeeme*
Worthy ſo rare a Nymph as ſhe had beene.
But I did finde that female foes would yeeld,
Though their relentleſſe breaſts at firſt were ſteeld:
Continuall drops will pierce the hardeſt ſtone.
Sap. *Did* Technis *finde her ſuch a ſtony one?*
Tech. Sappho *I did: yet though ſhe oft had vowd*
A veſtall life, and had my ſuit withſtood,
I found her of a better minde next day,
For ſhe had throwne her veſtall weed away.
Lin. *Thrice happy Shepheard!*
Tech. Linus, *ſay not ſo;*
If it be happineſſe to end in woe,
Thou mightſt enſtyle me happy;
Dory. *Was not ſhe*
Fully reſolued now to marry thee?
Tech. *Yes* Dorycles: *but when ſhe had conſented,*
Heare by what ſtrange miſchance I was preuented!
Vpon a time a Summering *there was,*
Where euery liuely Lad tooke in his Laſſe
To dance his Meaſure, and amongſt the reſt
I tooke me one *as frolike as the beſt.*
Dym. *What was ſhe man?*
Tech. *A Matron full of zeale,*
But pardon me, I muſt her name conceale.
Lin. *It was* Alburna *I durſt pawne my life.*

Tech. *I muſt confeſſe it was the Parſons wife,*
A luſty Trolops I may ſay to you,
And one could foot it giue the wench her due.
Lin. *Yea marry Sir, there was a Laſſe indeed*
Knew how ſhe ſhould about a Maypole tread.
Tech. *And I may ſay, if* Linus *had beene there,*
He would haue ſaid, we euenly matched were:
For I may ſay at that day there was none
At any actiue game could put me downe
And for a dance;
Sap. *As light as any fether,*
For thou didſt winne the Legge *three yeeres together.*
Tech. *And many ſaid that it great pittie was*
That ſuch a Parſon *had not ſuch a* Laſſe *:*
So as indeed all did conclude and ſay,
That we deſeru'd the Pricke and prize that day.
But hauing now our May-games wholly plaid,
Danc'd till we wearie were, and Piper paid:
Each tooke his wench he danc'd with on the Downe,
Meaning to giue her curt'ſie of the Towne.
Sim. *What curt'ſie* Technis?
Tech. *As our Shepheards vſe,*
Which they in modeſtie cannot refuſe:
And this we did, and thus we parted then,
Men from their women, women from their men.
Dory. *But didſt nere after with* Alburna *meet?*
Tech. *Yes, on a time I met her in the ſtreet,*
Who after kinde ſalutes inuited me
Vnto her houſe, which in ciuilitie
I could not well deny;
Dym. *True* Technis *true.*

Tech.

Tech. *And she receiu'd me, giue the wench her due,*
With such a free and gracefull entertaine,
As did exceed th' expectance of a Swaine.
Dory. *She had some reason for't;*
Tech. *None I may sweare,*
Saue that she ioyed much to see me there.
Dory. *Yet did;*
Tech. *Did eat, did drinke, and merry make,*
For no delight saue these did Technis *take.*
For I may say to you if so I had,
My lucke to Horse-flesh *had not beene so bad,*
As by some yeeres experience I haue found;
So as of your suspicion there's no ground:
But if I had, no fate could be more hard
Than that which I sustained afterward.
Corid. *Relate it* Technis.
Tech. *To my griefe I will,*
Hauing done this without least thought of ill,
This (as report doth new additions draw)
Came to the eare of Amarillida:
Who iealous of my loue (as women are)
Thought that Alburna *had no little share*
In my affection, which I may protest
Was nere as much as meant, much lesse exprest.
Sap. *Alas good Shepheard.*
Tech. *So as from that day*
I found her fancy falling still away,
For to what place soeuer I did come,
She fain'd excuse to leaue me and the roome.
Lin. *Yet she nere fix'd her loue on any one.*
Tech. *Yes* Linus, *else what cause had I to mone?*
Some few moneths after did she take a Mate,

I must confesse of infinite estate;
Yet in my minde (nor doe I speake't in spight)
He's one can giue a woman small delight,
For he's a very Erwig.
Lin. *What is he?*
Tech. *Petreius sonne;*
Lin. *The map of miserie.*
Tech. *Yet thou wouldst wonder how this dunghil worm*
When he encounters me, redarts a scorne
On my contemned loue:
Dym. *All this doth show,*
That he resolues to triumph in thy woe;
But how stands shee affected?
Tech. *'Las for griefe,*
Shee is so farre from yeelding me reliefe,
As shee in publique meetings ha's affaid
To glory in the trickes which shee hath plaid.
Dory. *O matchlesse insolence!*
Tech. *Yet shall my blisse*
In wanting her, be charactred in this;
" Hauing lost all that ere thy labour gain'd,
" Be sure to keepe thy precious name vnstain'd.
Corid. *A good resolue.*
Tech. *Yet must I neuer leaue*
While I doe liue, but I must liue to grieue:
For I perswade me, there was neuer Swaine
Was recompenc'd with more vniust disdaine.
Dym. *Indeed thou well mightst grieue.*
Dory. *Yet shall't appeare,*
I haue more cause, if you my Tale *will heare:*
For nere was story mixed with more ruth,
Or grounded on more Arguments of truth.

Corid.

Corid. *Let's haue it* Dorycles;
Dory. *With all my heart,*
And plainly too ; griefe hates all words of art.

The Argument.

Orycles *loues* Bellina;
Who esteemes
As well of him,
But proues not same she seemes.

The second Argument.

*Orycles* a youthfull Swaine,
Seekes *Bellina's* loue to gaine:
Who, so euen doth fancy strike,
Tenders *Dorycles* the like.
Yet obserue how women be
Subiect to inconstancie!
Shee in absence of her loue,
Her affection doth remoue,
Planting it vpon a *Swad*,
That no wit nor breeding had.

Whom

Whom she honours; but in time
Dorycles seemes to diuine,
Since her loue is stain'd with sin,
She'le ere long dishonour him;
For who once hath broke her vow,
Will infringe't to others too.
In the end he doth expresse
His disdainfull Shepherdesse:
Who, when she had iniured
Him and his, and cancelled
That same sacred secret oath,
Firmely tendred by them both;
She a Willow-garland sends
For to make her Swaine amends,
Which he weares, and vowes till death
He will weare that forlorne wreath.
With protests of lesse delight
In her *Loue*, than in her *Spight*.

THE SECOND EGLOGVE.

Dorycles tale.

Ome Shephherds come, and heare the wofulst Swaine
That euer liu'd, or lou'd on western plaine:
Whose heauy fate all others doth surpasse
That ere you heard;
Dym. *Say Heardsman what it was.*
Dory. *I must and will, though* Dymnus *I confesse,*
I'm very loth my folly to expresse,
Whose madding passion though it merit blame,

I

I will difplay't.
Tech. *To't then: away with fhame.*
Dory. *I lou'd a bonny Laffe as ere lou'd man,*
For fhe a middle had that you might fpan,
A mouing eye, a nimble mincing foot,
And mannerly fhe was, for fhe could lout:
And her I lou'd, and me fhe held as deare.
Corid. *But* Dorycles *where liu'd fhe?*
Dory. *Very neare:*
Knowft thou not Polychreftus?
Corid. *Who, the Swaine*
That with his fheepe doth couer all our Plaine?
Dory. *It feemes thou knowft him* Coridon;
Corid. *I doe:*
And feuen yeeres fince I knew his Daughter too.
Dory. *Who, faire* Bellina?
Corid. *Yes, the very fame.*
Dory. *And her I lou'd, nor need I thinke't a fhame.*
For what might moue affection or imply
Content of loue to any Shepheards eye,
Which fhe enioy'd not? For if choyce difcourfe
(As what more mouing than the tongue) had force
To infufe loue, there was no Heardfman neare her
Who was not rauifh'd if he chanc'd to heare her;
And for a beauty mix'd with white and red.
Corid. *I know 't was rare, good* Dorycles *proceed.*
Dory. *When I was young, as yet I am not old,*
I doted more than now a hundred fold:
For there was not a May-game *that could fhow it*
All here about, but I repair'd vnto it,
Yet knew not what loue meant, but was content
To fpend the time in harmleffe merriment.
                                                                    But

But at the laſt, I plaid ſo long with fire,
I cing'd my wings with heat of loues deſire.
And to diſplay my folly how it was
Without digreſſion, thus it came to paſſe.
Downe by yon Vale a Myrtle groue there is,
(Oh that I nere had ſeene it, I may wiſh)
Where Pan the Shepheards God to whom we pray,
Solemniz'd had his wonted holiday:
Whereto reſorted many noble Swaines,
Who flouriſh yet vpon our neighbour Plaines;
'Mongſt which Bellina with a youthfull ſort
Of amorous Nimphs, came to ſuruey our ſport.
Which I obſeruing (ſee the fault of youth)
Tranſported with vain-glory, thought in truth
Shee came a purpoſe for a ſight of me,
Which I with ſmiles requited louingly:
But howſoere, I know Bellina ey'de
My perſon more than all the ſwaines beſide.
When night was come, vnwelcome vnto ſome,
And each was now to haſten towards home,
I 'mongſt the reſt of Laddes, did homeward paſſe,
And all this time I knew not what Love was.
To ſupper went I and fell to my fare,
As if of loue I had but little care,
And after ſupper went to fire to chat
Of ſundry old-wiues tales, as this and that;
Yet all this while loue had no power of me,
Nor no command that euer I could ſee.
Hauing thus ſpent in tales an houre or two,
Each to his reſt (as he thought beſt) did goe,
But now when I ſhould take me to my reſt,
That troubled me which I did thinke of leaſt.

            Tech.

Tech. *Trouble thee Swaine!*
Dory. *Yes* Technis; *and the more,*
Becauſe I neuer felt ſuch pangs before.
This way and that way did I toſſe and turne,
And freeze and frie, and ſhake for cold and burne,
So as I wiſht a hundred times, that day
Would now approach my paſſion to allay.
Yet ſtill, (ſo weake was my diſtemper'd braine)
I thought Bellina *put me to that paine,*
Yet knew no cauſe why ſhee ſhould vſe me ſo,
Yet thought to aſke her if 't were ſhee or no:
So as next day, I purpos'd to repaire.
To ſee if ſhee could yeeld a cure to care.
But ſhe *(poore wench) was ſplit on fancies ſhelfe,*
All full of care, yet could not cure her ſelfe;
So as in briefe we either did impart,
The ſecret paſſions of a wounded heart,
Shot by loues ſhaft, for ſo't appear'd to be,
Which found, we vow'd a preſent remedie;
Yet to our friends both ſhee and I did feane,
As if we neuer had acquainted beene.
Dym. *A prety ſleight;*
Dory. *Though many times and oft,*
Plaid we at Barlybreake in Clytus *croft.*
And thus our loues continued one halfe yeere
Without ſuſpition, till one *neighboring neere,*
An equall friend vnto vs both, did make
A motion of our Mariage.
Tech. *Did it take?*
Dory. *Yes* Technis *yes, ſo as firſt day I went,*
My friends, to ſhew that they were well content,
Wiſh'd that all good ſucceſſe might vſher mee.

                                                    Lin.

Lin. *One should haue throwne an old shoo after thee.*
Dory. *Nay Linus that was done: and now to hie*
Vnto my Tale, *on went my* dogge *and I,*
Poore loaue-eard Curre.
Sapp. *Why* Dorycles, *hadst none*
To second thee?
Dory. *Too many (Swaine) by one:*
For trowst thou Lad, when I my suit should make
Vnto her friends, my dogge *he let a scape.*
Sapp. *Ill nurtur'd flitchell.*
Dory. *Now yee may suppose*
Bellina *tooke the Pepper in the nose,*
That to her friends when I should breake my minde,
The carrian Cur should at that time breake winde.
So as for halfe an houre I there did show
Like to a sensesse Picture made of dough:
Nor was my dogge *lesse 'sham'd, but runs away*
With taile betwixt his legs with speed he may.
At last my spirits I did call together,
Showing her friends the cause why I came thither,
Who did accept my motion; for that day
I was esteem'd a proper Swaine I say,
And one well left.
Cor. *We know it* Dorycles,
Both for thy wealth and person thou mightst please.
Lin. *For good mug-sheepe and cattell, Ile be sworne*
None could come neare thee both for haire and horne.
Dory. *Yee ouer-value me, but sure I am*
I had sufficient for an honest man:
Hauing thus free accesse to her I lou'd,
Who my affection long before had prou'd
Though she seemd nice, as women often vse,

When

When what they loue they seemingly refuse.
Not to insist ought longer on the matter,
They deemd me worthy, if they did not flatter,
Of her I su'd ; So as without more stay,
Appointed was this solemne Nuptiall day.
Sapp. *Happy appointment ;*
Dory. Sapphus *say not so,*
It rather was the subiect of my woe,
For hauing heard reported for a truth
She formerly had lou'd a dapper youth,
With whom she purpos'd euen in friends despight,
To make a priuate scape one winter night ;
I for a while thought to surcease my suit,
Till I heard further of this iealous bruit.
Tech. *Why didst thou so ?* Bellina *had consented*
To loue that youth, before you were acquainted.
Dory. Technis *'tis true ; But some there were auer'd,*
Though I'm resolu'd they in opinion err'd,
That these two were affide one to the other.
Sapp. *What hindred then the match ?*
Dory. Bellinas *mother :*
Who tender of th' aduancement of her childe,
And well perceiuing Crispus *to be wilde,*
(For so the youth was named) did withdraw
Bellina *from him by imperious awe :*
Which done, and he preuented of her daughter,
His Countrey left, he neuer sought her after.
Tech. *I knew that* Crispus.
Dory. *Then you knew a lad*
Of seeming presence, but he little had,
And that was cause he grew in disesteeme.
Sap. *Alas that want of meanes should make vs meane.*
Dory.

Dory. So did it fare with him; for to his praise
*(Though with his tongue he wrong'd me many waies,
But* tongues *inur'd to* tales *are nere beleeu'd)*
*He had from Nature choicest gifts receau'd,
Which might haue mou'd loue in a worthy creature,
If that his life had beene vnto his feature.
But promising out-sides like the* Panthers *skin,
Though faire without, are oft times foule within;
But heauens, I hope, to mercy will receiue him,
His wrongs to me are buried; so I leaue him.*
Corid. *But admit Shepheard they had beene affide,
Shee might reuolt, it cannot be denide.*
Dory. *I grant she might; and I confesse there be
Some that haue done 't are greater farre than we:
But goodnesse is the marke, not height of state
That meaner men by right should imitate.
I might produce store of examples here,
But lest I should be tedious, I forbeare,
What tragick Scenes from breach of faith are bred,
How it hath caus'd much guiltlesse bloud be shed.
This caus'd me for a time to hold my hand,
To see how all this businesse would stand,
And that I might my fancie better waine
From her I lou'd, to* Troynouant *I came.
Where I imploi'd my selfe no little time
About occasions for a friend of mine:
For I did thinke to be from place remou'd,
Would make me soone forget the wench I lou'd.*
Sap. *I rather thinke it would thy loue renew;*
Dory. Sapphus *it did; and farre more rigour shew:*
" *For true it is, when louers goe to wooe,*
" *Each mile's as long as ten, each houre as two.*

Whence

" *Whence each true louer by experience proues*
" *Man is not where he liues, but where he loues.*
For what delight, as all delights were there,
Could my enthralled minde refresh or cheere,
Wanting my Loue, *whose only sight could show*
More true content than all the world could doe?
Yet stay'd I still, expecting I should heare,
How in my absence, she herselfe did beare,
And whether those same rumours which I heard,
Were true or false, as I found afterward.
Lin. *How went they* Dorycles?
Dor. *Howso'ere they went*
I found Bellina *meerely innocent;*
Whence I inferr'd, that many times we wrong them,
By causelesse laying false aspersions on them:
For I peceiu'd she had beene woo'd by many,
But neuer yet affianc'd vnto any.
Coryd. *Thrice happie* Dorycles!
Dor. *Happie indeed,*
Till worse euents did afterwards succeed.
Coryd. *What fate?*
Dor. *Farre worse than ere on Shepheard leight.*
Tech. *Expresse it Heardsman;*
Dor. *So I purpose streight.*
Hauing thus heard all rumours to be vaine,
I streight resolu'd to returne backe againe
Into my Countrey: where I found my wench
The same I left her when I came from thence;
So as in briefe, so happie was my state,
I meant my marriage rites to consummate.
Which that they might be done more solemnly,
All our young Shepheards *in a company,*

Addrest

Addrefs'd themfelues to grace that day ; befide
The choiceft Damfels *to attend the* Bride,
For to preuent occafion of delay,
Set downe on both fides was the Mariage day.
Tech. *Me thinkes this cannot chufe but happen well;*
Dory. *Stay Technis heare, what afterwards befell!*
The Euen before that I fhould maried be,
One came in all hafte and acquainted me
How Cacus *that vnciuill loffell, would*
Carry the beft Ram *that I had to fold ;*
Wherewith incens'd withouten further ftay,
Going to th' fold I met him in the way:
Who of my Ram *not onely me denide,*
But vs'd me in difgracefull fort befide,
Which I diftafting, without more adoe
Reach'd my vnnurtur'd Cacus *fuch a blow,*
As he in heat of paffion aymd his Crooke
Iuft at my head to wound me with the ftroake :
Which I rewarded, fo as by our men
Without more hurt we both were parted then.
But fcarce had Phœbus *lodged in the Weft,*
Till He, whofe fury would not let him reft,
Sent me a challenge ftuffed with difgrace,
Length of his Weapon, Second, *and the* Place.
Dym. *Then we muft haue a field fought.*
Dory. *Without ftay ;*
I met him though it was my mariage day,
Though not on equall termes.
Tech. *More fit 't had bin*
T' encounter'd with Bellina *than with him.*
Sapp. *I would haue thought fo* Technis ;
Lin. *So would hee,*

If

If he had beene resolu'd as he should be.
Dor. *Shepheards 'tis true ; but now it is too late,*
For to exclaime against relentlesse fate,
Whose aduerse hand preuented that delight,
Which louers reape in a blest nuptiall night. (Swaine;
Cor. *Thou mightst with credit haue deferr'd it,*
Dor. *I know it,* Corydon : *but 'twas my aime*
To right my reputation, which did stand
Engag'd, vnlesse I met him out a hand,
Which I perform'd, and with my Second *too,*
To beare me witnesse what I meant to doe.
Dym. *And he perform'd the like ;*
Dor. *He vow'd he would,*
And so indeed by Law of armes he should,
But I perceiu'd his recreant spirit such,
To fight on equall termes he thought too much :
Neere to Soranus *caue there stands a groue,*
Which Poets faine was consecrate to Loue,
Though then it seem'd to be transform'd by fate,
From th' groue of Loue, *vnto the graue of* Hate ;
There we did meet : where he out of distrust,
Fearing the cause he fought for was not iust,
To second his iniurious act, did bring
A rout of desperate rogues along with him,
Who lurking, kept together till we met,
And so vpon aduantage me beset,
As fight or fall, there was no remedie,
Such was the height of Cacus *villanie.*
Tech. *Who euer heard a more perfidious tricke ?*
Dor. *'Tis true ; yet though my* Second *had been sicke,*
And much enfeebled in his former strength,
We held them play, till haplesly at length,
    P   *Through*

Through violence of fury, from him fell
His luckleſſe weapon.
Dym. *Oh I heare thee tell*
A heauy Scene!
Dor. *Yes* Dymnus *hadſt thou ſeene*
How our ſhed bloud purpled the flowrie greene,
What crimſon ſtreamlins flow'd from either of vs,
Thou wouldſt haue pitied, though thou nere did loue vs:
For hauing fought ſo long as we had breath,
Breathleſſe we lay as Images of death,
Bereft of ſenſe or Motion.
Sap. *'Las for woe,*
Any true Heardſman ſhould be vſed ſo.
Cor. *What boundleſſe ſorrowes were ye plunged in!*
Dor. *Tis true; and worſer farre had vſed bin,*
Had not Dametas *that well natur'd Swaine,*
Repair'd that inſtant to our forlorne Plaine;
Who ſeeing vs, and in what ſtate we were,
In due compaſſion could not well forbeare
From ſhedding teares, ſo ſoone as he had found
Our red-bath'd Corpes faſt glewed to the ground.
Oft did he reare our Bodies, *but in vaine,*
For breathleſſe they fell to the Earth againe;
Oft did he rub our temples to reſtore
That vitall heat, which was ſuppreſt before:
But without hope of life, though life was there,
As Men of Earth, did we on Earth appeare.
At laſt aſſiſted by a Swaine or two,
(See what the Prouidence of Heauen can doe)
We were conueyed to a Graunge *hard by,*
Whereto were Surgeons ſent immediatly,
Whoſe learned ſkill drain'd from experience,

Brought

Brought vs in time to haue a little senfe
Of our endanger'd state.
Dym. *But pray thee tell*
Whose hand exprest most art?
Dor. *Graue* Astrophel,
Whose knowne experiments of Art haue showne
More noble cures of late on this our Downe,
Than all our Mountebankes *could euer doe,*
For all these precious drugs they value so.
Sap. *Indeed I know He has much honour won*
For his admired Cures; good Shepheard on.
Dor. *Hauing long languish'd betwixt life and death,*
Remou'd from thought of loue for want of breath,
As men we liu'd expos' to dangers Sconce.
Lin. *Would not* Bellina *see thee?*
Dor. *Nere but once.*
For hauing heard there was no way but one,
And that in all mens iudgements I was gone,
Shee straight resolues to finde a cure for care;
That if I liu'd she might haue one to spare.
Tech. *Why, made shee choice of any but thy selfe?*
Dor. *Yes* Technis *yes, and of a dwarfish elfe,*
Whom she preferr'd, (though he could little please).
Before her first loue, haplesse Doricles.
Tech. *Inconstant Swainlin.*
Dor. *Hauing heard of this,*
You may conceaue how griefe augmented is:
I straight depriu'd of hope, began to raue,
And would not take what my Physician *gaue,*
But scorning all prescriptions valued death
Aboue a languishing distastfull breath;
Till by perswasion and recourse of time

P 2 *Those*

Thofe braine-ficke paffions and effects of mine
Depreffed were: fo as vpon a day,
The burden of my forrowes to allay,
And to expreffe the nature of my wrong,
I fet my hand to pen, and made a Song.
Dym. *Good* Dorycles *let's heare what it may be,*
It cannot but be good if't come from thee.
Dor. *Shepheards you fhall; and if you thinke it fit,*
I lou'd her once, fhall be the Tune *of it.*
Tech. *No* Tune *more proper; to it louely Swaine.*
Dor. *Attend then Shepherds to my dolefull ftraine.*

THe faireft faire that euer breath'd ayre,
  Feeding her Lambkins on this Plaine;
To whom though many did repaire,
  I was efteem'd her deareft Swaine.
To me fhe vow'd, which vow fhe broke,
  That fhe would fancie me or none,
But fince fhe has her Swaine forfooke,
  I'le take me to a truer one.

Had fhe beene firme, as fhe was faire,
  Or but perform'd what fhe had vow'd,
I might haue fung a fig for care,
  And fafely fwum in fancies flood;
But ô the ftaine of womanhood!
  Who breakes with one, keepes touch with none;
Wherefore in hate to fuch a brood,
  I'le take me to a truer one.

Was't not enough to breake her vow,
And quit my loue with fuch difdaine,

But scornfully deride me too,
With scoffes to gratifie my paine?
But since my labours are in vaine,
Ile spend no more my time in mone,
But will my former loue disclaime,
And take me to a truer one.

Who euer liu'd and shew'd more loue,
Or lesse exprest what she did show?
Who seeming firme so false could proue,
Or vow so much, and slight her vow?
But since I doe her nature know,
I am right glad that she is gone;
For if I shoot in *Cupids* bow,
I'le take me to a truer one.

More faithlesse faire nere spoke with tongue,
Or could protest lesse what she thought;
Nere Shepheard suffer'd greater wrong,
Or for lesse profit euer wrought;
But since my hopes are turn'd to nought,
May neuer Heardsman make his mone
To one whose mold's in weaknesse wrought,
But take him to a truer one.

(thee;
Cor. *May all poore Swaines be henceforth warn'd by*
But didst thou neuer since Bellina *see?*
Dor. *Yes, and her louely spouse* Archetus *too,*
Who seeing me (quoth he) There doth he goe,
Who on a time, as I enformed am,
Would lose his Lasse *before he lost his* Ram;
Which I retorted, saying, I thought best,

My butting Ram *should be his worships crest,*
Whose broad-spread frontlets did presage what fate
Would in short time attend his forked pate.
Sap. *Thou hit him home my* Dorycles; *but say,*
What said she to thee?
Dor. *Bit lip, and away;*
Though the next morne, my sorrow to renew,
Shee sent a Willow *wreath fast bound with* Rew,
Which I accepted, but that I might show
I neuer rue her breach of promise now,
The Rew *that tyde my* Wreath *I threw aside,*
And with Hearts ease *my* Willow *garland tyde.*
Lin. *A good exchange.*
Dor. *Now Shepheards you haue heard*
My faithfull loue, and her vniust reward;
Did euer Swaine enioy the light of Sunne,
That bare such iniuries as I haue done?
Tech. *Indeed thy wounds were great;*
Dym. *Yet mine as wide.*
Dor. *I mist my* Loue, *and lost my* bloud *beside.*
Dym. *Suspend thy iudgement, and thine eare incline*
Vnto my Tale, *and thou wilt yeeld to mine.*
Coryd. *Let's haue it* Dymnus;
Dym. *Heardsman so thou shalt,*
Yet if I weepe, impute it to the fault
Of my surcharged heart, which still appeares
The best at ease, when eyes are full'st of teares.

The

The Argument.

Ymnus Palmira
*Woes to be his Wife,
But ſhe had vow'd
To liue a ſingle life.*

The ſecond Argument.

*Ymnus* with long looking dim,
Loues the wench that lotheth him;
Price nor praier may not perſwade
To infringe the vow ſhe made;
Hauing meant to liue and die
Veſta's virgin votarie.
Yet at laſt ſhe seemes to yeeld
To her loue-ſick *Swaine* the field,
So that he will vndertake
Three yeares ſilence for her ſake:
Which hard Pennance he receaues,
And performes the taske ſhe craues.
But while he reſtraines his tongue,
Shee pretends the time's too long:
Wherefore ſhe doth entertaine
In her breaſt another *Swaine.*

Dymnus hauing heard of this,
Hies to th' place where th' marriage is,
Purpoſing to make a breach
By dumbe ſignes, though want of speech:
But alas they all command him
Silence, cauſe none vnderſtand him.
Thus he ſuffers double wrong,
Loſſe of *wench*, and loſſe of *tongue*,
For till three yeares were expir'd,
He nere ſpoke what he deſir'd,
All which time conſum'd in dolour,
He diſplayes her in her colour;
And concluding, wiſheth no man
Loſe his tongue to gaine a woman:
And to cheere his penſiue heart,
With a *Song* they end this *part.*

THE THIRD EGLOGVE.

Dymnus tale.

*Pon a time while I did liue on* Teeſe,
*I made loue to a wench my friends to pleaſe,
But (as my fate was ſtill) it would not be,
For wooe I knew not how, no more than ſhe:*
*Yet I can well remember this ſhe ſaid,
For ought ſhe knew, ſhe meant to die a Maid,
A* Veſtall *Virgin, or a Votareſſe,
A cloyſter'd Nun, or holy Prioreſſe;
To which I anſwer'd, if't were her deſire
To be a* Nun, *I meant to turne a* Frier,
*So might it chance that we againe ſhould meet,
Where th'* Nun *and* Frier *might play at Barly-breake.*
                                                    Cor.

Cor. *Where liu'd thy Loue?*
Dym. *Neere th' bottome of the hill,*
Betweene Pancarpus *temple and the mill,*
There liu'd my faire Palmira, *who I fay,*
'Mongst all our wenches bore th Palme *away:*
And her I lou'd and lik'd, and fu'd and fought,
But all my loue and labour turn'd to nought;
For fhe had vow'd which vow fhould nere be broke,
Shee'd die a Maid, *but meant not as fhe fpoke.*
Dor. *No* Dymnus, *no, the nicefl fure I am,*
Would liue a Maid if't were not for a man;
But there is none of them can brooke fo well,
To be a Beareward and leade Apes in Hell.
Dym. *True* Dorycles, *for in proceffe of time,*
I found her maiden humour to decline:
For fhe did grant the boone which I did aske,
Vpon condition of a greater taske.
Lin. *What heauie cenfure might this* taske *afford?*
Dym. *That for three yeeres I fhould not fpeake a word.*
Cor. *Alas poore Swaine, this* taske *which fhe prepar'd,*
In all my time the like was neuer heard.
Dor. *But this fame* filent taske *had harder bin,*
If fhe had prou'd what fhe enioyned him:
For none can doe a woman greater wrong,
Than barre her from a priuiledge of tongue.
Sap. *A womans tongue's a clapper in the winde,*
Which once a foot, can neuer be confinde;
But to thy taske, *good* Dymnus.
Dym. *To proceed,*
What fhe enioyn'd I did performe indeed:
For I appear'd as one depriu'd of fpeech,
Yet nere my friends vnto my aimes could reach;

But

*But much lamented that a Swaine so young,
And promising, should lose his vse of tongue.*
Tech. *I wonder how thou could expresse thy minde!*
Dym. *Onely by dumbe signes, so as I did finde
Within short time, a great facilitie
In that hard* taske *which she imposed me.*
Lin. *Hardest aduentures oft the easiest seeme,
Only for loue of such inioined them.* (ease
Dym. *And such were mine; when others talk'd with
Of this and that, I euer held my peace;
Others sung Carols of their fairest faire,
But I in silent measures had a share;
Others discours'd of pleasures of the time,
And I approu'd them with a secret signe.
Others could court, as Shepheards vse to doe,
Which I could doe as well, but durst not show:
For all my aymes and purposes did tend
To gaine my* Loue, *and for no other end.*
Cor. *Did not performance of this* taske *obtaine
That prize of loue which thou desir'd to gaine?*
Dym. *No* Corydon; *for though I did obey,
Shee thought three yeares too long a time to stay,
So as her* dumbe knight *she did straight disclaime,
And tooke her selfe vnto another* Swaine.
Sap. *Disloyall wench!*
Dym. *Yet 'las what remedie;
A mariage is intended solemnlie:
Which that it might more priuatly be caried,
In a retyred* Cell *they must be maried.*
Tech. *Vnhappy Swaine!*
Dym. *So did I then appeare:
For when the mariage came vnto my eare,*

I

I straight repair'd to th' Cell right speedily,
Where these sad rites solemniz'd were to be.
Straite was the Gate kept by a Porter *grim,*
Who guards the doore that none should enter in:
But I, as time requir'd, resolu'd to venter,
Did boldly knock, and knocking freely enter;
Where entring in, each casts his eye about,
Some full of feare, as others were of doubt,
What my approach should meane; but to be briefe,
(Short tales seeme long that doe renue our griefe)
The Priest pronouncing, iustly as I came,
Who giues her to be maried to this man?
I rush'd into the croud, their hands to breake,
And gladly would haue spoke but durst not speake:
At which attempt, some strange constructions had,
And verily imagin'd I was mad;
Others suspecting what I did intend,
Thought that my aymes were to no other end,
Than to preuent the Mariage for that time,
And afterwards perswade her to be mine.
Nor were their iudgements erring, for I thought
By my deuice to haue this Proiect wrought
Only by dumbe signes: sometimes would I show
With eyes heau'd vp to Heauen her breach of vow;
Sometimes in violent manner would I seeme
As if through loue I had distracted beene,
Pulling my deare Palmira *from his hand,*
Who to receiue her for his Spouse did stand.
Sometimes, as Men in sorrowes plunged deepe
And could not vtter them, I'gan to weepe,
And wash the Temple with a brinie flood,
Yet all this while I was not vnderstood:

For

For in despite of all that I could doe,
I was restrain'd, and she was married too.
Cor. What discontent might equall this of thine?
Dym. Yet though I bore it sharply for the time,
I afterwards, and haue done euer since,
Borne this disgrace with greater patience. *(end!*
Lin. Yet Dymnus *thou wast* dumbe *till three yeeres*
Dym. Yes Linus, and as truly did intend
What she enioyned me, as I desir'd
To marrie her, when those three yeeres expir'd:
Which comne and past, I then exprest my griefe,
Finding apt words to tender me reliefe;
" For woes doe labour of too great a birth,
" That want the helpe of words to set them forth.
Tech. But didst thou nere display her hatefull shame?
Dym. In generall I did, but not by name,
Nor euer will: my purpose is to liue
And laugh at loue, and no occasion giue
Of iust offence to her or any one,
Or silently consume my time in mone,
Frequenting shadie Lawnes in discontent,
Or to the Ayre my fruitlesse clamors vent.
Though I resolue, if ere I make my choice,
In better sort and measure to rejoyce
Than I haue done;
Dor. Or else I'me sure thy share
Though it decrease in ioy, will grow in care.
Dym. I know it will: Now as my wrong was great,
And greater farre than I could well repeat,
This shall be my Conclusion; There is no Man
Wife that will lose his tongue for any Woman:
For sure I am that they will be more prone

(Such

(Such is their guize) to triumph ouer one
When they haue drawne him headlong to their traine,
Than such as on more firmer grounds remaine.
" Fly Women, they will follow (still say I)
" But if ye follow women, they will fly.
Tech. *Rightly opinion'd* Dymnus; *but t'allay*
Thy grounded griefe, and to conclude the day,
Let's haue a Song.
Dor. Technis *with all my heart.*
Dym. *Though I'ue smal mind to sing, I'le beare a part.*
Cor. *And you too* Sapphus.
Sap. *Yes, and* Linus *too,*
Lin. *Yes, I my Art amongst the rest will show.*
Dor. *To it then freely: safely sing may we,*
Who haue beene slaues to Loue, but now are free.

Tech. TEll me Loue what thou canst doe?
Dor. Triumph ore a simple Swaine;
Dym. Binding him to such a vow;
Cor. As to make his griefe thy gaine.
Sap. Doe thy worst thou canst doe now;
Lin. Thou hast shot at vs in vaine.
All. For we are free, though we did once complain.

Dor. Free we are as is the ayre;
Tech. Or the siluer-murm'ring spring.
Dym. Free from thought or reach of care;
Cor. Which doe haplesse Louers wring.
Sap. Now we may with ioy repaire;
Lin. To our gladsome Plaines and sing;
All. And laugh at Loue, and call't an idle thing.

Dym.

Dym. Sport we may and feede our Sheepe,
Dor. And our Lamkins on this Downe;
Tech. Eat and drinke, and foundly fleepe,
Cor. Since thefe ftormes are ouer-blowne;
Sap. Whilft afflicted wretches weepe,
Lin. That by loue are ouerthrowne:
All. For now we laugh at follies we haue knowne.

Cor. Here we reft vpon thefe rocks;
Dym. Round with fhadie *Iuy* wreath'd;
Dor. Ioying in our woolly flocks;
Tech. On thefe Mountaines freely breath'd;
Sap. Where though clad in ruffet frocks,
Lin. Here we fport where we are heath'd;
All. Our only care to fee our Paftures freath'd.

Sap. Thus we may retire in peace;
Cor. And though low, yet more fecure,
Dym. Then thofe Men which higher preafe;
Dor. *Shrubs* than *Cedars* are more fure:
Tech. And they liue at farre more eafe,
Lin. Finding for each care a cure.
All. Their loue as deare and liker to endure.

Lin. For wherein confifts earths bliffe,
Sap. But in hauing what is fit?
Cor. Which though greater men doe miffe;
Dym. Homely Swaines oft light of it.
Dor. For who's he that liuing is,
Tech. That in higher place doth fit,
All. Whofe fly Ambition would not higher git.

Tech.

Tech. Let vs then contented be,
Dor. In the portion we enioy ;
Cor. And while we doe others fee,
Sap. Tofs'd with gufts of all annoy ;
Dym. Let vs fay this feele not we :
Lin. Be our wenches kinde or coy,
All. We count their frownes and fauours but a toy.

*Dor. Let's now retire, it drawes to Euening time,
Next* Tale *my* Corydon, *it muft be thine.*
Tech. *Which may be done next day we hither come,
Meane time, let's fold our flocks and hye vs home.*

A

A Paſtorall Palinod.

THeſe Swains *like dying* Swans *haue ſung their laſt*,
  And ioy in thinking of thoſe woes *are paſt ;*
For woes *once paſt, like pleaſing* paſtimes *ſeeme,*
And ioy vs more than if they had not beene. (Plaines,
Such Layes *become theſe* Launes, *ſuch* Plaints *theſe*
" *Great men may* higher *haue, no* heuier *ſtraines ;*
For Swains *their* Swainlins *loue, and wooe them too,*
And doe as much as brauer outſides doe.
But Heardſmen *are retired from their ſhade*
Of Myrtle *ſprayes and ſprigs of* Oſyer *made,*
With purpoſe to reuiſit you to morrow,
Where other three *ſhall giue new life to ſorrow:*
Meane time repoſe, leſt when the Swaine *appeares,*
You fall aſleepe when you ſhould flow with teares.

FINIS.

THE SHEPHEARDS TALES.

Too true poore shepheards *do this Prouerbe find,*
No sooner out of sight then out of mind.

[THE SECOND PART.]

LONDON,
Printed for Richard Whitaker.
1621.

HIS PASTORALLS
ARE HERE CONTINVED WITH THREE OTHER TALES;
hauing relation to a former part, as yet obfcured: and deuided into certaine Paftorall Eglogues, fhadowing much delight vnder a rurall fubiect.

The Argument.

*Ere* Corydon *proues,*
That nothing can be fent,
To croffe loue more,
Thē friends vnkind reftraint.

The fecond Argument.

*Orydon* coy *Celia* woes,
And his loue by tokens fhowes.
Tokens are thofe lures, that find
Beft acceffe to woman kind.
Long he woes ere he can win;

Yet

Yet at laſt ſhe fancieth him:
And ſo firme, as you ſhall heare,
Each to other troth-plight were;
But alas, where loue is moſt,
There it oft-times moſt is croſt.
For theſe two are cloſly pent,
Each from other by reſtraint;
He, vnto the plaine muſt go,
Loue-ſicke, heart-ſicke, full of wo,
Where he ſings ſuch chearefull layes,
In his chaſt choiſe, *Celias* praiſe,
That ſteepe mountaines, rocks and plaines,
Seeme entranced with his ſtraines:
But alas, while he does keepe,
Helpleſſe ſhepheard, hapleſſe ſheepe,
Celia for to ſeeke her *make*,
From her *keeper* makes eſcape,
And vnto the mountaine goes,
Where her ſelfe, her ſelfe doth loſe;
While one of *Lauerna'es* crew,
Seizeth on her as his dew,
Where by force, by awe, by feare,
She was long detained there,
And in the end affianc'd ſo,
As ſhe ends her life in wo.

THE SHEPHEARDS,
TALES.

The shepheards.
Technis. Dymnus. Dorycles.
Corydon. Sapphus. Linus.

THE FIRST EGLOGVE.

Corydons tale.

*N*ay *shepheards stay, there is no haſt but*
good,
We three are shepheards, and haue under-
ſtood
Both of your follies and your fancies too ;
Dor. *Why tell vs* Corydon, *what thou wouldſt do !*
Cor. *Shew my misfortune Swaines, as you haue done,.*
Tech. *Deferre it till to morrow* Corydon.
Cor. *No,* Technis *no, I cannot if I would,*
You'ue told your griefes, and now mine muſt be told:
What though the Sunne be drawing to the Weſt,
Where he intends to take his wonted reſt,
Tis Moone-light (lads) and if it were not light,
Welcome you are to lodge with me all night.
Dor. *Thankes* Corydon.
Cor. *Why thanke you* Corydon?
Simple and meane's the cottage where I won;
Yet well I wot, for cheſtnuts, cakes, and creame;
If you'le accept my welcome as I meane,
You shall not want, but haue sufficient ſtore,
With hearty welcome swaines, what would ye more ?
Dym. *More* Corydon! *t'is all that we can wiſh,*
But to thy tale, let's heare now what it is.
Dor. *Yes, do good* Corydon; *and we will ſtay;*

Cor. *Attend then shepheards, heare what I shall say.*
Sap. *And when you'ue done, I will begin with mine;*
Lin. *Which I'le continue in the euening time.*
Cor. *Well said, good shepheards, we are iustly three,*
To answer their three tales, and here for me.
There was a Maid, *and well might she be said,*
So chast, so choice she was, to be a Maid,
Where lillie white mixt with a cherrie red,
Such admiration in the shepheards bred,
As well was he that might but haue a sight
Of her rare beauty mirror of delight.
Oft would she come vnto a siluer spring,
Which neare her fathers house was neighboring,
Where she would eye her selfe as she did passe,
For shepheards vse no other looking-glasse.
Tech. *True* Corydon.
Cor. *But which may seeme more rare,*
This Maid *she was as wise as she was faire;*
So as discretion did so moderate
The safe condition of her low estate,
As enuie neuer wrong'd her spotlesse name,
Or soild her matchlesse honour with defame.
Dor. *Vnder a happie Planet she was borne,*
Cor. *She was indeed; nor did she euer scorne,*
The company of any country maid,
How meane soere or sluttishly araid:
But she would be their play-fare, to make chuse,
Of such poore simple sports as wenches vse.
Yea in their wakes, shroues, wassel-cups, or tides,
Or Whitson-ales, or where the country brides
Chuse out their bride-maids, as the custome is,
She seld or neare was seene to do amisse:
But so respectiue of her name and fame,

That though she blusht, she neuer blusht for shame
Of any act immodest, but retain'd
That good opinion which her vertues gain'd.
Dym. *Sure* Corydon *this was a Saintly woman ;*
Cor. *Indeed such Saints 'mongst women are not cōmon:*
But to my story ; her did many swaine,
By fruitlesse suite endeuour to obtaine,
As young Spudippus, *rich* Archymorus,
Actiue Amintas, *youthfull* Hirsius.
Dor. *It seemes sh'ad choice.*
Cor. *Yes Dorycles, she had :*
And some of these were good, and some as bad,
But neither good nor bad, nor rich nor poore,
Could her content, though she had daily store.
Yet from Pandoras *box did nere proceed,*
More hatefull poyson vpon humane feed,
Then from these forlorne louers, whose report,
(But iust is heauen, for they were plagued for't,)
Aspers'd this scandall on faire Celia,
That she had made her choice some other way.
Tech. *Vnworthy louers.*
Cor. *True indeed, they be*
Vnworthy th' loue of such an one as she ;
For Linus *you do know them ;*
Lin. *Yes, I do,*
But specially Spudippus, *whom I know,*
To be thē notedst cot-queane that's about him.
Tec. *Sure* Linus *thē she could not chuse but flout him.*
Cor. *Perhaps she did, yet with that modestie,*
As she did shadow it so couertly,
That he could scarce discouer what she ment.
Lin. *How ere* Spudippus *would be patient.*

Dor. Then he's some gull.
Lin. No he's a wealthy man,
And such an one as rightly, sure I am,
Knows how much milke crummock his cow will giue,
And can discerne a riddle from a siue.
Cor. Linus, it seemes thou knowes him passing well.
Lin. Las if I would, some stories I could tell,
Would make you laugh : for as it chanc'd one day,
Some with my selfe did take his house by th' way,
Where we an houre or two meant to remaine,
To trie how he his friends would entertaine.
Dor. And pray thee how?
Lin. I'le tell thee Dorycles :
Hauing an houre or two taken our ease,
And readie to depart (I pray thee heare)
He sent one of his Scullerie for some beare,
Which though long first, came in an earthen cup,
Which being giuen to me, I drunke it vp;
Which drunke.
Cor. How then good Linus, pray thee say?
Lin. The rest were forc'd to go a thirst away.
Dor. Had he no more?
Cor. Thou vs'd him in his kind.
Lin. May all be vsed so that haue his mind.
But much I feare me, I'ue disturbed thee,
Now Corydon shew what th'euent may be!
Cor. Long did these woe, but Celia could approue
Of nothing lesse then of these swainlings loue,
Yet would she faine to fancie one of these,
Whereby she might her bedrid father please.
Tech. Had she a father?
Cor. Yes, a surly Lout,

Who

Who long had laine decrepit with the gout,
And liu'd for all the world, and so did die
Like to a hog, *that's pent vp in a* stie.
Dor. *Some cancred erwig.*
Cor. *True, a very elfe,*
Who car'd not who staru'd, so he fed himselfe.
He, as the want of one sense is exprest,
By giuing more perfection to the rest,
For euen his sense of feeling *did decline,*
Though he had bene a nigglar *in his time,*
Yea all those mouing, actiue faculties,
Which in the heate of youth are wont to rise,
Gaue way vnto suspition, lest his daughter
Through those loue-luring gifts which many brought
Should set her Maiden honor at whole sale. (her,
Tech. *Age h'as an eare indeed for euery tale.*
Cor. *True,* Technis *true, for no affection can*
Haue more predominance ore any man,
Then iealousie *a selfe-consuming rage,*
Is said to haue ore men of doting age.
Dor. *Thy reason* Corydon *?*
Cor. *That disesteeme*
Of being now more weake then they haue bene,
Makes them repine at others now that may,
And are as able to beget as they.
Tech. *Tis rightly noted* Corydon.
Lin. *Yes, he*
Knowes by obseruance whence these humors be,
Cor. Linus *I do, and better had I bene,*
If I had neuer knowne what these things meane;
But shepheards you shall heare the reason, why
I should this Dotards humour thus descrie.

Sap.

Sap. *Yes, do good Swaine.*
Cor. *It chanc'd vpon a night,   (bright,*
A Moone-light night, when Moone and starres shine
That I with other shepheards did repaire
To th'old-mans house, and found faire Celia *there,*
Whom I in curtsie with a kind salute,
Kist, & with speaking heart though tongue was mute,
Wish'd, ô what wishes do possesse a mind,
That dare not vtter how his heart's inclind !
She might be mine, thrice blest in being mine.
Dor. *Why didst not woe her Swaine, for to be thine?*
Cor. *Yes* Dorycles *I woed her, though not then,*
For Maidens they are bashfull amongst men,
And dare not well in modestie impart,
What they could giue consent to with their heart;
So as to tell thee truly Dorycles,
We past that night in making purposes,
Singing of catches, *with such knowne delights.*
As young folke vse to passe ore winter nights.
And at that time, I may be bold to tell thee,
For such conceits I thought none could excell me.
For well you know, I was in Hyble *bred,*
And by the sacred sisters *nourished,*
So as being stor'd by Nature, help'd by art,
There was no straine I bore not in some part:
Which gaue faire Celia *such entire content,*
As she discouerd after, what she ment.
Though I may sweare, for fiue months I came to her,
And with some termes of art assaid to woe her:
During which time, all th'anfwer I could get,
Was this; she did not meane to marrie yet.
Tech. *That's all the answer these young women haue,*
                                                While

While they reiect what after they receiue.
Cor. Technis, *indeed I did perceiue as much,*
Though all young wenches humours be not such:
But th'greatest cause of Celias *distaste,*
Which made me many times the lesser grac't,
Proceeded from that chrone *her dogged father,*
As after by coniectures I did gather:
Perswading her, that she should plant her loue
On such whose hopefull meanes might best approue
Her discreet choice: and that was not to be
Affianced to such an one as me. (*faith,*
Dor. *Alas poore Swaine; 'tis true what th' Prouerbe*
We aske not what he is, but what he hath.
Cor. *And yet perswasions which her father vs'd,*
Could not preuaile with her, for she had chus'd,
In heart I meane.
Tech. *Whom did she dote vpon?*
Cor. *Will ye beleeue me!*
Tech. *Yes.*
Cor. *Twas* Corydon.
Lin. *Thrice happie swaine.*
Cor. *Thrice happie had I bene,*
If I had slept still in this golden dreame;
But afterwards occurrences there were,
Which thus abridg'd my hopes, as you shall heare.
Such deepe impression had affection made,
As there remained nothing vnassaid,
To consummate our wishes, but the rite.
Tech. *Yes something else.*
Cor. *What* Technis!
Tech. *Marriage night.*
Sap. *They had enioyed that, you may suppose.*
                                                    Cor.

Cor. *No,* Sapphus *no, she was not one of those:*
So modest, chast, respectiue of her name,
Pure and demure, as th' sweetnesse of her fame,
Aboue the choifest odors that are sent
From spicie Tmolus *flowrie continent,*
Sent forth that fragrant and delightfull fauour,
As none ere heard, and did not seeke to haue her.
For sundrie choise discourses haue we had,
And I nere knew that ought could make her glad,
Which had least taste of lightnesse.
Tech. *Sure thou art,*
So much thy praises relish true desert,
Worthy such vertuous beautie.
Cor. Technis *no,*
Albeit Celia *esteem'd me so,*
As long and tedious seem'd that day to be,
Which did deuide her from my companie.
So as in silent groues and shady launes,
Where Siluans, water-nimphs, fairies, *and* faunes,
Vse to frequent, there would we sit and sing,
Eying our beauties in a neighbour spring,
Whose siluer streamlings with soft murmring noise,
To make our consort perfect, gaue their voice.
And long did we obserue this custome too,
Though her consent did bid me ceasse to woe:
For now I was no woer, but her loue,
And that so firmely linkt, as nought could moue,
Alter or sunder our vnited hearts,
But meagre death, which all true louers parts.
Tech. *Then* Corydon, *to me it doth appeare,*
That you were troth-plight.
Cor. Technis *so we were.*

But

But see (good shepheards) what succeeded hence:
This loue she bore me did her sire *incense,*
So as discurteously he pent his daughter
In such a vault, I could not see her after.
Which when my friends perceiu'd, they grieued were,
That th' loue which I his Celia *did beare,*
Should be rewarded with contempt and scorne,
Being for parentage equally borne,
With best of his, as most of you can tell.
Lin. *Proceed good* Corydon, *we know it well.*
Cor. *For was I not of* Polyarchus *line,*
A noble shepheard!
Sap. *True, who in his time*
Solemniz'd many wakes on this our downe,
And ere he dide was to that honour growne,
As all our plaines resounded with his laies,
Sung by our Swaines in Polyarchus *praise.*
Cor. *It seemes thou knew him* Sapphus: *but attend*
For now my storie draweth neare an end.
My friends distasting this repulse of mine,
Forc'd me from th' course whereto I did incline:
So as my hopes confin'd, I'me driuen to go
From Adons *vale vnto a mount of wo.*
Lin. *Vnhappie shepheard.*
Cor. *And vnhappie sheepe,*
For ill could I my heards from worrying keepe,
Though to that charge my friends enioyned me,
When I could scarcely keepe my owne hands free,
From doing violence vpon my selfe:
So as one day vpon a ragged shelfe,
Wreath'd round with Iuie, as I sate alone,
Descanting Odes of sorrow and of mone,

I

I chanc'd on my mishap to meditate,
Celias restraint, and my forlorne estate;
Which done, I vow'd if speedy remedy
Gaue no reliefe vnto my maladie,
That very cliff where I repos'd that day,
Should be the meanes to take my life away.
Tech. *O* Corydon *this soundeth of despaire.*
Cor. *It does indeed: but such a watchfull care,*
Had gracious Pan *of me, that in short time,*
These motiues to despaire 'gan to decline,
And lose their force: so as when griefes grew ripe,
I vs'd to take me to my oaten pipe.
Dor. *But ere thou proceed further, tell vs Swaine,*
Where all this time thou vsed to remaine.
Cor. *A broad-spread* oake *with aged armes & old,*
Directs the passenger the way he would,
Neare Cadmus *rising hillocks, where the spring*
Of golden Tagus *vseth oft to bring*
Such precious trafficke to the neighbour shore.
As former times through blindnesse did adore
Those curled streames, wherein they did descry
Their loue to gold, by their Idolatrie:
That shady oake *I say, and that blest spring,*
In my distresse, gaue me such harboring;
As night and day I did not thence remoue,
But waking mus'd, and sleeping dream'd of loue.
Tech. *Who euer heard the like!*
Dor. *How didst thou liue?*
Cor. *On hope.*
Tech. *Weake food.*
Cor. *Yet did it comfort giue,*
To my afflicted mind, which did desire,

Euer

Euer to finge her wings in fancies fire.
For many weekes in this diftreft eftate,
Wretched, forlorne, helpleffe and defolate,
Sate I deiected, mufing on defpaire,
And when thofe drerie clouds would once grow faire:
But las the more I did expect reliefe,
The leffe hope had I to allay my griefe,
So as in th' end, as you fhall after heare,
All meanes for my redreffe abridged were.
But that you may perceiue what loue can do,
And how effectually her paffions fhow,
I who before I louely Celia *kent,*
Knew not what th' Heliconian *Mufes ment,*
Addreft my felfe;
Lin. *To what good* Corydon?
Cor. *To write of loue, and thus my Mufe begun.*
Tech. *Pray thee kind Swaine let's heare what thou didft write.*
Dor. *Yes do: for well I know it will delight*
S[h]epheards to heare, of fhepheards amorous toyes;
Sap. *On then good* Corydon.
Cor. *Haue at ye Boyes.*

 Celia fpeake, or I am dombe,
 Here I'le foiorne till thou come,
 Seeke I will till I grow blind,
 Till I may my *Celia* find.
 For if *tongue-tide*, ftring would breake,
 If I heard but *Celia* fpeake;
 And if *blind*, I foone fhould fee,
 Had I but a fight of thee;
 Or if *lame*, loue would find feete,
 Might I once with *Celia* meete;

        Or

Or if *deafe*, should I but heare
Loues sweete accents from thy eare:
Thy choice notes would me restore,
That I should be *deafe* no more.
Thus though *dombe, blind, deafe,* and *lame,*
Heard I but my *Celias* name,
I should *speake, see, heare,* and *go,*
Vowing, *Celia* made me so.

Tech. *Beshrow me* Corydon, *if I had thought,*
That loue such strange effects could ere haue wrought.
Cor. *Yes* Technis, *yes,* loue's *such a wondrous thing,*
That it will make one plungd in sorrow sing,
And singing weepe, for griefe is wont to borrow
Some strains of ioy, that ioy might end in sorrow.
For what is woe (as we must needs confesse it)
Hauing both tongue and teares for to expresse it,
But a beguiling griefe, whose nature's such,
It can forget, lest it should grieue too much.
Dor. *Indeed such sorrow seldome lasteth long,*
But say good Swaine, heard Celia *of thy song?*
Cor. *I know not,* Dorycles: *but twas her lot,*
That from her keeper afterwards she got.
Tech. *Happie escape.*
Cor. *Ah* Technis, *say not so,*
For this escape gaue new increase to wo;
Lin. *How could that be?*
Cor. *Heare but what did ensue,*
She was preuented by a ruffin-crue,
As she vpon the mountaines rom'd about,
Through desart caues to find her shepheard out.
Tech. *Alas poore wench; what were they* Corydon?
Cor. *Such as did haunt there, and did liue vpon*

Rapine

Rapine and violence, triumphing in
Impunitie, sole motiue vnto sin.
In briefe, they were, for so they did professe,
Of braue Lauerna'es *crue, that patronesse*
Of all disorder, and each euening time
Offer'd stolne booties to her godlesse shrine.
Tech. *Mishap aboue mishaps.*
Cor. *True, so it was;*
My lasse she lost her lad, the lad his lasse.
And sundry daies, this rout did her detaine,
While haplesse, helplesse she did sore complaine
Of their inhumane vsage, but her griefe,
Sighs, sobs, teares, throbs, could yeeld her small reliefe:
For in the end one of this forlorne crew,
Seiz'd on my long-lou'd Celia *as his dew,*
To whom espous'd whether she would or no,
She ends her life, her tedious life, in wo.
Lin. *A sad euent: but can she not be freed?*
Cor. *To what end* Linus, *she's dishonoured!*
Tech. *Vnhappie fate.*
Cor. *Besides, she now is tide,*
And by enforcement, made anothers Bride.
Come shepheards come, and say if euer time,
Made heardmens woes so ripe, as't hath done mine.
Sap. *Yes* Corydon, *though thou thy griefes hast showne,*
Which makes thee thinke none equall to thine owne,
I haue a Tale *will moue compassion too,*
If Swaines haue any pittie.
Dym. *Pray thee how?*
Sap. *Nay I will not be daintie; but attend,*
And then compare our stories to the end,

And

*And you'le conclude that neuer any Swaine
Did loue so well, and reape so small a gaine.*

The Argument.

*Apphus woes Siluia,
Yet he thinks it ill,
To take to that,
Which he did neuer till.*

The second Argument.

He, whose sweet and gracefull speech,
Might all other shepheards teach:
She, whom countries did admire,
For her presence and attire:
She, whose choise perfections mou'd,
Those that knew her to be lou'd.
She, euen *Siluia*, for saue she,
None so faire, and firme could be;
When she should be *Sapphus* Bride,
And their hands were to be tide
With their hearts in marriage knot,
Sapphus heares of *Siluias* blot.
Whereby *Sapphus* doth collect,
                                    How

How hard it is for to affect,
Such an one as will reioyce,
And content her in her choice;
He concludes, since all things be
Certaine in vncertaintie,
Who would trust what women say,
Who can do but what they may.
,, Forts are won by foes assault,
,, If Maids yeeld, it is Mans fault.

THE SECOND EGLOGVE.

Sapphus tale.

 *Had a* Loue *as well as any you,*
And such an one, as had she but her due,
Deseru'd the seruice of the worthiest swaine
That ere fed sheepe vpon the Westerne *plaine.*
Dym. *Good* Sapphus *say, what was thy lasses name?*
Was it not Siluia*?*
Sap. *The very same;*
It seemes thou knew her.
Dym. *Yes exceeding well,*
And might haue knowne her, but I would not mell,
In more familiar sort.
Sap. *Vnworthy Swaine,*
Did her affection merit such a staine?
Suppose she threw some looser lookes vpon thee,
And thou collected thence she would haue won thee,
Is this th' requitall of the loue she bore?
Dym. *Nay on good* Sapphus, *I'le do so no more.*
Sap. *No more! why now I sweare, and may be bold*
That Dymnus *would haue done it if he could.*

S   Why

Why sir, what parts were euer in you yet,
That she on you such fancie should haue set?
Tech. *Fie, shepheards fie, we come not here to scold:*
Come Sapphus, *tell thy tale as we haue told.*
Sap. Dymnus *doth interrupt me.*
Lin. Dymnus *ceasse.*
Dym. *Nay I haue done, so he will hold his peace.*
But to vpbraid me, that I had no part
To gaine her loue, I scorne it with my heart:
For Ile auouch.
Tech. *Nay then the strife's begun.*
Dor. Dymnus *for shame.*
Dym. *Nay shepheards, I haue done.*
Dor. *Pray then proceed good* Sapphus.
Sap. *Willingly:*
Though I can hardly brooke this iniury.
Dym. *Why* Sapphus, *I am sure thou know'st all this,*
That she was light.
Sap. *I know she did amisse,*
Yet I must tell you Dymnus, *'t had bene fit,*
That rather I then you had noted it:
For it concern'd me most.
Dym. *Pray let it rest,*
I did not know so much, I may protest.
Sap. Dymnus, *enough: and thus I do proceed;*
Vpon a time when I my flocks did feed,
Her father Thyrsis *chanc'd to come that way,*
And to obserue me more, a while made stay
Vpon the Downe, *where I did feede my sheepe:*
Who eying me, how duely I did keepe
My woollie store (as I had care) from worrien,
Scab, sought, the rot or any kind of murren:

Tooke

Tooke such a liking on me, as to say
The very truth, vpon next holy day,
He did inuite me to his house, where I
Found what was loue in louely Siluia's *eye.*
In briefe, I lou'd her, I may boldly tell,
And this her father notes, and likes it well:
For oft vs'd he to say, right sure I am,
A penny in a man then with a man,
He did esteeme more of, which he applide
Vnto that care which he in me descride.
Dym. *A iolly Swaine he was.*
Sap. *He was indeed,*
And on these Downs *more frolicke* rams *did breed,*
Then any Swainling that did dwell about him,
And truth to say, they would do nought without him.
Dor. *Tis said that* Thirsk *frō* Thirsis *tooke her name,*
Who thither with his heards a grazing came,
And plaid vpon his pipe such pleasant straines,
As he yet liues vpon the neighbour plaines.
Sap. *This know I* Dorycles, *that in my hearing,*
He pip'd so sweete, that many shepheards fearing
Th'melodious straines which issued from his reed,
Would so amaze their flocks they could not feede:
Ioyntly together in a secret caue,
Where Palms *and* Mirtles *their increasing haue,*
They so contriu'd an harbour *for the nonst,*
That he might from the scorching Sunne be sconst,
And sing at pleasure, while his accents raising,
Heardsmen were hearing, and their heards were gra-
For curious seats hewne from the solid stone, (*zing.*
Were aptly fram'd for Swaines to sit vpon,
Who in his voice conceiu'd such choice delight,

As a whole Sommer day from morne to night,
Seem'd but an houre, so sweetly did he sing,
While euery day he found out some new *spring.*
But all too long digression haue I made;
Falling in loue with Siluia *as I said,*
I saw *and perishd,* perishd, *for it cost*
My libertie, which I by seeing lost.
Dor. *Deare was that sight.*
Sap. *Yet dearer may I sweare,*
Was she to me, then any senses were:
For other obiects I did wholly shon,
Chusing her selfe for me to looke vpon.
Neither was I hope-reft, for she did seeme
To fancie me, howse'euer she did meane;
And I deseru'd it, as I thought that day,
For clothed in my suite of shepheards gray,
With buttond cap and buskins all of one,
I may assure you (heardsmen) *I thought none*
On all our Downe *more neate or handsome was,*
Or did deserue more kindnesse from his lasse.
Dym. *A good conceit doth well.*
Sap. *And truth was this,*
She shew'd me all respect that I could wish,
And vndissembled too, I am perswaded,
Though afterwards all that affection faded.
For on a day, (this I thought good to tell,
That you may thence perceiue she lou'd me well)
In a greene shadie harbour *I repos'd,*
With Sycamours *and* Iunipers *enclos'd,*
She priuately into the harbour *crept,*
Which seene, I fain'd asleepe, but neuer slept.
Tech. *A faire occasion!*

Lin.

Lin. *How did she reueale*
Her loue?
Sap. *If you had felt, what I did feele,*
You neuer would awakt, but wisht do die, [to
In such a foule-beguiling phantasie.
For first she eyed me, nor contented so,
With nimble pace she to my lips did go:
And calls, and clings, and clips me round about,
Vsing a soft-sweete dalliance with her foote,
Not to awake me from my chearefull dreame,
But to impart what she in heart did meane;
Wherewith I seem'd to wake.
Tech. *Why didst thou so?*
Sap. *Technis, I thought she trod vpon my toe,*
But as I wak'd, she without further stay,
Dying her cheekes with blushes, stole away.
Dym. *This shew'd she lou'd thee.*
Sap. *So I know she did,*
But who can perfect what the fates *forbid?*
For long we liued thus, and loued too,
With vowes as firme as faith and troth could do,
That nought should ere infringe that nuptiall band,
Confirm'd betwixt vs two with heart and hand.
So as with Thirsis *knowledge and consent,*
After so many weekes in loue-toyes spent,
It was agreed vpon by either side,
That I should be her Bridegroome, *she my* Bride.
And th'day of Solemnization was set downe,
So as the choisest youths in all the towne,
Addrest themselues, for I was valued then
Amongst the chiefest Swaines, to be my men.
Lin. *I know it* Sapphus, *both thy wealth and worth,*

Were

Were both of power enough to fet thee forth.
Sap. *In briefe, for I your patience might wrong,*
To ſtand vpon theſe marriage rites too long;
To th' Church we went, fuſpecting I may ſweare,
No ſuch euents as after did appeare.
Tech. *What ſad euents, good* Sapphus?
Sap. *Being now*
Come to do that which we could nere vndo,
The Prieſt pronounc'd a charge, whereby was ment,
If either of vs knew impediment,
Why we ſhould not be ioyned, then to ſpeake,
That we in time might ſuch a wedlocke *breake;*
Or any one there preſent ſhould ſhew cauſe,
Why we might not be married by the lawes:
There to declare, in publicke one of theſe,
Or elſe for euer after hold their peace.
God ſpeed them well, ſaid all, ſaue onely one,
Who ſtood from thence ſome diſtance all alone,
Crying, aloud in open audience,
Sapphus *forbeare, there is no conſcience,*
That thou ſhould ioyne thy hand to one *defil'd;*
At leaſt prouide a father *for her* child,
Which ſhe kind pregnant wench is great withall,
And, who ere got it, will thee father *call.*
Tech. *This was a ſtrange preuention.*
Sap. *I confeſſe it,*
But if y'ad heard how Meuus *did expreſſe it,*
(For ſo his name was) you would haue admir'd
His frontleſſe impudence.
Dym. *Sure he was hir'd,*
To fruſtrate these ſolemnities.
Sap. *Ah no,*

Beleeue

Beleeue me Dymnus *it was nothing so:*
For she was fruitfull long before her time,
But th' fault was hers, it was no fact of mine:
So as her neighbours iudg'd and censurd on her,
That she begun by time to take vpon her.
But this shall be in silence past for me,
Onely she's shadowed in my *Omphale.   * *A Poem enti-*
And so charactred, as the time may come,   *tled* Omphale.
Siluia shall be as Flora *was in* Rome.
Dor. *But what succeeded hence?*
Sap. *Vpon this voice*
There streight arose a strange confused noise,
Some Meuus *tax'd, and said he was to blame,*
To blemish any modest Maidens name;
Others were doubtfull, lest it should be true,
And thus they thought, and thus it did ensue.
I now suspicious of this foule dishonour,
Which Meuus *publickly had laid vpon her:*
Resolu'd those solemne spousals to delay,
And put them off vntill another day:
Meane while, (attend me Swains) when th' day came on
That I should marrie, Siluia *had a sonne.*
Cor. *God blesse the boy.*
Dym. *Who might the child begit?*
Sap. *Nay* Dymnus *sure, who euer fatherd it.*
Dym. *Who I!*
Sap. *Nay blush not man, for you haue told,*
You might oft-times haue done it if you wold;
But I do wish her all the good I can,
And praise her choise, though I be not the man.
Tech. *Vnhappie choice!*
Dor. *Hard fate!*

T'is nothing so,
You'le heare a choise more fatall ere you go.
These were but toyes to entertaine the time,
Prepare your handkerchers if you'le haue mine.
All. *What, must we weepe?*
Lin. *Shepheards a while forbeare,*
And if there be no cause, iudge when you heare.

The Argument.

Inus *doth* Lesbia *loue,*
And woe, and win,
And after by her
Lightnesse wrongeth him.

The second Argument.

Ouely *Lesbia*, who might be,
For birth, beauty, quality,
Styled Natures Paragon,
Fram'd for *Swaines* to dote vpon;
In a word for to expresse,
Feature of this *Shepheardesse*,
If you would her stature know,
She was neither high nor low;

But

But of such a middle size,
As if Nature did deuise,
(For as't seemeth so she ment)
To make her, her president;
With a Sun-reflecting eye,
Skin more smooth then iuory;
Cherrie lip, a dimple chin,
Made for loue to lodge him in;
A sweete chearing-chafing sent,
Which perfum'd ground where she went;
A perswasiue speech, whose tongue
Strucke deepe admiration dombe.
She, euen she, whom all approu'd,
Is by liuely *Linus* lou'd,
And at last (what would ye more)
Though she was betroth'd before
To *Palemon*, that braue Swaine,
Who quite droupes through her disdaine,
Is with rites solemnized,
Vnto *Linus* married;
Whom he finds (as heauen is iust)
After, staind with boundlesse lust,
So as he laments his state,
Of all most vnfortunate,
That he should in hope of pelfe,
Wrong both others and himselfe.

THE

THE THIRD EGLOGVE.

Linus tale.

*Lou'd a* laſſe, *alas that ere I lou'd,*
Who as ſhe ſeem'd to be, if ſhe had
    prou'd,
A worthier Swaine *the countrey*
    nere had bred,
And her I woing won, and winning wed.
Tech. *I like thee* Linus, *thy preamble's ſhort ;*
Lin. Technis, *indeed I am not of that ſort,*
Who for a thing of nought will pule and crie,
And childiſhly put finger in the eye ;
The burden of my griefe is great to beare.
Dor. *What is it* Linus, *pray thee let vs heare ?*
Lin. *The* Maid *I got, and* Lesbia *was her name,*
Was to another troth-plight ere I came.
Cor. *How ſhould ſhe* Linus *then be got by thee ?*
Lin. *It was my fate, or her inconſtancie.*
Hows'ere I haue her, and poſſeſſe her now,
And would be glad to giue her one of you.
Tech. *Art wearie of thy choice ?*
Lin. Technis, *I am,*
For I'me perſwaded ſhe'd wearie any man.
So ſeeming ſmooth ſhe is and euer was,
As if ſhe hardly could ſay Michaelmas :
But priuately ſo violently fierce,
As I'me afraid her name *will ſpoile my verſe.*
Cor. *This is ſome* hornet *ſure.*
Lin. *A very* waſpe,

                                          Whoſe

Whose forked tongue who euer should vnclaspe,
Would find't a taske to charme it.
Dym. *Is't so tart;*
Lin. *O Dymnus, that thou didst but feele a part*
Of my affliction, thou wouldst surely mone,
And pittie me, that's matcht to such an one;
For tell me shepheards was there ere so rare,
A crime, wherein my Lesbia *doth not share?*
Proud, (though before as humble to the eye
As ere was Maid) so as one may descrie,
Euen by her outward habit what she is,
And by her wanton gesture gather this:
If thou be chast, thy body wrongs thee much,
For thy light carriage faith, thou art none such.
Sap. *Some fashion-monger I durst pawne my life.*
Lin. *Sapphus 'tis true, such is poore Linus wife,*
Though ill it seemes a country Shepheardesse,
Such harsh fantasticke fashions to professe:
One day vnto a Barber *she'de repaire,*
And for what end but this, to cut her haire,
So as like to a Boy *she did appeare,*
Hauing her haire round cut vnto her eare.
Cor. *Good Linus say, how lookt that* Minx *of thine?*
Lin. *Like to a fleecelesse Ewe at shearing time.*
So cowd she was, as next day she did show her
Vpon the Downs, *but not a Swaine could know her;*
So strangely clipt she seem'd, and in disguise,
So monstrous ougly, as none could deuise
To see one clad in lothsomer attire:
And this she knew was farre from my desire,
For I did euer hate it.
Tech. *Pray thee Lad*

Tell

Tell vs in earnest how she might be clad!
Lin. *There is a fashion now brought vp of late,*
Which here our country Blouzes imitate,
The cause whereof I do not thinke it fit,
If I did know't, for to discouer it,
But sure I iudge, some rot's *in womans ioynts,*
Which makes them faine to tye them vp with points.
Dym. *With points!*
Lin. *Yes Dymnus, that's the fashion now,*
Whereof I haue a tale, *right well I know,*
Will make you laugh.
Dor. *Let's heare that tale of thine.*
Lin. *Shepheards you shall; it chanc'd vpon a time,*
That Lesbia, *whose spirit euer would*
Obserue the fashion, do I what I could,
Bearing a port far higher in a word,
Then my abilitie could well afford:
That she I say into this fashion got,
(As what was th'fashion she affected not)
Of tying on with points *her looser waste;*
Now I obseruing how her points *were plast,*
The Euen before she to a wake *should go,*
I all her points *did secretly vndo,*
Yet therewithall such easie knots did make,
That they might hold till she got to the wake,
Which she not minding.
Cor. *On good* Linus, *on.*
Lin. *She hyes her to the* wake (*my* Corydon)
Where she no sooner came, then she's tane in,
And nimbly falls vnto her reuelling,
But see the lucke on't, while she scuds and skips,
Her vnderbody falls from off her hips,
                                                    Whereat

*Whereat some laught, while others tooke some ruth,
That she vncas'd, should shew the naked truth.
But heare what happen'd hence, ere th'setting Sunne
Lodg'd in the West, she heard what I had done;
So as resolu'd to quite me in my kind,
Next morne betime, she* Hylus *chanc'd to find.*
Sap. *Who,* Clytus *boy!*
Lin. *Yes* Sapphus, *selfe-same Lad,
Who was a good boy, ere she made him bad.*
Tech. *Pray* Linus *how?*
Lin. *Through her immodestie,
She him allur'd for to dishonour me.*
Tech. *Disloyall* Lesbia; *but pray the shew,
Did* Hylus *(harmelesse youth) consent thereto?*
Lin. *Technis, he did;*
Dor. *How shouldst thou know as much?*
Lin. *She did display't her selfe.*
Dor. *Is her shame such?*
Lin. *Yes, and withall defide me to my face,
With such iniurious speeches of disgrace,
As patience could not beare.*
Tech. *And didst thou beare them?*
Lin. *Yes,* Technis *yes, & smild when I did heare them
For this is my conceit, it seemeth no man,
To shew his violence vnto a woman.*
Dym. Linus *sayes well, but womans nature's such,
They will presume if men do beare too much.
For if the tongue vpon defiance stand,
The tongue should be reuenged by the hand.*
Lin. *Some would haue done it* Dymnus, *but I thought
If I reuenge by such base meanes had sought,
The worled would condemne me; she could blind*
                                                Most

Moſt men with an opinion, ſhe was kind,
But in a modeſt ſort: for on a time,
Rich Amphybæus *offring to the ſhrine*
Of Panaretus *(as there went report)*
Sought for her loue in a diſhoneſt ſort,
With price, with prayer, yet nere attain'd his aime,
To ſoile her honour, or her vertues ſtaine;
Sap. *Women are nice when ſimple heard-men craue it,*
And will ſay nay, when they the fainſt would haue it.
Lin. *'Tis right; and now good ſhepheards tell me true,*
Haue I not cauſe, for I'le be iudg'd by you,
To mone my hard miſhap?
Tech. *Thou haſt indeed.* (bleed;
Cor. *Thy woes, friend Linus, make my heartſtrings*
Lin. *I thanke you all; but will you heare a ſong,*
Penn'd in the meditation of my wrong?
Dor. *For loues-ſake do!*
Lin. *Iudge if the* deſcant *fit*
The burden *of my griefe, for this is it;*
As for the note *before I further go,*
My tune *is this,* and who can blame my woe?

    If *Marriage* life yeeld ſuch content,
    What heauie hap haue I,
    Whoſe life with griefe and ſorrow ſpent,
    Wiſh death, yet cannot die;
    She's bent to ſmile when I do ſtorme,
    When I am chearefull too,
    She ſeemes to loure, then who can cure,
    Or counterpoize my woe?

    My marriage day chac'd you away,

                                        For

For I haue found it true,
That *bed* which did all ioyes difplay,
Became a *bed* of rue ;
Where *afpes* do brouze on fancies floure,
And beauties bloffome too :
Then where's that power on earth may cure,
Or counterpoize my woe?

I thought *loue* was the *lampe* of life,
No *life* without'en *loue*,
No *loue* like to a faithfull *wife* :
Which when I fought to proue,
I found her birth was not on earth,
For ought that I could know ;
Of good ones I perceiu'd a dearth,
Then who can cure my woe?

Zantippe was a iealous fhrow,
And *Menalippe* too,
Fauftina had a ftormie brow,
Corinna'es like did fhow ;
Yet thefe were Saints compar'd to mine,
For mirth and mildleffe too :
Who runs diuifion all her time,
Then who can cure my woe?

My *boord* no difhes can afford,
But *chafing difhes* all,
Where felfe-will domineres as Lord,
To keepe poore me in thrall ;
My difcontent giues her content,
My friend fhe vowes her foe :

How

How fhould I then my forrowes vent,
Or *cure* my endleffe woe?

No *cure* to *care*, farewell all ioy,
Retire poore foule and die,
Yet ere thou die, thy felfe employ,
That thou maift mount the skie;
Where thou may moue commanding *Ioue*,
That *Pluto* he might go
To wed thy *wife*, who end't thy life,
For this will cure thy wo!

Dym. *I iudge by this, that thou wouldft faine forfake
And freely giue her any that would take her.* (her,
Lin. Dymnus *I would, but I my* croffe *muft beare,
As I haue done before this many yeare;
But fince our griefes are equally expreft,
Let's now compare which is the heauieft!*
Tech. *I loft my* Amarillida;
Dor. *But fhe
Was nothing to* Bellina.
Dym. *No, nor fhe
Like to my faire* Palmira.
Cor. *Nor all three
Equall to* Celia;
Sap. *Let* Siluia *be
The onely faire.*
Lin. *Admit, they all were faire,
Your griefes with* me, *may haue no equall fhare,
For you are free, fo as perhaps you may
Make choice of* fome, *may be as faire as they;
But I am bound, and that in fuch a knot,*

             As

As onely death may it vnloofe, or not.
Tech. *To* Linus *muſt we yeeld ; but who are theſe?*
Dor. *Two iollie ſhepheards, that do hither preſe,*
With ribbon fauours, and roſemary ſprigs,
Chanting along our Downes *their rurall ijgs,*
As to ſome wedding boun ;
Sap. *You may preſume,*
For Iohn vnto the May-pole *is their tune,*
And that's their bridall note.
Lin. *Let vs draw neare them,*
Cloſe to this ſhadie Beech, *where we may heare them.*

The ſhepheards holy-day, reduced in apt meaſures to Hobbinalls Galliard, or Iohn to the May-pole.

Forth of a curious Spinet *graced with the beſt rarities of Art and Nature,* Mopſus *a ſhepheard, and* Marina *a ſhepheardeſſe, ſinging a Nuptiall hymne in the way to the Bridall.*

Opſo. *Come* Marina *let's away,*
For both Bride *and* Bridegroome *ſtay,*
Fie for ſhame are Swaines ſo long,
Pinning of their head-geare on?
  Pray thee ſee,
  None but we,
Mongſt the Swaines are left vnreadie,
  Fie, make haſt,
  Bride is paſt,
Follow me and I will leade thee.
           T   Mar.

Mar. *On my louely* Mopsus, *on,*
I am readie, all is done,
From my head vnto my foote,
I am fitted each way to't ;
    Buskins gay,
    Gowne of gray,
  Best that all our flocks do render,
    Hat of stroe,
    Platted through,
  Cherrie lip and middle slender.

Mop. *And I thinke you will not find*
Mopsus *any whit behind,*
For he loues as well to go,
As most part of shepheards do.
    Cap of browne,
    Bottle-crowne,
  With the leg I won at dancing,
    And a pumpe
    Fit to iumpe,
  When we shepheards fall a prancing.

And I know there is a sort,
Will be well prouided for't,
For I heare, there will be there
Luueliest Swaines within the Shere :
    Ietting Gill,
    Iumping Will,
  Ore the floore will haue their measure :
    Kit *and* Kate,
    There will waite,
  Tib *and* Tom *will take their pleasure.*
                                  Mar.

Mar. *But I feare;*
Mop. *What doeſt thou feare?*
Mat. Crowd *the fidler is not there:*
And my mind delighted is,
With no ſtroake ſo much as his.
    Mop. *If not he,*
      There will be
  Drone *the piper that will trounce it.*
    Mar. *But if* Crowd,
      Strucke aloud,
  Lord me thinks how I could bounce it!

Mop. *Bounce it* Mall, *I hope thou will,*
For I know that thou haſt skill,
And I am ſure thou there ſhalt find,
Meaſures ſtore to pleaſe thy mind;
    Roundelayes,
    Iriſh-hayes,
  Cogs and rongs and Peggie Ramſie,
    Spaniletto,
    The Venetto,
  Iohn come kiſſe me, Wilſons fancie.

Mar. *But of all there's none ſo ſprightly*
To my eare, as tutch me lightly:
For it's this we ſhepheards loue,
Being that which moſt doth moue;
    There, there, there,
    To a haire,
  O Tim Crowd, *me thinks I heare thee,*
    Young nor old,
    Nere could hold,
  But muſt leake *if they come nere thee.*

Mop. *Blush* Marina, *fie for shame,*
Blemish not a shepheard's name;
Mar. Mopsus *why, is't such a matter,*
Maids *to shew their yeelding nature?*
  O what then,
  Be ye men,
That will beare your selues so froward,
  When you find
  Vs inclin'd,
To your bed *and* boord *so toward?*

Mop. *True indeed, the fault is ours,*
Though we tearme it oft-times yours;
Mar. *What would shepheards haue vs do,*
But to yeeld when they do wo?
  And we yeeld
  Them the field,
And endow them with our riches.
  Mop. *Yet we know,*
  Oft-times too,
You'le not sticke to weare the breches.

Mar. *Fooles they'le deeme them, that do heare them*
Say, their wiues are wont to weare them:
For I know there's none has wit,
Can endure or suffer it;
  But if they
  Haue no stay,
Nor discretion (as tis common)
  Then they may
  Giue the sway,
As is fitting to the woman.
                                            Mop.

Mop. *All too long* (deare loue) *I weene,*
Haue we ſtood vpon this theame:
Let each laſſe, *as once it was,*
·*Loue her* Swaine, *and* Swaine *his* laſſe :
    So ſhall we
    Honor'd be,
In our mating, in our meeting,
    While we ſtand
    Hand in hand,
Honeſt Swainling, *with his* Sweeting.

Dor. *How ſay you* ſhepheards, *ſhall we all repaire*
Vnto this wedding, *to allay our care?*
Dym. *Agreed for me.*
Tech. *And I am well content.*
Cor. *On then, let's make our life a merriment.*
Sap. *See where they come !*
May Hymen *aye defend them.*
Lin. *And far more ioy then I haue had God ſend them.*

FINIS.

T 3

OMPHALE,
OR,
THE INCONSTANT
SHEPHEARDESSE.

Perijſſem, niſi perijſſem.

LONDON,
Printed for RICHARD
WHITAKER.
1621.

To her in whofe chaft breaft
choifeft vertues, as in their
Abſtract, are feated :

The accomplifhd Lady P. W. *wife to the*
Nobly-defcended S.T.W. Knight :
and daughter to the much
honoured, S.R.C.

*All correfpondence to her worthieft
wifhes.*

OMPHALE,
OR,
THE INCONSANT
SHEPHEARDESSE.

N bondage free, in freedome bound
    I am,
A hopeleſſe, hapleſſe, loue-ſicke,
    life-ſicke man;
When I write ought, ſtreight loue
    preuenteth me,
And bids me write of nought but Omphale:
When I ride Eaſt, my heart is in the Weſt,
Lodg'd in the center of her virgin-breaſt.
The homelieſt cell would chearefull ſeeme to me,
If I in it might liue with Omphale.
My youth growes ag'd, for though I'me in my prime,
Loue hath made furrowes in this face of mine;
So as laſt day (aye me vnhappie elfe)
Looking in th' glaſſe, I ſcarce could know my ſelfe.
And I, from whom theſe ſharpe extreames did grow,
Was not content, but I muſt tell her too,
Which made her *proud*, for few or none there are,
(If women) but they'r proud if they be faire.
All this laſt Sommer hath it bene my hap,
To ſport, toy, play, and wanton in her lap,

                      And

And euer th'more I plaid, if so I could,
Or strength admitted meanes, the more I would:
For truth confirmes that Maxime, *where we find*
A louing, loyall, well-disposed mind,
Prest for encounter, there we loue to plant,
Feeding on Loues delights in midst of want;
For Loue contemnes all want, and counts't a gaine,
To purchase one houres ioy with two yeares paine.
Alas how oft (too oft thou well may say)
Haue I in priuate spent with her *the day,*
Inuoking th' Sunne, plants, heauen, and earth and all,
If fall I should, she did procure my fall?
And still she vow'd, and bit her lip, and slept
Apart from me, and wip'd her eyes and wept,
And stood and chid, and call'd me most vniust,
To harbour in my bosome such distrust.
And I (too credulous I) as one dismaid,
Was forced to recant what I had said,
Swearing I was resolu'd that th' constancie,
Of *Hypemnestra *match'd not* Omphale.
Thus did I gull my selfe to sooth my loue,
Who prou'd a Serpent, *though she seem'd a* Doue:
For vowes, protests, and all that she had spoken,
Were by her light affection quickly broken.
And whence came this? not fr̄o me, heauen thou knowes,
But from my loue who triumphs in my woes;
My loue; raze out that name: she was indeed,
When thou *and* she *your lambkins vs'd to feede*
On Arnus *flowrie banks, being wont to make*
Posies and nosegaies for her shepheards sake,
And bind them to his hooke; *but let that passe,*
She is not she *nor time the same it was.*

* *Or Hypermnestra, one of the fiftie daughters of Danaus, who out of a tender nuptiall affectiō, saued her husband Lynceus from that great slaughter which was committed by her sisters, in slaying their husbands.*

For

For then (ô then) fufpicious eyes were free,
And none but heauenly bodies lookt on thee;
(Too faire fpectators,*) though we now and then*
Difpence with Gods fight rather then with men.
And can fhe thinke on this and not relent,
Or thinking not of this, can fhe confent
To leaue Admetus? *Yes, why can fhe not!*
Now loues fhe Cloris, *and I feare his lot*
Will proue as fatall, for her very eye
Tells me fhe meanes to tread her fhoe awry.
And this I faw before, and durft not fee,
For th' loue I bore to her, perfwaded me
She could not be fo thankeleffe, as requite
My faithfull feruice with fuch ftrange defpite:
Yet I perceiu'd, not by fufpicious feare,
But by the Organs both of eye and eare,
That loue was fained which to me fhe bore,
Referuing others *to fupply her ftore.*
And I confeffe in th' end I iealous grew,
For fome *had many fauours, I but few;*
Others *had fmiles, I frownes, fo as I fay,*
I found her former fancie fall away,
Which gaue increafe to griefe, caufe to my eye
To looke into her fteps more narrowly;
So as poore foole (fo vainely did I erre)
I thought each bufh *did play th' Adulterer,*
So violent was this paffion; which to fhow,
Though of Actæons *there be ftore enow,*
I briefly meane, (and let all others paffe)
To tell you how my iealous humour was.
Each thing I ey'd, did reprefent to me,
The louely feature of my Omphale,

                                                                     Yet

Yet ſo, as ſtill that precious forme I ſaw,
Did by attractiue power another draw,
To make her forme more complete, for we know,
Number can ne're conſiſt of leſſe then two.
Streight did I ſee, (ſuſpition made me ſee)
My ſelfe made cuckold in a phantaſie,
Which in my thoughts ſuch deepe impreſſion tooke,
As now and then I threw away my booke,
Calling my ſelfe an Aſſe, to pore on that
Which gaue my wench time to cornute my pate;
And to confirme the height of my diſgrace,
Suffer the riſing of her common place.
Sometimes in ſilent nights, when hoarie care
Is charm'd aſleepe, and men exempted are
From day-bred paſſions, would I ſtart from bed,
And ſweare, the night had me diſhonoured;
While ſhe (ſleepe-lulled ſoule) did thinke no harme,
But lay entwining me with arme in arme:
Yet hearing me ſhe wakt, and chid me too,
For doing (humerous foole) what I did do,
And as ſhe chid I wept, yet inward faine,
My dreames prou'd falſe. I went to bed againe.
If I but found her in diſcourſe with any,
I ſtreight renounc'd her loue, and ſwore too many
Were factors in my Pinnace, yet one frowne
Sent from her brow, ſubdude me as her owne.
If ſhe receiu'd a letter from a friend,
I ſtreight conieɤlur'd what it did intend;
Suppoſing (vaine ſuppoſe) where th' place ſhould be,
That witneſſe might the ſhame of Omphale:
To which I vow'd reuenge, though nothing were,
But my owne thoughts that miniſtred this feare.

Oſt

Oft would I faine (for what were all my thoughts,
But fictions meerely) that she played nought
With her owne shadow, *and* Narciffus-*like,*
That in her forme she tooke such quaint delight,
As forced now to surfet on her store,
She prou'd this true: Much plentie made her poore.
Thus did her presence cause me to admire her,
Her absence like occasion to desire her;
Without whose presence, though the Sunne shone faire,
All seemed darke, because she was not there.
Last time we parted with teare-trickling eye,
Hand ioyn'd in hand right ceremonially,
I calld the heauens and sacred powers aboue,
To witnesse with me my vnfained loue,
And vow'd withall, if ere it should appeare,
I broke the faith which I had plight to her,
Or entred any bed lasciuiously,
Intending to play false with Omphale,
Or entertain'd least thought of disrespect
To her *or* hers *in nature of neglect,*
Or euer cancell'd th' deed, which (heauens you know,
Was seal'd and was deliuer'd twixt vs two)
Or euer chang'd my fancie, to deuide
My shared loue vnto another Bride,
Or ere disclaim'd what I in secret vow'd,
Or disallow what Hymen *had allow'd;*
If this or that, or any of these all,
Should censure me of lightnesse, that my fall
Might recompence my shame (which heauens forbid)
And this I vow'd to do, and this I did.
Nor did she *spare to second me in this,*
But wish'd if ere she chanc'd to do amisse,

With

With an intent of ill, or violate
Those solemne hests our loues had consummate,
Or stain'd that spousall rest, *that* blest repose,
Where two encountred, yet were neither foes;
Or disesteem'd my loue, or prized it
Lesse then a constant louer did befit,
Or let one day or night passe carelesly,
Without recalling me to memory,
Or giue occasion to the world to say,
She loues another when her loue's away,
Or entertaine a fauour, *or descry*
Least of affection by alluring eye,
Or riot in my absence, or consort
With any that might blemish her report,
Or frequent publicke presence, which might moue
A subiect *for varietie of loue:*
If this *or* that, *or any should begin*
To taxe her life, might vengeance plague her sinne.
Thus we both vow'd, and thus we parted too,
But heare how soone my loue infring'd her vow;
No sooner had the region *of the* West,
Remou'd me from my loue, and rest me rest,
Where steepie mountaines ragged and vneuen,
Ossa *and* Pelion-*like do menace heauen,*
Where scalpie hils and sandie vales imply,
The ploughmans toile's requited slenderly;
Where their course feeding and their homely fare,
Makes their wits lumpish, and their bodies spare:
Then she (inconstant she) forgot me cleane,
And all her vowes, as if I had not bene.
Distance of place, made distance in our loue,
And as my body mou'd, her loue did moue

From

From her first center: thus euen in my Prime,
Did my loue change, when I did change my clime.
Thus like blind Cupids *ball (by fancie crost)*
Was I to euery hazard strangely tost;
Thus was my seruice guerdon'd with disgrace,
While Cloris *crept into* Admetus *place:*
And can her height of sinne be thus forgot?
No, wanton no, who is it knowes it not?
So as thy crime thy nature will display,
And make thy storie worse then Cressida,
Who in contempt of faith, (as we do reade)
Reiected Troilus *for* Diomede!
Canst thou make shew of loue to me or any,
That art expos'd to louing of so many?
Canst thou haue heart to vow, when thou forsooke,
And didst infringe the oath which thou first tooke?
Canst thou haue face to come in open light,
That hast incurr'd reuenge in his pure sight,
Whose vengeance thou inuok't? canst thou repaire
Vnto thy sex, or taste the common ayre,
Hauing, (by making of thy faith so common)
Infected th' ayre, *impeach'd the* Sex *of women?*
Canst thou looke on that faithlesse hand of thine,
And giue it to another being mine?
Canst thou, and see that face, not blush to see
Those teares thou shed, and vowes thou made to me?
Or canst embrace another in thy bed,
Hearing thy first *espoused friend not dead?*
Suppose I should surprize thee, could I long
Restraine my hand, and not reuenge my wrong?
Could I allay my passion vnexprest,
Or see th' Adulterer *sleepe within thy brest?*

            Could

OMPHALE.

Could I endure my bed *should be abus'd,*
Or see her strumpeted, whom I had chus'd?
Could I content my selfe to see my shame,
And coward-like, not to redresse the same?
No, no insatiate thou, sooner could time
Leaue his gradation, or the Sunne *to shine,*
Light bodies to ascend and leaue their center,
Riuers their downeward course, then I should venter
My patience on that odds: but foolish I,
That gaue no credit to mine eare or eye,
But made my senses *all* Cassandra'es, *where*
Mine eare *presag'd, yet I'de not trust mine* eare:
Such strange distempers doth this Circe *breed,*
This phrensie-*fancie in a louers head,*
That though he heare, see, taste, *and* touch, & smell
His loues vnkindnesse, yet he dare not tell,
But must renounce th' instruction of all these.
Yea, (euen himselfe) that he his wench may please.
O why should man tearme woman th' weaker kind,
Since they are stronger, *as we daily find,*
In will, *and* head, *although their husbands browes,*
Oft to a harder kind of temper growes?
So as for all that we do style them weaker,
They oft become to be their husbands maker!
But now Admetus, *wilt thou pine and die,*
And waste thy selfe for her inconstancie?
Wilt thou lament the losse of such an one,
As hath resolu'd to keepe her faith with none?
Or canst thou dote on her, *that longs to be*
Affected of each youth that she doth see?
No, no Admetus, *since she proues vntrue,*
Shed not one teare nor sigh, for none is due,

But

OMPHALE.

But offer Pan *the chiefe of all thy flocke,*
That thou art rid of such a weathercocke.
Now maist thou pipe vpon thy oaten reede,
Whilest thy Mug-sheepe *on* Arnus *pastures feede:*
Where bonnie Clytus *will attend on thee,*
And Mopsus *too will keepe thee companie.*
There the late-freed Capnus *will repaire,*
And ioy to taste the freedome *of the ayre;*
Where he will descant on no rurall theame,
But on Ambitions *curbe,* the golden meane.
And ioy he may, for who did euer heare
Such alterations as in him *appeare?*
Where long restraint hath labour'd to restore
That loue *to* him *which he had lost before.*
With whom Admetus *may in consort ioyne,*
Comparing of your fortunes one by one;
He to regaine the loue *which he had lost,*
Thou to forget her loue that wrong'd thee most.
And well would this befeeme Admetus *straine,*
" For shepheards should not laugh at others paine,
But in compassion of their grieues and them,
To imitate their passions *in the same.*
And this's a better course, and safer too,
Then to do that which thou so late didst do,
Pining and puling, wishing death *appeare,*
Which for thy wishes was no whit the neare.
" For death (whē we are happie) will come nie vs,   Iole in Oet. Her.
" But if we wretched be, then death will flie vs.
How oft hath my experience made this good,
When wishing death, I was by death withstood?
For still I thought my woes would haue an end   * Mors sola portus, dabitur
If *Death *arriu'd, afflictions welcome friend.*   ærumnis locus. ibid. Deian.

U   But

But th' more I sought, the more he *fled from me,*
To make me riper in my miserie:
" For griefe is of that nature, as it growes
" In age, so new effects it daily showes.
Yet now thou *liues (and thanks to th' powers aboue)*
Hast neare by this, suppress the thoughts of loue.
Now canst thou feed, *and* sleepe, *and* laugh, *& talke,*
Sport, *and tell tales, refresh thy selfe, and walke*
In flowrie Meedes, whilest thou seest Cloris *hing*
His iealous head to heare the Cuckow sing.
Alas (poore man) what bondage is he in,
To serue a Swaine that's cauteriz'd in sin,
Expos'd to shame, and prostitute to lust,
In whom nor's grace, nor faith, nor loue, nor trust?
And heauen I wish, she may in time reclaime
He'r former course, and rectifie the same:
But th' Pumice stone will hardly water yeeld,
Or grace appeare in such a barren field :
For such light mates *encompasse her about,*
As Vertue's choak't before it can take roote.
O Cloris, *if thou knew* Admetus *mind,*
And th' hard conceit he h'as of womankind,
Whose fairest lookes, *are* lures, affections, baits,
Words, wind, vowes, vaine, *and their* protests deceits,
Songs, charms, teares, traines *to trace vs to our end,*
Smiles, snares, frowns, fears, *which to our ruine tend:*
Then wouldst thou (Cloris) *censure* Omphale,
The pregnant mirror of inconstancie,
And curbe thy fancie, ere it haue least part
In one *can vow so often with one heart.*
For heare me (Cloris) *she did neuer show*

More

More loue to thee, *then she to others too:*
Yet what art thou (if man) maist build thee more
Vpon her faith then others did before?
What art thou canst perswade thy selfe of this,
She'le not tread right, h'as trod so long amisse,
Or that she'le now proue constant, that h'as prou'd,
So faithlesse to the most, that she has lou'd?
No, Cloris, *no, the* Prouerbe *it is true,*
And is confirm'd in her whom thou doest sue;
" To wash the Moore, is labouring in vaine,
" For th'colour that he h'as, is di'd in graine.
So th'more thou striues to make her blacknes *white,*
Thou drawes heauens curtaine to display her night.
Her night *indeed, saue that no starres appeare,*
(No lights of grace) within her hemi-spheare,
But th'changing Moone, whose lightnesse doth expresse
That light-inconstant mind of Omphales :
" *Where* Vertue *seemes at* Nature *to complaine,*
" *That* vice *should be at* full, *and she at* waine.
Yet Nature answers, she h'as done her part,
And that the fault is rather in her heart,
That is so spacious, to entertaine
The wauering loue of euery wanton Swaine.
And I assent to Nature, for it's showne,
By her rare workemanship, what she h'as done,
In giuing beautie lustre, her *content ;*
In forming her, her selfe to represent.
And reason good ; for when I thinke vpon,
That Zeuxes, Phydias, *and* Pigmalion,
(Those natiue artists) *who indeed did striue*
To make their curious statues *seeme aliue,*
Reducing art *to* Nature ; *then I find,*

U 2 *Nature*

*Nature had cause to satisfie her mind
In something aboue* art, *that after-time
Might moue* her *to reioyce,* art *to repine.
And what more mouing* patterne *could there be,
Then the admired forme of* Omphale,
Whose feature equall'd Nature, *and did show
The very* Spring *whence fancie's said to flow?
For first her stature's seemely, which I call,
Neither too dwarfish low, nor giant-tall;
Her* front *a rising mount, her* eyes *two lamps,
Which, wheresoere she lookes impression stamps;
Her* cheeke *twixt rosie red and snowie white,
Attracts an admiration with delight;
Her* nose *nor long nor short, nor high nor low,
Nor flat, nor sharpe, the token of a shrow;
Her* mouth *nor ferret-straite, nor callet-broade,
But of an apt proportion, as it should;
Her* breath *the fragrant odour, which loue sips
From these two cherrie portels of her lips;
Where those two iuory pales or rowes of teeth,
Accent her speech, perfumed by her breath;
Her* chin *th' inclining vale, deuided is,
By th' daintie dimple of loues choisest blisse,
Which, as maine flouds from smallest currents flow,
Deriues her sweets to th' riuelings below;
Her* necke *a rocke enazur'd with pure veines
Of orient pearle, which with amorous chaines
Of lou's desir'd embraces, charmes the eye,
And tyes it to her* obiect, *when she's by;
Her* breasts *two Orbs or Mounts, or what you will
That may include perfection, which to fill
The world with admiration, are layd out,*

To

To worke the feate her lightnesse *goes about;*
Two prettie nipples, one oppos'd gainst t'other,
Challenge the name of Nurse *aswell as Mother:*
Though some (for state makes loue to children worse)
Scorne, being mothers to become their nurse.
In briefe her *all, (because I'le not descend,*
In praise of that, *where praises haue no end)*
Is beauties faire Idæa, *which implies*
Height of content, to loues amazed eyes.
And yet this she, *the modell of delight,*
Though outward faire, seemes to my inward sight,
As spotted as the Ermine, *whose smooth skin,*
Though it be faire without, is foule within.
For what more foule then vice? *but chiefly that*
Which makes a woman to degenerate,
From her more shamefast Sex, where modestie
Should sit vpon her cheeke, *to verifie*
What th'Comick said: *straid thoughts find neuer (rest,
"*But shamefast lookes become a woman best.*
Indeed they do; for there is greater sence,
That shame *should moue man more then* impudence;
For bashfull lookes adde fuell to loues fire,
While th'spirit of lust *doth with her flame expire.*
Which makes me wonder, that th' interiour light
Whence man resembles God, should lose his sight,
By doting on an Idoll, that can take
To charme loues dazled eyes a Syrens *shape,*
Making Art *vye with* Nature *for the best,*
And foiling that which should surpasse the rest.
For what is faire, *if that be all there is,*
But an eye-pleasing thing, that yeelds no blisse,
Wanting that inward faire, *which who enioyes,*

* Errant, nec
sedem repetunt
serenam Quæ
petulanti corde
resurgunt, &c.

Esteemes

Esteemes all outward ornaments as toyes,
Compared to that beauty, which no Art
Could euer equall, or expresse in part?
Indeed the grace of vertue is more rare,
And exquisite, when she *that's good is faire,*
For she *becomes most complete well we know,*
That's grac'd with vertue and with beautie too.
Whence that experienst [*] *Morall vs'd to reach*
A looking glasse to such as he did teach;
Wherein, if such were faire themselues did eye,
He would exhort them rather to apply
Their minds to vertue, for great pittie twere,
Foule soules *(quoth he)* should haue a face so faire:
But if deform'd, he streight would counsell them,
With wholesome precepts to supply the same;
For fit it were *(quoth he)* a face so foule,
Should be prouided of a beauteous soule.
But rare's this composition, for we find,
Seldome that double blisse in woman-kind,
Where she *that's faire can soone admire her owne,*
And knowes what Nature for her selfe hath done:
Yea she by this can learne another straine,
Put on coy looks, and th'fashion of disdaine, (breath,
Minf-speech, huff-pace, sleeke-skin, *and* perfum'd
Goats-haire, brests-bare, plume-fronted, fricace-
All which infuse new motions into man, (teeth,
Late borrow'd of th' Italian Curtezan.
But now to thee *thou wanton, will I come,*
To taxe, not visit that polluted tombe,
Of all infection, which to giue it due,
Is now become no Temple *but a* stue;
Tell me, disdainfull faire, if I ere wrong'd,

Or

[*] Socrates.

Or thee, *or any that to thee belong'd!*
Haue I incurr'd dishonour, or deuoted
My loue to many, whereby I am noted?
Haue I bene too profuse in my respect,
To otherfome, and blancht thee with neglect?
Haue I incurr'd a merited difgrace,
In begging loue when thou was out of place?
Haue I by courting any, ere expreft,
My felfe ought leffe then what I ftill profeft?
Didft euer fee a fauour worne by me,
But that poore bracelet *I receiu'd of thee,*
Twifted with gold, and with thy faithleffe haire,
Which now I'ue throwne away with all my care?
Did I ere vow and breake, as thou haft done,
Or plight my faith (faue thee) to any one?
Why then fhouldft thou infringe that facred oath,
Which with a kiffe was fealed to vs both,
When fcarce one houre *did vs occafion giue,*
(So fhort was time) to take our lafting leaue?
But I can gueffe where thou wilt lay the blame;
Not on thy felfe, *but on* them *whence thou came.*
That luftfull flocke *I meane, which gaue beginning*
To thee of being firft, and then of finning.
It's true indeed, we know a poifoned fpring,
Can feld or neuer wholefome water bring,
Nor can we looke that any barren field,
Should ought faue tares *or fruitleffe Darnell yeeld:*
For this from Scripture may collected be,
" Such as the fruite is, fuch is ftill the tree.
Too late I find this true, and heauens I wifh,
My former harmes may caution me *of this;*
For what is ill defcendeth in a blood,

Sooner

Sooner and surer too, then what is good.
" For th'fathers vertues still attend his bere,
" And being dead, with him lie buried there;
" But th'vices which he had are not content
" To die with him, but liue in his descent.
*So natiue is thy ill, hauing her birth
From that corrupted* stock *which brought thee forth,
As sooner may the Æthiope become white,
Th' Cymmerian pitchie shade transparent light,
The* Tiger *leaue his nature, th'*Wolfe *his prey,
The* Sunne *to guide the chariot of the day,
The* * Pellican *her desart, or the* * Craine,
That nat'rall loue which in her doth remaine
Vnto her parents; then thy parents shame,
Got by their* sinne, *be wiped from thy name.
No wanton, no, thy darknesse is displayd,
Which can by no meanes re-disperse her shade,
But shall suruiue all time; for it's the will
Of Powers aboue,* there should be life in ill,
As well as good: *that th' memory of the first
Might make succeeding ages count her curst.
For I haue red (and thou was cause I red)
Some fickle* Dames *in stories mentioned,
Whose small respect to th' honour of their name,
Hath made them since the lasting* heires *of shame:
And such were* Messalina, Martia,
Faustina, Lays, Claudia, * Portia,
*Two of which name there were of different kind,
In th' various disproportion of their mind;*
" *One good, one ill, one light, one constant prouing,*
" *One spousall-lothing, one her honour louing.*
But which of these *can equall* Omphale?

             Or

---

* Queis pario perio; quod acerbæ prolis imago Extitit, & teneræ nota parentis erit. vid. Alcyat.
* Quæ parenti confecto ætate consulit, eique præstando natale officium, proprijs alis gerit. vid. Basil. in Homil.

* Portia the famous Curtizan; and that noble Ladie, an eminent patterne of modestie, wife to Port. Cato the Senatour.

Or which of these *liue more licentiously?*
All patternes in their time (as well they might)
And cautions too, to moue vs tread aright
That do succeed them: yet obserue this staine,
This wedlocks-blemish, and you will complaine,
Of th' present times, that they'r more ripe in sinne,
And breach of faith, then former times haue bin.
More ripe *indeed, for where's that age become,*
" Folke di'd for loue, as we haue red of some,
Who their affections so implanted haue,
As nought could bury fancie but their graue?
But these were childish times; indeed they were,
For rather then for her *I'de shed one teare,*
That disesteemes my loue, or send one grone,
Or sigh, or sob, or pule, or make a mone,
Or fold my armes, as forlorne louers vse,
Or grieue to lose, when she doth others chuse,
Or breake my sleepe, or take a solemne fast,
I wish that taske *might be* Admetus *last.*
No Omphale, *though time was when I mourn'd,*
That time is chang'd, and now my humour's turn'd;
So as I scarce remember what thou art,
That once lay neare and deare vnto my heart.
Now is my Pasture *greene and flourishing,*
And poore Melampus *which was wont to hing*
His heauie head (kind curre) for's maisters sake,
Begins his sullen humour to forsake.
Now is my bottle mended, and my hooke,
My bag, my pipe, so as if thou should looke,
And see Admetus *with his woollie store,*
Thou'de say, he were not th' man he was before;
And iudge him too, (to see him now reuiue,

And

*And change his note) the happieſt man aliue.
And ſo I am, to liue and leaue to loue,*
(Though faithfull mates would flinty natures
Whoſe rare effects the Poet *ſeemes to ſhow,*   moue)
When wiues expreſſe th'affections which they owe.
" * Turtle with Turtle, husband with his mate,
" In diſtinct kindes one loue participate.
*But ſince affection is ſo rare to find,
Where th'face weares not the liuerie of the mind,
And womans vowes (as* * *th*'Satyre *rightly ſaith)
Be rather made for complement then faith ;*
Be free from loue Admetus : *if not free,
At leaſt* from loue of ſuch as Omphale.

* Turture ſic turtur iungit amanda ſuo.

* Sic iurare ſolent, ſed non feruare puellæ. *Lucian.*

FINIS.

A Poem defcribing the leuitie of a
woman: referuing all generous refpect
to the vertuoufly affected of
that Sexe.

Irft I feare not to offend,
A very thing of nothing,
Yet whom thus farre I commend,
She's lighter then her clothing:
Nay from the foote vnto the crowne,
Her very Fan will weigh her downe:
And marke how all things with her Sexe agree,
For all her vertues are as light as fhe.

1.

She chats and chants but ayre,
A windie vertue for the eare,
T'is lighter farre then care,
And yet her fongs do burthens beare.

2.

She dances, that's but mouing,
No heauie vertue here fhe changes,
And as her heart in louing,
So her feete in conftant ranges.

She foftly leanes on ftrings,
She ftrikes the trembling lute and quauers:

Thefe

These are no weightie things,
Her strokes are light, so are her fauours.
Those are her vertues fitting to her kind,
No sooner showne, but they turnd all to wind.

Then to you, O Sexe of fethers,
On whose browes sit all the wethers,
I send my Passion weau'd in rimes,
To weigh downe these light emptie times.

Descript.

What are you, O heires of scorning,
But like Dew that melts each morning;
Euening vapours, and nights prize,
To answer our voluptuous eyes:
And but to screene that sinnes delight,
I thinke there neuer had bene night.

Nor had we bene from vertue so exempt,
But that the tempter did leaue you to tempt.
You bit the Apple first that makes vs die,
Wheres'ere we looke the apple's in our eye,
And death must gather it; for your turn'd breath,
And mortall teeth e'en to the core strucke death.

FINIS.

HIS ODES:
OR,
PHILOMELS
TEARES.

Odes *in ſtraines of ſorrow tell
Fate and fall of euery* fowle,
Mounting Merlin, Philomel,
Lagging Lapwing, Swallow, Owle;
*Whence you may obſerue how ſtate
Rais'd by* pride, *is raz'd by* hate.

LONDON,
Printed for Richard Whitaker.
1621.

TO THE G,ENEROVS,
INGENIOVS, AND IVDICIOVS
PHILALETHIST, *Thomas Ogle* Esquire: the
succeeding issue of his diuinest wishes.

Nknowne to you I am, yet knowne I am
To th'better part of you, your vertuous
   name;
Which like a precious odour *hath infus'd*
Your loue *so much in* me, *as I haue chus'd*
Your selfe, to patronize what I haue writ,
Whose name I thought had power to shelter it.
I grant indeed, Smooth * Eagle *for your* name,
Includes that Sun-reflecting (Anagram)
These birds *which in my* Odes *their fates display,*
Are some *night-birds, as* others *of the day;*
Which in my iudgement, tenders more delight,
To see how sin's orecurtained by night,
Whereas the day *sends forth his golden raies,*
And shewes such birds *as chant their* maker's *praise.*
Which Morall, *as it suites these times of ours,*
I do disclaime my right in't, it is yours,
If you esteeme it worthie to obtaine
Your approbation : This is all our ayme.

* Sic tereti cursu
repetit spiracu-
la montis
Aquila, quæ
valles spernit,
vt alta petat.
Sol radios mit-
tit, radiosq; re-
flectit ocellis;
Aquila sis visu
semper (Amice)
tuo. *Alcyat. in*
Emblem. Samb.
ibid. Plin. in Nat.
Hist. Ælian.
ibid. Greg. in
Mor. expo. in
Iob.

R. B.

THE
TRAVELLOVR,
DILATING VPON THE
sundrie changes of humane affaires,
most fluctuant when appearing
most constant.

AN ODE.

Ell me man, what creature may
Promise him such safe repose,
As secure from hate of foes,
He may thus much truly say,
Nought I haue I feare to lose,
No mischance can me dismay;
Tell me, pray thee (if thou can)
If the *woreld* haue such a man!

Tell me, if thou canst discerne
By thy reasons excellence,
What man for his prouidence,
Of the *Pismire* may not learne:
Yet that creature hath but sense,
Though she do her liuing earne,
Spare, not costly, is her fare,
Yet her *granar* shewes her care!

Tell me, canſt thou ſhew me him,
That exact in each deuice,
Is at all times truly wiſe,
And is neuer ſeene to ſwim
(For in this his iudgement lies)
Gainſt the current of the ſtreame,
But ſeemes to haue full command,
Of each thing he takes in hand!

Tell me, was there euer knowne
Such a man that had a wit,
And in ſome part knew not it,
Till at laſt conceited growne,
He grew prowder then was fit,
Euer boaſting of his owne;
For that *Maxime* true we know,
" *He that's wittie, knowes him ſo!*

Tell me, is that *man* on earth,
Whoſe affaires ſo ſtable are,
As they may for all his care,
Fall not croſſe and crabdly forth,
And of ſorrowes haue no ſhare,
Which deſcend to man by birth;
What is he can promiſe reſt,
When his mind's with griefe oppreſt!

Tell me, is there ought ſo ſtrong,
Firmely-conſtant, permanent,
Or on *earth* ſuch true content,
As it fadeth not ere long:
Is there ought ſo excellent,

As

As it changeth not her fong,
And in *time* that all deuoures,
Mixeth fweets with fharpeft foures !

Tell me, who is he that fhines
In the height of Princes loue,
Sitting minion-like with *Ioue*,
Glorying in thofe golden times,
But he feares fomething may moue
His diftaft by whom *He* climbes :
Wherefore he that feares to fall,
Should forbeare to climbe at all !

Tell me, where is *Fortune* plac'd,
That fhe may not men beguile,
Shrowding frownes with fained fmile ;
Where is *He* fo highly grac'd,
Shewing greatneffe in his ftile,
Hath not bene in time out-fac'd,
By fome *riuall*, where ftill one
Striues to put another downe !

Tell me, then what life can be
More fecure, then where report
Makes vs onely knowne to th' Court,
Where we leade our liues fo free,
As we're ftrangers to refort,
Saue our priuate familie ;
For I thinke that *dwelling beft*,
Where leaft cares difturbe our reft !

THE NIGHTINGALL.

2. *ODE.*

Vg, *IVg;* faire fall the *Nightingall*,
    Whofe tender breaſt
Chants out *her* merrie *Madrigall*,
    With *hawthorne* preſt:
Te'u, Te'u, thus ſings ſhe euen by euen,
And reprefents the melodie in heauen;
  T'is, T'is,
   I am not as I wiſh.

Rape-defiled *Phylomel*
  In her ſad miſchance,
Tells what ſhe is forc'd to tell,
  While the *Satyres* dance:
Vnhappie I, quoth ſhe, vnhappie I,
That am betraide by *Tereus* trecherie;
  T'is, T'is,
   I am not as I wiſh.

Chaſt-vnchaſt, defloured, yet
  Spotleſſe in heart,
Luſt was all that *He* could get,
  For all his art:
For I nere attention lent
To his ſuite, nor gaue conſent;
  T'is, T'is,
   I am not as I wiſh.

                          Thus

Thus hath faithleſſe *Tereus* made
  Heartleſſe *Phylomele*
Mone her in her forlorne ſhade,
  Where griefe I feele :
Griefe that wounds *me* to the heart,
Which though gone, hath left her ſmart;
  T'is, T'is,
  I am not as I wiſh.

THE LAPWING.

3. ODE.

Vnhappie I to change my *aeric* neſt,
For this ſame *mariſh* dwelling where I reſt,
  Wherfore my ſong while I repeate,
    I'le cloſe it vp ;
    Rue yet, rue yet.

Euery Cowheard driuing his beaſts to graze,
Diſturbs my reſt, *me* from my *neſt* doth raiſe,
  Which makes my young take vp this ſong,
    To wreake my wrong ;
    Rue yet, rue yet.

Thou ſubtile *Stockdoue* that haſt cheated me,
By taking vp thy *neſt* where I ſhould be,
  Haſt me and mine in perill ſet,

Whose song is fit;
Rue yet, rue yet.

Solely-retired, see I liue alone,
Farre from recourse or sight of any *one*,
  And well that life would suite with me,
    Were I but free;
    Rue yet, rue yet.

Young-ones I haue, that thinking I am fled,
Do leaue their *nest*, and run with *shell* on *head*,
  And hauing found *me* out *we* cry,
    Both they and I;
    Rue yet, rue yet.

Crest-curled mates why do you beare so long
The *Stockdoues* pride, that triumphs in your wrong
  Let vs our signals once display,
    And make him say;
    Rue yet, rue yet.

Too tedious hath our bondage bene I wis,
And onely patience was the cause of this,
  Where if we would contract our power,
    We'de sing no more;
    Rue yet, rue yet.

March on then brauely, as if *Mars* were here,
And hate no guest so much as *slauish feare*,
  Let the proud *Stockdoue* feele your wing,
    That he may sing;
    Rue yet, rue yet.

                                        Let

Let none escape, though they submissiue seeme,
Till you haue spoil'd and quite vnfether'd them,
  So you shall make them vaile the wing,
    And henceforth sing;
  Rue yet, rue yet.

THE OWLE.
4 ODE.

A Kings daughter, see what *pride* may do,
In fatall *yewe* takes vp my for-
    lorne seate,
The cause wherof was *this*, if you
    would know,
I would haue better bread then grew on wheate,
Though now a *Mouse* be all the food I eate,
And glad I am when I can feed of it.

Ruff-curled necke, see I reserue some show
Of what I was, though far from *her* I was,
Wherein my boundlesse *pride* so farre did grow,
That as in place I did the rest surpasse,
So in the purest *beautie* of my face,
Courting my selfe in fancies looking-glasse.

Milke-bathed skin, see *wantons* what I vs'd,
To make my *skin* more supple, smooth, & sleeke,

Wherein my natiue hue by *Art* abus'd,
I lay a new *complexion* on my cheeke,
Sending my *eyes* abroad futers to feeke,
And vying fafhions with each day i' th weeke.

Nought I affected more then what was rare,
" Beft things (if common) I did difefteeme,
Seld was I breathd on by the publike ayré,
" *For thofe are moft admir'd are feldome feene,*
Which is, and hath a cuftome euer bene,
" Such as come oft abroad, we vulgar deeme.

Thus felfe-admir'd I liu'd, till thus transform'd,
I got a *feature* fitting with my *pride:*
For I that fcorned others, now am fcorn'd,
Had in difgrace, and in purfuite befide;
May the like *fate* like fpirits aye betide,
So worthleffe honour fhall be foone defcride.

For *ruff* thick-fet, a curle-wreathed *plume,*
Round 'bout my necke I weare, for *tyres* of gold
A downie *tuft* of *feathers* is my crowne,
For *fan* in hand my clawes a pearch do hold,
And for thofe cates and dainties manifold,
" *A moufe I wifh, but wants her when I would.*

Be well aduis'd then *Minions,* what you do,
" Portray my *feature,* and make *vfe* of it,
What fell to *me* may likewife fall to you,
And then how daring-high fo ere you fit,
Nought but difhonour fhall your *pride* begit,
" Dead to report of *Vertue* as is fit.

THE

THE MERLIN.

5. *ODE*.

Hence *Nisus*, whence,
   Is this the fate of kings,
For arme on Scepter,
   To be arm'd with wings?
Poore speckled *bird*, see how aspiring may
Degrade the high, and their estate betray.

  Once Fortune made
   Nisus her fauorite,
  And rer'd his throne
   To such vnbounded height,
That forreine states admir'd what *he* possest,
Till slie *ambition* nestled in his breast.

  Till then how blest,
   And after see how base
  His *greatnesse* fell,
   When reft of Princely grace;
Those many fleering *Parasites* he gain'd,
In his successe, not one in want remain'd

  Chesses he weares
   Now on his downie feete,

                              Where

Where once *guilt spurs*,
　　With store of pearle set
Adorn'd his nimble heeles, and *hooded* now,
His *beuer* wants: this can *ambition* do.

Vp still *he* mounts,
　　And must a pleasure bring,
　That once was king,
　　To meaner then a king;
Where *he*, who once had *Falkners* at command,
Is faine to picke his meate from *Falkners* hand.

Imperious *fate*,
　　What canst not thou effect,
　When thou perceiues
　　In man a dif-respect
Vnto thy honour, which we instanc'd see,
In no one *Nisus* better then in thee!

But *flow* bird *flow*,
　　See now the game's a foote,
　And white-maild *Nisus*,
　　He is flying to't;
Scepter, Crowne, Throne & all that Princely were
Be now reduc'd to *feathers* in the ayre.

THE

THE SWALLOW.
6. ODE.

Ou chatt'ring *Fleere*, you *Faune*,
    you *fommer-friend*,
  Not following vs, but our fuc-
    ceffe,
Will this your flatt'ring humour
    nere haue end,
Of all other meritleffe?
  Flie I fay, flie, be gone,
  Haunt not here to *Albion:*
She fhould be fpotleffe, as imports her *name*,
But fuch as *you* are borne to do her fhame.

How many faire protefts and folemne vowes,
  Can your hatefull conforts make,
Wheras (heauen knows) thefe are but only fhows
  Which you do for profit-fake?
    O then leaue our coaft and vs,
    Blemifh'd by your foule abufe,
Vertue can haue no being, nor could euer,
Where th'*Parafite* is deem'd a *happy liuer*.

Tale-tattling goffip, prone to carrie newes,
  And fuch newes are euer worft,
Where falfe report finds matter, and renewes
  Her itching humour till it burft,
                           Where

Where each euen finds tales enough,
  All the gloomie winter through,
To paſſe the night away, and oft-times tries,
That *truth* gets friendſhip ſeldomer then *lies.*

Spring-time when flowers adorne the chearefull
  And each *bird* ſings on her ſpray,   (mede,
When flowry groues with bloſſoms checkered,
  And each day ſeemes a marriage day,
    Chatt'ring *Swallow* thou canſt chuſe
    Then a time to viſit vs;
Such are theſe fained friends make much vpon vs,
When we are *rich*, but being *poore* they ſhun vs.

The ſtormie *winter* with his hoarie locks,
  When each branch hangs downe his head,
And icie flawes candies the ragged rocks,
  Making *fields* diſcoloured,
    Driues *thee* from vs and our coaſt,
    Where in *ſpring-time* thou repo'ſt;
Thus thou remaines with *vs* in our delight,
But in our diſcontent th'art out of ſight.

Time-ſeruing *humoriſt* that faunes on Time,
  And no merit doeſt reſpect,
Who will not loath that fees that vaine of thine,
  Where deſerts are in neglect,
    And the *good* is priz'd no more
    Then the *ill*, if he be poore?
Thou art the rich mans claw-backe, and depends
No more on men, then as their *trencher-friends.*

                                        Go

Go turne-taile go, we haue not here a *Spring*
   For fuch temporizing mates,
Pan's in our Ile, and he fcornes *flattering;*
   So thofe *Guardians* of our States,
     Who are early vp and late,
     And of all, this *vice* doth hate :
Flie tell-tale, flie, and if thou wilt, complaine thee,
That Albyon's harfh, and will not entertaine thee.

THE FALL OF THE LEAFE.

7. *ODE*.

*Lora* where's thy beauty now,
Thou was while'om wont to fhow?
Not a *branch* is to be feene,
Clad in *Adons* colour *greene;*
Lambkins now haue left their fkip-
Lawn-frequenting *Fauns* their tripping;   (ping,
Earths bare breaft feeles winters whipping,
And her brood the North-winds nipping.

Though the *Boxe* and *Cypreffe* tree,
Weare their wonted liuerie,
And the little *Robin* fcorne
To be danted with a ftorme,
Yet the *Shepheard* is not fo,
When *He* cannot fee for fnow,
Nor the *flocks* which he doth owe,
And in drifts are buried low.

                           Nor

Nor the *Grazer*, difcontent
That his fodder fhould be fpent,
And when winter's fcarce halfe-done,
All his ftacks of hay are gone ;
Nor the *Lawyer*, that is glad
When a *motion's* to be had,
Nor poore *Tom*, though he be mad ;
" Cold makes *Tom* a *Bedlam* fad.

Nor the *Webfter*, though his feete
By much motion get them heate,
Nor the knaue that curries leather,
Nor the crofſ-ledgg'd *Taylor* neither,
Nor at *glaſſ-worke*, where they doubt
Left their *coftly fire* go out,
Nor the carefull carking *Lout*,
That doth toyle and trudge about.

No nor th' *Ladie* in her coach,
But is muff'd when *frofts* approach,
Nor the crazie *Citizen*,
But is furrd vp to the chin,
Oifter-callet, flie *Vpholfter*,
Hooking *Huxfter*, merrie *Malfter*,
Cutting *Haxter*, courting *Roifter*,
Cunning *Sharke*, nor fharking *foifter*.

Thus we fee how *Fall of th'leafe*,
Adds to each condition griefe,
Onely two there be, whofe wit
Make hereof a benefit ;
Thefe, conclufions try on man,

Surgeon

"*Surgeon* and *Phyſician*,
While it happens now and than,
Kill then *cure* they ſooner can!

Now's their time when trees are bare,
Naked *ſcalps* haue loſt their haire,
Teeth drop out and leaue their gumms,
Head and eyes are full of rheumes,
Where if *Traders* ſtrength do lacke,
Or feele *aches* in their backe,
Worſe by odds then is the racke,
They haue *drugs* within their packe.

Thus the harſheſt ſeaſons come
In good *ſeaſon* vnto ſome,
Who haue knowne (as it is meete)
Smell of gaine makes labour ſweet:
But where labour reapeth loſſe,
There accrews a double croſſe;
Firſt, fond cares his braine doth toſſe,
Next, his gold reſolues to droſſe.

FINIS.

To my knowing and worthie esteemed friend AVGVSTINE VINCENT, all meriting content.

*Augustines
Vincentius.
Tute vincas
ingeniosus.*

May you be in
Your actions prosperous,
And as *ingenious*,
So victorious;
So may your *fate*,
Smile on your happie name,
And crowne you with,
A glorious *Anagram*:
While *Vertue*,
(Mans best lustre) seemes to be,
That *style*, which stamps
You deepe in *Heraldrie*.

BRIT.

BRITTANS BLISSE:

A Pean of thankſgiuing for our long enioyed peace vnder a gracious Soueraigne.

Eace, Plentie, Pleaſure,
Honour, Harbour, Health,
Peace, *to encreaſe*
In ſubstance and in wealth;
Plentie, *to praiſe,*
Heauens Soueraigne the more,
Pleaſure, *to ſolace vs*
Amidſt our ſtore,
Honour, *to guerdon*
Merit in our time,
Harbour, *to fit*
Each vnder his owne vine,
Health, *to enioy*
A bleſſing ſo deuine,
Deriu'd from Ieſſes *roote*
And Dauids *line.*

Health, Harbour, Honour,
Pleasure, Plentie, Peace,
Which from our Soueraigne
Haue their prime increase;
Health, *to performe*
Our distinct offices,
Harbour, *to shroud vs*
From extremities,
Honour, *to crowne*
The temples of desert,
Pleasure, *to cheare*
The intellectuall part,
Plentie, *to store*
Our hopes *with all successe,*
Peace, *to accomplish*
Our full happinesse.

All which, by heauens hand powr'd on *Albyon,*
Make vp a Catalogue to looke vpon;
That for so many quiet *Halcyon* dayes,
Her precioust *prize,* might be her Makers praise.

Pacis, honoris, amoris, Edena Britannica nostri,
Rege regente bono, leta trophæa gerit.

Vpon

*Vpon the worthie and sincere Proficients
and Professants of the common Law;
an Encomiastick Poem.*

L*Aw* is the *line*,
Whose leuell is dispatch,
A *lampe*, whose light shewes
Iustice what is right,
A *larke*, whose vnseal'd eyes
Keepes early watch,
A *loome*, whose frame
Cannot be sway'd by might,
A *list*, where truth
Puts iniury to flight;
Streight *line*, bright *lampe*,
Sweete *larke*, strong *loome*, choice *list*,
Guide, shine, shield, guard,
And liue truths Martialist.

Law is the *sterne*,
Which steares the ship of state,
The glorious *stem*
Whence *Iustice sciens* spring,
The chearefull starre,
Which early shines and late,

The *ſtaffe*, whoſe ſtay
Supports the languiſhing,
The *ſtreame*, whoſe ſpring
Is euer cheriſhing;
Rare *ſterne*, rich *ſtem*, cleare *ſtarre*,
Firme *ſtaffe*, pure *ſtreame*,
Steere, cheare, direct, ſupport,
Refreſh the *meane*.

Bleſt then are *you*,
Who labour to redreſſe
The poore mans caſe,
And meaſure your contents
By ſhielding th'weake
From awfull mightineſſe,
Like graue *Profeſſants*,
Good *Proficients*,
Clozing with *equitie*
Your ioynt conſents;
'Tis you, 'tis you,
Who in this blemiſhd time,
Send out your lights
While other ſtarrs decline.

When Greece in glory flouriſh'd,
She did reare
Some *Images* neare
Iuſtice ſacred throne,

        Which

Which to be *lame* and *blind*
Portrayed were,
As proper obiects
To be look'd vpon,
Implying what
In *Iustice* should be done;
Blind to distinguish
Friend or foe, and *lame*,
From taking bribes,
To staine *Astræas* name.

Cleare *lights*, pure *lamps*,
Rare *stemms*, rich *streames* of life,
Who shine, beame, spring,
And draine your christall course
From *Iustice* throne,
To coole the heate of strife,
By curbing *aw* with *law*,
With *censure*, force,
To chastise with *restraint*,
Cheare with *remorse* ;
Long may *you* liue,
Since by your life *you* giue
Iustice new breath,
And make *her* euer liue.

Salus ciuitatis sita est in legibus.

IN MOMVM.

QVid carpendo premis tua viscera ferrea Mome?
    Momus, Mimus eris dum mea scripta premis.
Haud curo inuidiam, mea spes tenuissima tuta est,
    Nam tuta est tenuis vena, sed alta minus.
Anguis es, & viridi latitans sub fronde, venenum
    Eijcis, exiguo tempore inermis eris.
Non sum cui fortuna nocet, vel fata inuabunt,
    Fata canunt magnis, non cecinere meis.
Non cecinere meis, licet ista poemata magnis
    (Si mihi vota fauent) sint relegenda locis.

Me paucis malle à sapientibus esse probatum.

IN ZOILVM.

TExit vt exiguam subtilis Aranea telam,
    *Zoile sic scriptis tela retorque meis.
Torque, retorque, manet mea laus, mea gloria maior,
    Quo magis exhausta est gloria maior erit.
Vlciscar scriptis: tua mens tuus vltor adibit,
    Inuidiæ stimulis mens tua puncta tuis.
Pone miser miseræ monumenta miserrima vitæ,
    Vixisti misero more, miserq. mori.

* Mercurium in lingua, non in pectore geris.

IN PARONEM.

PAro parem, nec habet nec habere optat,
    Impar est præmijs, impar & laboribus;
Opera carpit mea studijs assiduis,
Tacet, attamen aliena carpit;

Inuisurum facilius quam imitaturum. Zeuxes.

O quantæ tenebræ tenuere locum,
Tuum, *Cymmerijs* inuolutum vmbris?
Vt minus afflares aliorum operibus,
Opera corrigis, emendare nequis;
Oleum & operam perdidit *Paro*
Per aurea fecula tranfeat *Maro*.
Non plura referam, reticere iuuat,
Si tu maleuolam reprimes linguam,
Sin male dicendo pergas difpergere
Hifce teterrima crimina fcriptis,
Scribam, liuorem irritare magis
Torquendo rigidi vifcera *Paronis*.

Vid. Martial. in. Lib. 3. Epigr. in Zoilum. Conuiua quifquis Zoili poteft effe, &c.
——rumpantur ilia *Codri* inuidia.

Crefcant & crepant. Vid. Apotheg.

AD INVIDVM.

Exeat Menippus.

INuidus vlcifcens vltor fibi maximus effet,
Nam ftupet ille malis fic periendo fuis.

AD SEIPSVM.

Intret Ariftippus.

TV tibi res folitus non te fubiungere rebus,
Me peritura doces fpernere, fpreta pati.

FINIS.

Danc'd are my Measures, *now I must repose,
(Retire at least) and laugh at vertues foes,
Who let them frowne, fume, fret, this is my* Mot,
My spirit's *aboue their* spite; *I feare them not.*

Faults are as obuious to bookes in Presse, as misconstruction after. Do me the fauour to correct such escapes with thy *pen* as are past in the *Print:* for *such* as are more consequent they are here noted, for the impertinent they are to thy discreeter iudgement referred.

Errata.

Pag. Tab. for subihct, reade in some coppies subject. pag. 48. line vlt. for liuer. leaue. pag.. 51. l. 15. for thas, r. that p.68.l.16.for suppressed, r. suppreft. p. 79. l. 14. for heare, r.feare. p. 110. l. vlt. for marks, marts. p. 160. l. 8. for excellent, r.exquisite. p. 161. l. 1. adde, are euer to be. p. 164. for eminent, r.imminent. ibid. tit. ψεσδολ. ψεσδοφ. πολιγοτ. p. 209. in marg. adde, issue.

www.ingramcontent.com/pod-product-compliance
Lightning Source LLC
Chambersburg PA
CBHW020223240426
43672CB00006B/399